OUR PARLIAMENT

The Churchill Arch

Revised and enlarged edition

Strathearn Gordon

OUR PARLIAMENT

PUBLISHED FOR
THE HANSARD SOCIETY BY
CASSELL · LONDON

CASSELL & COMPANY LTD
35 Red Lion Square · London WC1
and at
MELBOURNE · SYDNEY · TORONTO
JOHANNESBURG · CAPE TOWN · AUCKLAND

First Edition October 1945
Sixth (revised and enlarged) edition 1964

Printed in Great Britain
by Ebenezer Baylis & Son, Ltd.,
The Trinity Press, Worcester, and London
1263

Contents

Contents (continued)

Illustrations

Illustrations (*continued*)

'I pray that, with God's blessing, this light will shine henceforth not only as an outward and visible sign that the Parliament of a free people is assembled in free debate but also, that it may shine as a beacon of sure hope in a sadly torn and distracted world.'

Mr. Speaker's words on re-lighting the lantern above Big Ben on 24th April, 1945.

The 'Ayrton Light', named after a First Commissioner of Works, Mr. Acton Smee Ayrton, M.P., has shone since 1885 to show when the House of Commons is sitting.

Acknowledgements

The author wishes to thank Mr. Michael Padev for allowing him to quote an extract from his book *Dimitrov Wastes No Bullets* (Eyre & Spottiswoode, 1948). The facsimiles on pages 91, 93, 112–114, 116, 126–127 and 135 and the illustration facing page 84 are Crown copyright and are reproduced by permission of the Controller, H.M. Stationery Office.

Foreword

Of all the institutions for which the British are famous, of all the contributions this island people have made to the business of living, there is none more noteworthy or renowned than that of Parliament.

Emerson wrote that an institution is the lengthened shadow of one man. Of the institution of Parliament it may truly be said that it is the lengthened shadow of a nation. It has been the dynamic centre from which the principles and practices of the free way of life have radiated forth beyond the confines of Britain. Always changing, yet changeless in its spirit and purpose, Parliament has its roots in history, yet its branches reach out towards the days still to come.

Parliament is part of the birthright of every citizen, the mirror of the people's minds and the guardian of their liberties. We are, each and all of us, the custodians of the dignity of this famous national institution. Its efficiency as an instrument of governance depends upon the quality of its members and this, so far as the Commons are concerned, depends upon the skill, judgement and political honesty with which citizens discharge their electoral responsibilities. Democratic government enables the citizen to enjoy *rights*. Every right carries with it a corresponding *duty*.

It is the high duty of each one of us to be informed about Parliament and its purposes and to be concerned with its operations.

The book you are now reading has run through five editions in English, and has also been published in French, Spanish, Italian, German, and Japanese. Though the work is intended for the general reader it is hoped that it will be respected by the expert as a competent and useful introduction to a great subject. A short reading list has been added for those who wish to pursue this subject a little further.

STEPHEN KING-HALL

Author's note to the 1964 revised edition

This edition has been completely revised and I hope that no parliamentary change of importance which has occurred since 1958 has been overlooked.

I am extremely grateful to Dr. David Menhennet, who works with me in the House of Commons Library, for his valuable advice and unstinted help in bringing this book up to date.

S. GORDON

Chapter I
OUR PARLIAMENT

'Disinterested intellectual curiosity is the life-blood of real civilization.'
G. M. Trevelyan, *English Social History*.

Not long ago a mutual disappointment brought home to me how unfamiliar Parliament may be to some of the electors. I had got an elderly farmer friend into the gallery of the House of Commons to hear a debate. He is an old-fashioned type, a man of sense and judgement founded on experience rather than on books, a good neighbour and an excellent member of society. It was a long-standing promise. My friend walked through the lobbies and up the stairs to his seat with an expression of respect and keenest anticipation. The debate was quite up to the average in interest and incident. But when he came out it was evident that he had received a staggering disappointment. The picture he had conceived of the House of Commons, whatever it was, had been rudely shattered. 'Well, I *never*,' he kept repeating, 'fancy us being governed by such a set of *ordinary*-looking fellows! A lot of bald heads and *ordinary* talk; I *am* disappointed.'

I felt just as disappointed myself, as though I had taken him to such an extravagantly dull play that he had come out yawning. I tried to find out what was wrong. He was far too intelligent to have expected to see magnificent figures in powdered wigs and satin breeches delivering brilliant orations like those which made Fox and Sheridan famous some 170 years ago. But I think he may have imagined a House still peopled with the politicians of his Victorian youth—the frock coats, silk hats and resounding formal speeches of a bygone age. At any rate he had completely failed to imagine Parliament as it is.

This book is an attempt to explain in simple terms how Parliament has grown up, what it is and how it works and affects people's lives today. It is offered to my friend who expected something so much less ordinary, to foreign visitors who still flock to Westminster, to all fellow citizens who have never found time to attend a debate in the House of Commons, and above all to the young people of Britain.

The subject should be approached without prejudice. Parliament has many qualities, but I wish most to point out its quality of *fairness*—its capacity, if properly worked, to ensure fair conditions of discussion and decision by our representatives of all the problems which affect our daily lives. Fashions have changed since the days of 'I reckon it's true: I seen it in print'. Many of the people who might have said that now seem to approach such a subject as Parliament, if they approach it at all, in a mood of thorough-going cynicism. Nothing is to be believed unless it is base. 'The Government' is the enemy: a set of clever fellows seated in London, who manipulate the strings of power and tax the people—probably mainly for their own selfish interests. 'Why can't the Government pay our income tax for us?' was an earnest question put in perfectly good faith not long ago at a political meeting. It betrays a complete ignorance of the 'system' which is so freely criticized, and an unhappy sense of antagonism. If even a few of those who think and speak so bitterly about 'them' and 'their Parliament', can be brought to feel about it as 'us' and 'our Parliament' (especially when their own party is *not* in power) then the purpose of this book will be amply satisfied.

If, too, these people will put aside their certainty that Parliament is a tyrannical and incompetent sham, and all politicians nest-feathering scoundrels, until they have read these pages, they may then know the answers to some of the questions which perplex them most, which I believe to be as follows (the references show where the answers are to be found):

1. *Why doesn't Parliament* do *more? Why do they only* talk? (pp. 33–39).
2. *Why don't Members work harder? They always seem to be going for long holidays* (pp. 56–59).
3. *Why have Parties at all? Why not choose 'the best men' and let them do what is best for the country?* (pp. 75–78).
4. *Why is procedure so complicated that even Members themselves don't understand it?* (pp. 96–97).
5. *Why not abolish the House of Lords?* (pp. 144–153).
6. *Why does Parliament allow so much 'red tape' and bureaucracy in Whitehall?* (pp. 170–171).

So much for what we may call 'the opposition to Parliament'. Now for the others, who probably form the majority in Britain. They are more or less dimly aware that Parliament is a great and famous institution, hundreds of years old. They believe that it is also 'the Government'; and that it is somehow responsible for British liberties and freedom as well as for the income tax. They are proud of it as being part of their country and traditions; but just how old it is, how it works and how exactly it affects their own lives they have probably been too busy, too far away, or too uninterested to inquire.

Such readers should take note of the following facts. A famous writer on Parliament in the last century, Walter Bagehot, used to divide the features of the Constitution into the *dignified* parts which existed to impress and remind people, and the *efficient* parts which did most of the work. It is easy to stare at the Sovereign driving in her gilded coach to the opening of a new Parliament, or to peer down from one of the galleries of the House of Commons—without being able to make head or tail of what is going on—at the Speaker with his long wig and buckled shoes sitting behind the mace. But it is far more important to come to grips with the basic principles of the Constitution and especially to grasp the system of its inner working parts—the Prime Minister, the Cabinet, Parliament, the Parties and the Government Departments. To put it in another way, Big Ben's chime and bell would not be so famous if it did not also keep perfect time.

This book is partly a history book, since Parliament itself is in so many ways pure history. Every sentence spoken under its great sounding-board—perhaps in the reader's presence—passes into the annals of the nation. Future generations will refer to the great speeches of Churchill, Attlee and other eminent contemporaries with the same respect accorded today to the words of Burke and Disraeli. Equally, it should be remembered that the centuries of political development which lie behind us make *our* Parliament a precious legacy, which it is our high duty to understand. *Our* Constitution, said Burke, is 'an entailed inheritance derived to us from our forefathers—to be transmitted to our posterity—an estate specially belonging to the people of this kingdom, without any reference whatever to any other more general or prior right.'[1] Finally, and perhaps most important of all, it is impossible to understand Parliament as it is today without some knowledge of its historical development; and only by carefully using the lessons of its long experience can Parliament carry out its tasks with efficiency. The antiquity of our Parliament is one of the secrets of its survival in a world where democracy is very much on trial.

[1] *Reflections on the French Revolution*, Everyman's Library, 1951 edition, p. 31.

Chapter II
THE COMING OF PARLIAMENT

'The roots of the present lie deep in the past.'
Bishop Stubbs (1825–1901).

In primitive societies a single man—the chief or king—could himself supply all the powers of government. He could declare the necessary rules of conduct or laws, supervise their execution, and judge whether they had been broken. He could also decide quarrels, devise a policy to enable his people to defend themselves and improve their way of living, and act as their formal head, protector, and spokesman. But in larger and more civilized states these powers are commonly separated and given the following names. The body of people who make the laws are known as the *Legislature* (late Latin: Legislatio—proposing of a law); those who carry them out—and in general *execute* the country's policy—are called the *Executive* (medieval Latin: Exsecutare—to execute); while the judges who decide whether the laws have been infringed form the *Judiciary* (Latin: Judices—judges). The *Constitution* of a country means the way in which it is governed or organized. The Constitution regulates the powers possessed by each of the parts mentioned above, and their relationship to one another, and the term includes the rights and duties of subjects in relation to the supreme power in the state. The name of the Constitution is often taken from the nature of this supreme power. Thus, where it belongs to a king the constitution is an *Absolute Monarchy*; to a Dictator, a *Dictatorship*; to a few men, an *Oligarchy*; and to the best citizens or to the nobles, an *Aristocracy*. The word *Democracy* (Greek: demos—people) means a state wherein the supreme power belongs to the people or to their representatives. It is one of the purposes of this book to show that Parliament is the chief instrument through which that power can be kept where it belongs.

The British Constitution is a Democracy with a constitutional monarch at its head, by which is meant that although the supreme power lies in the hands of the people and the representatives whom they elect, the formal head of the state is a Sovereign whose powers are restricted by constitutional laws and customs. We shall return to the British Constitution in the next chapter, and in the meanwhile, with but two more definitions—of politics and Parliament—we can set out upon our researches. *Politics* means the science and art of government, and a politician is one skilled or engaged or interested in that art. In the last restricted sense it is the duty of every man or woman living in a democratic state to be a politician. But what exactly is meant by *Parliament*? Originally, the word, meaning a talk, was applied to the after-dinner gossip of monks in their cloisters, which was condemned by the authorities as unedifying. It came into use for the national assemblies after the middle of the thirteenth century, and soon became established. Legally, it now consists of the Queen, the House of Lords and the House of Commons, *acting together*, but colloquially it is used for the House of Commons with a conception of the House of Lords in the background, or, still more loosely, for 'the Government'. This last is an inaccurate use of the term; the Government is the Executive, which Parliament controls. I propose to choose the middle one of these three definitions—the two Houses of Parliament—and since the House of Commons is so much the predominant partner, the space and attention devoted to it will be proportionately large.

All authorities remark upon the haphazard and 'accidental' appearance presented by the growth of our Constitution. But though often misunderstood by those who were concerned in its evolution, it is the product of a natural development. However, a scrutiny of conditions at any stage inevitably involves an examination of their causes, so that the only safe method is to begin at the beginning.

If we search among the earliest records for a starting-point of Parliament, we are bound first to notice the *Witenagemot* (or *Witangemot*), that famous assembly of the wisest of our Anglo-Saxon forefathers, who were summoned to give rede (counsel) to kings with names like Alfred, Edward, Athelstan and Edmund, long years before the Conqueror fixed the immortal date of 1066 in our history. Even in those early times it was an English principle—similar conventions existed in most primitive European communities—that in important matters such as the interpretation of laws, the King ought not to act alone but should first obtain the advice and consent of the wisest of his people, and it was on this principle that he held 'deep speech' with the witan, or council of the wise men, two or three times a year. Sometimes the meetings were attended by gatherings of the ordinary folk, who, after hearing the speeches of the leaders, gave a vote for or against the proposition by clashing their arms against their shields. But the characteristic witan seems to have been a small aristocratic body, of variable composition, with enormous powers, surpassing in some respects those of the modern House of Commons. 'It can elect kings and depose them,' says one of our most brilliant historians.[1] 'The king and witan legislate; it is with the counsel and consent of the witan that the king publishes laws; the king and witan nominate the ealdormen and bishops, make grants of the public lands, impose taxes, decide on peace and war, and form a tribunal of last resort for causes criminal and civil. It is a supreme legislative, governmental and judicial assembly.' So that a free assembly, not elected, but representative in the limited sense that it was summoned from all parts of the country, existed in England over 1,000 years ago.

It should also be remembered that a form of local government was well established at this time. The country was organized in the 'shires' we know so well (and in smaller units), with an ealdorman who commanded the local forces and belonged to the witan, and a sheriff who represented the King's interests and presided in the shire court. Both sheriff and court survived the Conquest and are of high importance in the history of Parliament.

The Normans were despots and they ruled as despotically as they dared in the face of their turbulent followers, but they gave a basis to

[1] F. W. Maitland, *Constitutional History of England*, 1931 ed., p. 58.

the English Constitution in the shape of a strong kingship, making for national unity. William I emphasized the feudal system in England—the system under which the King made grants of land to his nobles in return for a promise of allegiance and of active help in time of war; and by which, similarly, the nobles became overlords to their tenants, promising them justice and protection in return for services rendered in peace and war. He insisted that every landholder, however small, must owe him direct allegiance, which qualified the man's oath to his immediate overlord and made loyalty to the King the supreme and universal duty of all English freemen.

William and his successors held 'Great Councils' which were probably assemblies of the King's tenants-in-chief, that is to say those who held land directly from him. The Saxon Chronicle of the Conqueror states that 'Thrice a year King William wore his crown every year he was in England; at Easter he wore it at Winchester, at Pentecost at Westminster, and at Christmas at Gloucester; and at these times all the men of England were with him—archbishops, bishops and abbots, earls, thegns, and knights.' 'All the men of England' probably meant the greatest of them only, but it seems certain that the few legislative acts of the period were done with the advice and consent of these Councils. It must be remembered that even the despotic Normans had no standing armies, no police and no civil service to support and defend the state. They were dependent upon the general public, and it was natural for them to carry on an immemorial tradition common to Normandy and to England, by governing with the help and consent of the greatest and the wisest of the free men whose lords they were.

It next becomes important to watch the transformation of these purely feudal bodies of great vassals called the Great Councils into something more representative of the whole nation. And here the first beginnings become visible of a connexion between taxation and direct representation, when Henry II, in imposing the famous Saladin tithe on belongings in 1188 for the expenses of a crusade, got it assessed in each district by a jury of neighbours. Incidentally, it was also probably the first attempt to tax personal property. It should be remembered that the medieval King (and his feudal subordinates) was normally expected to live 'of his own'. Hereditary revenues and customary dues, services and 'fees' were supposed to suffice. All taxation (in our modern sense) was extraordinary. Hence the feeling that when the King asked for more, he was asking for something to which he was not entitled as a matter of course.

Magna Carta was the last great landmark before the first Parliaments in the modern sense. It was to prove of momentous importance to the liberties of Englishmen, largely owing to the optimistic interpretations placed upon it by later generations; but for our purpose it is enough to note that on a stormy day in 1215 on the marshy islet of Runnymede, a committee of twenty-five angry nobles extorted from their reluctant King a promise that in future he would adhere to the law of the land by refraining from imposing any feudal aid (tax), except the three customary ones for redeeming the King's body from captivity, for knighting his eldest son, and for marrying his eldest daughter, *save by the common council of the realm*. Thus was the doctrine of the necessity of consent firmly re-established. Further, something like a distinct definition of the common council was provided. It was to consist of prelates and great nobles summoned by name, and of tenants-in-chief summoned collectively through the sheriffs. The effect of the Charter upon King John seems to have been startlingly dramatic. 'They have given me five-and-twenty over-kings,' he shouted, flinging himself upon the floor and furiously gnawing the sticks and straw which were the carpet of the period.

The idea of representation, particularly in the organization of the Church, for judicial purposes in connexion with juries, and for tax assessments, had long existed. Knights were probably first summoned to Westminster to give evidence in connexion with legal cases brought up from their own County Courts and other affairs of local government. In 1213 John summoned four knights from each shire to Oxford 'to speak with us about the business of our Kingdom'. The business was almost certainly financial. But in 1254 a great advance in the conception of parliamentary representation was marked when each sheriff was bidden to send two knights, chosen by the county, *to consider what aid they would give to the King in his great necessity*. The knights now came as delegates, no longer in their personal capacity as tenants-in-chief.

There, in the power to *grant or withhold supplies*, lies the lever which time and again has served the people to increase their control over the King and his executive government. Even today, the ability of governments to rule despotically is limited (with other safeguards) by the necessity for securing votes of supply in the House of Commons.

In 1265 Simon de Montfort summoned his famous Parliament, famous because for the first time representatives were called from the cities and boroughs as well as from the shires.

Several other Parliaments were held during the next thirty years, usually with no 'townsmen' in attendance. But in 1295,[1] Edward I provided the model towards which all previous experiments had been tending and which slowly crystallized into the type of modern Parliaments. The process was very gradual. Many Great Councils were called after 1295 in which the Commons or the clergy or the knights were not represented; and throughout the Middle Ages many important statutes were passed without the consent of the Commons.

The Model Parliament, as it later came to be called, was convoked to deal with yet another great national emergency.[2] It consisted of the archbishops, bishops and greater abbots, eight earls and forty-one barons, all summoned by name. The prelates were directed to bring representatives of the lesser clergy and the sheriffs to cause two knights of each shire, two citizens of each city, and two burgesses of each borough, to be *elected*. Thus, the assembly had ceased to be a feudal court, dependent entirely upon land tenure, and was becoming a body in which every class and interest had a voice. It was an assembly of the 'Estates' of the realm—clergy, barons, and commons, or, as Maitland calls them, 'those who pray, those who fight and those who work'. When these diverse Englishmen (numbering some 400 in all) were brought together their discussions were bound to help towards forming a national as opposed to a sectional policy. They made friends (and quarrelled, no doubt), learnt each other's local conditions and difficulties, and exchanged points of view. Today these functions of Parliament are still as vital for the national well-being as they were in 1295.

By 1300, therefore, representative institutions were established, much on the lines of our present Parliaments, except that only the archbishops and bishops now remain as representatives of the Church. But it should be repeated that although the growth of Parliament, as outlined here, sounds simple and straightforward, on closer study it resembles a piece of tapestry of the period. The effect of the finished pattern is clear

[1] Some authorities choose the Great Council of 1275 as the first true predecessor of modern Parliaments.

[2] The French had landed at Dover, and there were wars with Wales and Scotland.

enough, but a nearer scrutiny reveals all kinds of beginnings, interweavings and unfinished ends, and the tracing of each single thread has occupied many a constitutional historian's whole life-time.

There are three essential ideas to be grasped about these early Parliaments.

1. *Parliament as a Court of Justice.* The original unit, out of which everything developed, was the King's Court with its varying functions. Parliament, in its beginnings, was regarded as the highest court of royal justice, and even under Edward III the dispensation of justice was still looked upon by contemporaries as its primary function. That is why the expression 'The High Court of Parliament' may be echoing somewhere at the back of your mind. The only remaining judicial function of Parliament, apart from questions of 'Privilege' (see pp. 109–110), its duties in connexion with Private Bills (p. 106) and the obsolete process of Impeachment, is today exercised by the Lords as the highest court of appeal for the whole country—and even that function is left in practice to its specialist judges. But the idea of Parliament as the highest dispenser of justice for all grievances and for rich and poor alike remains to this day, as we shall see in a later chapter.

2. *Representation and Consent to Taxation.* We have just watched the first steps by which representatives of the people were summoned to Parliament to grant money to the King. The doctrine of *consent* to taxation (in the Great Council of the realm) was a feudal one. It is likely that a virtual *consent* to taxation was necessary in the shire courts long before representatives of these courts were summoned to Westminster. At first it was *advice* which was sought by the Sovereign in Parliament, particularly in the case of the Commons, but better returns were produced when it was *consent* which was invited. The practice of *representation* had been developed independently for other purposes, such as the assessment and collection of taxes imposed by the King in his Council. The two ideas were now linked together in the famous principle first affirmed in the Justinian Code and repeated in the writ of summons to the Model Parliament—'*Quod omnes tangit, ab omnibus approbetur*' ('What touches all should be approved by all'). Thus, the beginnings of the idea of financial responsibility to the electors, which is the essential element of a modern Parliament, and (as we have said), the basis of modern parliamentary sovereignty, were born with the earliest representative Parliament, over 650 years ago.

3. *The Failure of the Estates System in England.* The Model Parliament owed much to Edward I's wish to broaden the basis from which he drew counsel and help. It was convenient for the King to keep in close touch with the communities whose goodwill was so indispensable for the smooth running of government and the collection of taxes, and, once granted a place in the assembly, the humbler representatives soon took part in its development. Nor was it long before the nobles found occasion to desire their support. Both when Edward II was deposed by a Parliament, and Richard II by an assembly of Estates, the great men were clearly glad to share with the lesser the responsibility for such revolutionary actions. But the idea of the three Estates did not flourish in England, since from an early date the clergy as a body preferred to meet and to discuss their contributions of taxes in their own convocations. There is no evidence that the lesser clergy attended Parliament after the end of the fourteenth century, and in 1664 their subsidies to the state ceased and they were taxed with the laity. (It is typical of our irregular methods that this momentous constitutional change was first settled by a verbal agreement between Archbishop Sheldon and the Lord Chancellor Clarendon, without any express law.) The prelates remained in their capacity as feudal landlords and continued to sit with the greater barons. 'Baron' in this sense meant a military tenant-in-chief. The 'greater barons' were entitled to individual writs of summons to Parliament, and became the House of Lords. The knights of the shire were usually chosen from among the lesser barons. They were generally gentlemen of birth but not necessarily of the military rank of knighthood. They were elected in the full shire court under the superintendence of the sheriff, whose writ also charged him to arrange for the return of the city and borough representatives in his shire.

After a period of uncertainty as to which of the lesser barons were entitled to a separate summons and as to how the new representatives would group themselves, the knights of the shire, possibly owing to jealousies of the greater barons engendered in local shire affairs, threw in their lot with the citizens and burgesses and sat separately (for purposes of deliberation) from those summoned by name. This separation dates at least from the middle of the fourteenth century and possibly earlier.

It is here that the importance of the county court in the development of the English Parliament shows itself. Henry II, by insisting on juries of knights to represent all the freemen of these courts, forced the knights to become the representatives of the Commons. Later, they found it natural to co-operate with the burgesses. French historians usually see in the county court (peculiar to this country) the ultimate cause of the difference in the development of the English Parliament as compared with its continental equivalents. Hence the development not of three Estates, as in France until 1614, but of two Houses, the Lords spiritual and temporal, and the Commons. Thus were avoided, probably by chance, all the dangers of the permanent separation of our political society into Estates or classes. The name 'Commons' signified originally the organized communities from which came the representatives, but this meaning has been overlaid by a later notion of the common people who are represented—'The Commons of England'. The origin of the expression 'House of Commons' has been ascribed to the year 1450 and 'House of Lords' to the reign of Henry VIII.[1]

Before leaving the momentous period of the Model Parliament, two other points should be noted. Hitherto most of the arrangements we have been describing were tentative and uncertain. Parliament did not always meet in the same place. York was a favourite alternative to Westminster—for political or sanitary reasons. The decision as to who should be summoned, both to the Great Council and to Parliament, lay with the King and to some extent with the sheriffs, and depended upon the locality of the meeting and the needs of the moment. Attendance was often expensive and onerous and absences were frequent. The whole system was highly variable and bristled with exceptions. But after 1295 usages gradually became fixed. Parliaments upon that first model were frequently summoned, and with their consent the King enacted statutes.[2]

The second point to be noticed is that Parliament was an expansion for temporary purposes of the King's Great Council, which not only continued to meet in its old form without the representatives of shire, city and borough, but gradually split up into functional parts such as the King's Courts of Justice and the Privy Council containing the great officers of state. It is a relic of those old days when some of the judges of the Supreme Court take their seats, as advisers, among the peers at

[1] K. R. Mackenzie, *The English Parliament*, 1963, p. 20.

[2] A statute is a written law of a legislative body, *i.e.*, an Act of Parliament. Throughout its early stages, while it is passing through Parliament, it is called a Bill.

the opening of Parliament, although the courts in which they preside were long ago separated from Parliament.

These early Plantagenet Parliaments have been likened by Sir Courtenay Ilbert, in his *Parliament*, to an oriental durbar, a state audience with the King on his throne surrounded by his Great Council, hearing the petitions of his subjects and deciding how they should be met. The vital principle of 'grievances before supply' was thus already established. The King asked for some special financial aid and his people naturally chose the moment to strike a bargain with him regarding the redress of their grievances, which were presented by or through Parliament in the form of petitions.

Several of the vital principles of financial procedure were beginning to be established in the fifteenth century. As early as 1407 Henry IV acknowledged that grants of supply must originate in the Commons and that the report of such grants should be made to him through the Speaker of the Commons.[1] (It is interesting to note that the practice is still maintained, over 500 years later, when Bills for granting aids or supplies to the Crown are handed by the Speaker to the Clerk of the Parliaments to receive the Royal Assent.) But the grantors preferred to restrict their grants to the necessities of the occasion, both through normal parsimony and in order to keep a weapon wherewith to ensure the redress of their grievances. Frequent Parliaments were therefore required, sometimes two or more in one year, in each case involving a fresh election. It is said that Richard II, who packed his Parliaments with well-disposed adherents, devised the method of sessions and prorogations, to avoid the dispersal of an obliging assembly. The custom then followed that a Parliament once called remained in existence, unless dissolved, until the demise of the Crown. This system lasted until the Triennial Act of 1694, and is another typical example of the seemingly haphazard development of our Constitution.

The change from legislation by petition to legislation by statute was completed in the sixteenth century. There had been many complaints that the statutes drafted by the King's Council in satisfaction of petitions did not in fact tally with them, and Parliament having been dissolved, the Commons had no redress. In 1414 Henry V gave a vague promise that 'nothing be enacted to the petition of the Commons contrary to their asking', but it was not until Henry VIII's reign that the practice

[1] Bishop Stubbs, *Constitutional History*, 1880, Vol. III, p. 65.

was established of sending up Petitions (apart from those for Private Bills) to the King in the form of statutes, so that he could but assent or dissent.

The customs of Parliament gradually became more settled and its power increased, until Sir Thomas Smith, Queen Elizabeth's Secretary of State, was able to declare that 'the most high and absolute power of the realm of England consisteth in the Parliament', by which he meant, in the Sovereign in Parliament. It was true, but nevertheless the most dominating of the Tudors contrived to have their own way, Henry VIII by overawing and using Parliament, Elizabeth I by a mixture of scolding and tact.

In 1547 the House of Commons, which since before 1376 had usually sat in the Refectory or Chapter House of the Abbey, was allotted St. Stephen's Chapel in the Palace of Westminster, by Edward VI, and there it sat until the fire of 1834 destroyed the chapel. Two fortunate results of much constitutional importance ensued from this more or less accidental Tudor decision. The comparatively small size of the chapel permitted a conversational tone of discussion and a cut and thrust of debate which are impossible in the large chambers commonly used by such assemblies, where a single speaker at a time mounts a rostrum and delivers an oration in a loud, unnatural voice. Secondly, the rectangular shape of the chapel in later days encouraged a system of two opposed 'parties' sitting face to face, instead of the more numerous groups of opinion shading from left to right round the semi-circular benches so often seen in foreign chambers.

Under the Tudors, also, the House of Commons (slightly later than the Lords) started to keep Journals, which form an unbroken record of their proceedings to the present day. The main lines of procedure, including the committee system, grew up under Elizabeth I and James I; they were enormously elaborated and stereotyped in the eighteenth century, and remained in force until the Reform Bill of 1832. The procedure described in 1844 in the first edition of Sir T. Erskine May's famous treatise on *The Law, Privileges and Usage of Parliament*—which in its later editions has remained the prime authority on the subject of procedure—was essentially the same as that in use by the Long Parliament.

The great civil war, ending in the defeat and subsequent execution of

Charles I on the scaffold in Whitehall, was fought upon an issue which had in fact already been decided—whether the sovereignty should belong to the King or to the King in Parliament. But in vanquishing royal despotism, the country also showed decisively its rejection of all other forms of despotism, whether of an individual, of committees, or of Parliament itself. It was found in practice that the Government could not be efficiently carried on except through persons enjoying the confidence of Parliament. Hence the gradual development of the system whereby the Executive has become a kind of committee of the Legislature.

The restored monarchy broke down when James II was suspected of trying to foist his religion upon an unwilling country, and it gave place to an early form of the constitutional Monarchy we know. It would have been unnatural for the country not to try to mark their constitutional claims on the occasion of a change of monarchs in such circumstances as the revolution of 1688.

William III desired the Crown of England, but he was not so interested to hear about limitations of his power, and when, standing with his queen under a canopy of state in the banqueting room of Whitehall, he had to listen to the reading of the Declaration of Rights before the formal offer of the Crown was made, he replied with a 'laconic and jejune' little speech, without directly noticing the Declaration. However, the Declaration became the Bill of Rights, and another landmark was passed in the history of Parliament.

The Revolution Settlement, and in particular the Bill of Rights, says Maitland, placed the Sovereign distinctly below statute. He was to have no power to suspend or dispense with statutes; to create any new offence by proclamation; to exact money or to keep a standing army in peacetime without Parliament's consent. The judges were no longer to hold office during his pleasure. The people were to have a free choice of representatives in Parliament. Both Houses were confirmed in their right of liberty of debate. Moreover, the right of the people through their representatives to set whom they would on the throne was established. All theories of any rights to the throne independent of the law were abolished and all subsequent Sovereigns have occupied the throne by virtue of an Act of Parliament.

The two principal characteristics of the modified Monarchy were the party system and the Cabinet. Speaking of these great innovations Sir Courtenay Ilbert says: 'They were silent changes, not brought about by any act of legislature; gradual in their operation; developed, modified, deflected, retarded by strong personalities, like Walpole, Pitt, George III; imperfectly appreciated, misinterpreted, misunderstood.'

Whether the division of opinion which produced the two historic parties can be more truly ascribed to the reign of Charles II, or of Charles I, or whether it should be dated back to the Reformation is still a matter of argument, but it can be said that broadly the Tory Party of country squires and their dependents supported 'Church and King', while the Whig landlords with the rising commercial classes stood for toleration and the supremacy of Parliament. The Revolution of 1688 confused the Tories and gave a clear advantage to the great Whig families who had brought over the new Sovereigns. Moreover, William had plenty to occupy him outside the kingdom. It is not surprising that the years after the Revolution showed important constitutional progress. The Bill of Rights confirmed the House of Commons in the sole right to tax the nation which they had formally claimed under Charles II, and when the House resolved to grant only annual supplies to the Crown, it achieved the supreme power in the state—because the King had to come to Parliament every year for his 'aids'—though it did not for many years add to itself the power to control public policy. The Cabinet developed as a committee of the King's Privy Council, which can in turn be traced back at least to the beginning of Henry III's reign. Charles II tended to trust very few of his fifty or so Councillors with the dubious business which often occupied him, and a kind of inner council of five developed, which became known as the Cabal, since the initial letters of the participants' names at one time spelt this word. This system of an inner council persisted and crystallized into an institution, thus furnishing another example of a common development in our Constitution, whereby when a body becomes too large for effective action, its functions are gradually assumed by a smaller internal 'management committee' of its own members. The process has been repeated in the War Cabinets and 'Inner Cabinets' so familiar in the critical days since 1914.

All possibility of Cabinet government was almost prevented at an early stage by Parliament itself. The efforts of the Crown to wield influence by conferring pensions and 'offices of profit' upon Members of the House of Commons soon caused alarm, and the Act of Settlement in 1701 provided that 'no person who has an office or a place of profit under the King shall be capable of serving as a member of the House of Commons'. This provision would have made Cabinet government impossible, but it was repealed before taking effect.

It is interesting to note that the framers of the American Constitution also dreaded that corrupt influence might be secured to the Executive by these means. But they persisted with their remedy and the result has been one of the main differences between the American system of government and our own. Members of the President's Cabinet cannot be members of Congress. Consequently, Ministers in America do not have to face a daily battery of questions on the most delicate subjects of administrative policy to which Ministers here are constantly submitted. Under the United States Constitution the Executive is divorced from the Legislature and there is no such close relationship and no intimate control by the representatives of the people over the country's policy as exist here.

The subsequent history of the Cabinet is largely due to two circumstances—the desire of Parliament to take a constantly greater part in the Government, and also the accident that George I and George II could not speak fluent English and interested themselves less in the affairs of England than in those of Hanover. George I ceased to attend meetings of the Cabinet, and none of his successors resumed the Sovereign's seat, though George III tried hard to regain the executive power. The decision was vital; retirement from the Cabinet turned out to mean relinquishment of all real part in the determination of national policy. Most people still felt that the King was entitled to govern the country; but in practice he found that he could hardly do so unless he controlled the House of Commons. Hence the system of corruption—which was thought to be undermining the Constitution.

It was some time after the emergence of the great parties before all the members of an Administration came to be chosen from the same party. When such a Ministry was formed, in 1696, it received the disapproving title of 'the junto'. Most of Queen Anne's Ministries were mixed, as distinguished from coalitions, and it was Sir Robert Walpole's Whig Ministry of 1715 which first really established the practice of party solidarity.

The principle of the collective responsibility of a Ministry was of much slower growth. At first individual Ministers frequently dropped out for one cause or another. In the early days of parties the House of Commons disliked the presence of Ministers, and it was only gradually that it became resigned to their presence and finally grew to regard them as a whole body, to be attacked or defended as representatives of the party in power, rather than the King's Ministers. From their own point of view, also, collective responsibility became an advantage to the Cabinet. It was a good defence in early days against a King who might hesitate to dismiss a Minister he disliked if it was to involve the resignation of all; against their opponents in Parliament if they stood united in face of the common foe; and even against one another if it was made impossible for individual Ministers to dissociate themselves from policies agreed upon in Cabinet which later came to grief.

Side by side with the development of party and Cabinet came the emergence of the Prime Minister. The twin requirements of a chairman for the Cabinet when the King no longer attended, and of a leader and spokesman for the Government both inside and outside Parliament, with a particular ability to control the House of Commons, have tended naturally to produce this central figure of our constitutional system.

Such are the bare bones of Parliament's history. How can this great array of facts best be summarized in a sentence or two? Perhaps we can say that England has been singularly fortunate in her political development. She has had autocratic Sovereigns, but they never achieved the power of tyrannical despots such as other countries have suffered. From early Saxon days there existed a Great Council of the wise men of the realm, which after 1295 slowly crystallized into Parliament divided into Lords and Commons, approximately as it is today.

The executive power passed gradually, over a period of about 400 years, and if not smoothly, certainly at the cost of much less bloodshed than in other countries, from the King and his few aristocratic adherents to the King in his Privy Council, and finally to a committee of that Privy Council presided over by a Prime Minister. Meanwhile the powers of the House of Lords were being whittled away, and the authority to tax, to grant supplies, and to appropriate those grants passed more and more completely to the Commons, bringing inevitably with it an increasing control over the Executive, until the political centre of gravity had entirely altered and reached its present position at the 'top' of the House of Commons and dependent inevitably on the support of the majority in the House and in the country.

One unhappy civil war, culminating in the execution of the Sovereign in 1649, played its part in this process of development. Much more was achieved, however, not by the fierce test of arms and bloodshed, but by the slower, rational and more durable test of argument, of persuasion and of experience gained from peaceful trial and error. Sir Winston Churchill once said that the British Constitution was 'mainly common sense'; and this description may also be applied, in large measure, to the history of Parliament itself.

Chapter III
THE CONSTITUTION TODAY

1576

'. . . let us compare it [the English system of government] with common wealthes, which be at this day in esse . . . to see who hath taken the righter, truer, and more commodious way to governe the people as well in warre as in peace.'

Sir Thomas Smith, *De Republica Anglorum.*

1945

'. . . this House of Commons, which has proved itself the strongest foundation for waging war that has ever been seen in the whole of our long history . . . the strength of the Parliamentary institution has been shown to enable it at the same moment to preserve all the title deeds of democracy while waging war in the most stern and protracted form.'

Sir Winston Churchill, *in the House of Commons, on Victory Day, 8th May, 1945.*

Before me lies open a copy of 'The Constitution of the United States of America', starting with the words:

> We, the people of the United States, in order to form a more perfect union, establish justice, insure domestic tranquility, provide for the common defence, promote the general welfare, and secure the blessings of liberty to ourselves and our posterity, do ordain and establish this CONSTITUTION for the United States of America.

It runs to sixteen small pages and can be purchased anywhere in America. If you ask for the address of a shop where you can buy a copy of the British Constitution, the answer is that no such document exists. Our Constitution is based upon a certain number of statutes, such as the Bill of Rights, the Act of Settlement, the Habeas Corpus Acts and the Parliament Acts of 1911 and 1949,[1] but to a much greater extent upon judicial decisions and upon customs and conventions. It is described and discussed in countless textbooks, but no one has ever sat down in this country to 'ordain and establish' a Constitution, as did fifty-five American delegates in 1787.

Let us take a single example. Section I (1) of Article II of the American Constitution reads:

> The executive power shall be vested in a President of the United States of America. He shall hold his office during the term of four years, and together with the Vice-President, chosen for the same term, be elected as follows: . . .

In our Constitution, on the other hand, the chief executive office, that of the Prime Minister, though in existence since 1721, was not formally recognized by the Legislature, even in a subsidiary connexion, until the Chequers Estate Act of 1917 endowed him with a country house, and he was not defined as the principal Minister of State until the Ministers of the Crown Act of 1937. The first thing to notice therefore about our Constitution is that it is mainly unwritten.

Unwritten Constitutions are usually found to be far less 'rigid' than those which have been written down, and the flexibility which the British Constitution thus enjoys brings enormous advantages with it. Our Constitution has never stopped growing and is still going strong. Not having been cast into written form at any period, it has the more easily developed to meet new requirements. Think of a few of the issues which have faced it during the last four hundred years alone. Two countries—Scotland and Northern Ireland—have been linked to the original Kingdom. The Kingdom has been linked with an Empire; Colonies have been founded, some of whom have rebelled and drawn apart. Many others have now achieved full Commonwealth status. Three times invasion has threatened. One King was executed and succeeded by a Dictator: another fled from the Kingdom, dropping the Great Seal into the Thames in his flight: a third went mad: a fourth

[1] See p. 31.

abdicated. In none of these cases was the continuity of the Constitution wholly broken.

But if we can proudly say that our Constitution is efficient and successful, we cannot claim that it is any more logical or tidy than others. 'It is,' says Sir William Anson,[1] 'a somewhat rambling structure, and, like a house which many successive owners have altered just so far as suited their immediate wants or the fashion of the time, it bears the marks of many hands, and is convenient rather than symmetrical.'

Nor is the Constitution easy to describe or the terms of its phraseology any longer convenient. To borrow Bagehot's vivid similes, which are often as apt today as when he used them in 1867:

> When a great entity like the British Constitution has continued in connected outward sameness, but hidden inner change, for many ages, every generation inherits a series of inapt words—of maxims once true, but of which the truth is ceasing or has ceased. As a man's family go on muttering in his maturity incorrect phrases derived from a just observation of his early youth, so, in the full activity of an historical Constitution, its subjects repeat phrases true in the time of their fathers, but now true no longer. Or, if I may say so, an ancient and ever-altering Constitution is like an old man who still wears with attached fondness clothes in the fashion of his youth: what you see of him is the same; what you do not see is wholly altered.

The last and most important general characteristic of the British Constitution which we should notice is what is known as the Rule of Law, the fact that no exercise of arbitrary or unrestrained power by the Sovereign, the servants of the Crown, or anyone else is possible, at any rate for long. The law, administered by independent judges, is supreme. It is true that the law-makers, Members of Parliament, can *alter* the laws, but once they come out into the streets they are as subject to all the laws of the land as the humblest private citizen.

This attribute was the especial envy and admiration of continental observers in the eighteenth century, when arbitrary power was widely exercised. 'When Voltaire came to England', says Dicey,

> —and Voltaire represented the feeling of his age—his predominant sentiment clearly was that he had passed out of the realm of despotism to a land where the laws might be harsh but where men were ruled by law and not by caprice.[2]

[1] *Law and Custom of the Constitution*, 5th ed., 1922, Vol. I, p. 1.
[2] *The Law of the Constitution*, 10th ed., 1959, p. 189.

It is interesting to note how this independent status of the law, which has now become so strong a buttress of our Constitution, was built up by common sense and compromise, rather than by rigid political theory. Since the days of Edward III it was held that the Crown ought not to interfere with the Judiciary. Everyone remembers the legend of how King Henry V, as a young man, attempted by violence to free one of his servants who was a prisoner in the Court of King's Bench; of how Judge Gascoigne, after vainly pleading with the furious prince, committed him to prison; and of how Henry submitted with a good grace and thereby delighted his royal father. But as long as judges held office during the pleasure of the Sovereign their conduct often varied with his needs, and as late as the reign of Charles II the judgements of the courts were frequently influenced by dismissals and new appointments.[1]

By the Act of Settlement of 1701, however, the real independence of the judges was secured. Their salaries were fixed, they were to hold office 'during good behaviour' instead of 'during pleasure', and to be removable, only in case of gross misconduct, by the formidable process of an Address of both Houses of Parliament to the Crown. This procedure has indeed been used on occasion (Sir Jonah Barrington, a judge of the Irish Admiralty Court, was removed in 1830 for corruption), but, since 1700, judges have enjoyed almost complete independence. Their position has been subsequently protected by statutes which have placed their salaries and pensions on the Consolidated Fund. This provides for their regular payment without question, and avoids the necessity for review and possible interference by Parliament in the annual Estimates.

The separation of the Judiciary from the Executive and the Legislature is, however, by no means so rigid as certain political theorists would like. Parliament can interfere to remove a judge, and is expressly charged with the supervision of the courts. No judge may sit in the House of Commons, though some sit in the House of Lords as Lords of Appeal. The judges are appointed by the Sovereign, on the advice of the Lord Chancellor, who is a member of the Government; but although his attention may naturally be attracted to the talents of prominent legal figures in his own party, it is a proof of the exceptionally high level of ability and integrity reached by the profession that the appoint-

[1] A similar situation has very recently been reflected in France.

ments which are made suffer very little criticism from any quarter. As a result the laws of England are administered as fairly (though perhaps not as cheaply) as anywhere in the world, and that is one of the best of all securities for the protection of the subject.

Let us glance now at the separate elements which compose this largely unwritten and obscure, but living, flexible and above all, efficient Constitution.

THE SOVEREIGN

It is one of the pleasantest surprises in our constitutional history that, after the Sovereign has gradually been deprived through the centuries of most powers and reduced almost to the position of a figurehead, she has still an unexpected and valuable part to play. The oldest of all the *dignified* parts is seen to be after all an *efficient* part. It has been well said that 'the Queen reigns, but she does not govern'. But by virtue of her central position and continuous office the Sovereign has still enormous potential influence through the discussions which proceed incessantly between herself and the leading figures of the nation. She is perpetually in touch with the Government. You may have noticed how, when vital business is afoot, the principal Ministers are to be found calling at Buckingham Palace. Whatever crises may arise have first to be brought before the Sovereign. The triumphs and sorrows alike of the nation impose their separate demands on the royal attention. 'A constitutional monarchy,' Earl Attlee has said, 'depends for its success to a great extent on the understanding heart of the monarch.' She is the fount of honour, who dispenses to her people (usually on the advice of her Ministers) the titles and decorations which are the reward for honourable service to the State. Such experience is likely to develop very special qualities of sympathy and humility which inevitably serve to focus the loyalty of the country and the Commonwealth upon the Sovereign. It is said that the late King George V, after driving to St. Paul's Cathedral through scenes of extraordinary affection on the occasion of his Jubilee in 1935, remarked to the Archbishop of Canterbury, 'I can't understand it. After all, I'm quite an *ordinary* sort of fellow.'

Bagehot has said that the Sovereign has three rights—the right to be consulted, the right to encourage, the right to warn. He adds that a Sovereign of great sense and sagacity would want no others. The Sovereign's main constitutional functions are in appearance very limited. First, she appoints the Prime Minister, though generally the choice is already made, for the Prime Minister ought to be the leader of the party for the time being commanding the majority, and in the event of a choice between two or more persons, there will probably be the advice of the outgoing Prime Minister to be considered. Exceptionally, however, the Sovereign may have a real and a vital decision to make in this respect.

The second prime function of the Sovereign is to grant or refuse the Prime Minister's requests for a dissolution of Parliament. There is a latent prerogative power in the Crown to insist upon a dissolution, if it appeared, for instance, that the Ministry or House of Commons no longer represented the wishes of the people; but in almost every conceivable case she ought as usual to act upon the advice of her Ministers—here of the chief Minister. It has been stated that it has become customary for the Sovereign to grant one dissolution to every Prime Minister. If thereafter, however, it seemed that the request was being improperly made, as for instance, if the Prime Minister had differed from the majority of his Cabinet, and had advised a dissolution for that reason alone, the Queen might possibly be justified in withholding her consent. Similarly, she might refuse to give a contingent assurance to create the necessary peers to secure a majority in the House of Lords (such an undertaking was given by King George V to Mr. Asquith at the height of the struggle over the Parliament Bill in 1910) if it plainly seemed that the opinion of the country had not declared itself in favour of such a decision.

But it must be emphasized that the Sovereign could only take these steps in the most exceptional circumstances, since an alternative Prime Minister must be at hand to accept responsibility for the action, and he in his turn could not remain in office without the support of the House of Commons.

Finally, there are certain dormant powers of the Sovereign—such as the refusal of the Royal Assent to a Bill—whose revival is almost inconceivable, since the Cabinet in effect controls the entire legislative programme and the Sovereign acts only upon the advice of her Ministers.

THE PRIME MINISTER

The prestige and authority of the Prime Minister in power have constantly increased since the time of Sir Robert Walpole, both by reason of the shrinkage of the Sovereign's powers, and of the enormous increase in the volume and variety of the national business. His position has been well described by Lord Morley: 'The Prime Minister is the keystone of the arch. Although in Cabinet all its members stand on an equal footing and speak with equal voice . . . yet the head of the Cabinet is *primus inter pares* ["the first among equals"] and occupies a position which, so long as it lasts, is one of exceptional and peculiar authority. It is true that he is in form chosen by the Crown, but in practice the Crown is pretty strictly confined to the man who is designated by the acclamation of a party majority. . . . The Prime Minister, once appointed, chooses his colleagues and assigns to them their respective offices. . . . The flexibility of the Cabinet system allows the Prime Minister in an emergency to take upon himself a power not inferior to that of a dictator, provided always that the House of Commons will stand by him.' It should be added that when he resigns it is customary for all other Ministers to resign with him.

As has so often been noticed, many of the most important relationships and arrangements of our system are indefinite, intangible, and still in process of development.

But in any consideration even of such a powerful figure as the Prime Minister, it is indispensable to remember that the supreme control resides in the people's representatives in the House of Commons and behind them in the people themselves.

In the moulding of their Constitution, Englishmen have not only adhered to the principle expressed by Lincoln in 1854 when he remarked that 'no man is good enough to govern another man without that other's consent', but they have also been careful to claim for themselves the right to revoke that consent. They will allow their rulers to wield enormous powers—but only temporarily, and always subject to criticism and the ultimate sanction of dismissal. So it is with all authorities in the land, from the Sovereign downwards: Parliament, responsible to the people, can unmake them all.

THE CABINET

It is one of the principal *conventions* (as opposed to *laws*) of the Constitution that practically all the executive powers required to govern the country are exercised by the Cabinet and their subordinate

Ministers and civil servants. The Cabinet is really a committee of the Sovereign's Privy Council, or a committee of Parliament, whichever way you choose to look at it; (though modern critics demur to the description on the ground that the Cabinet is appointed by the Prime Minister and not by the parent body—the House of Commons). In its origins it belongs to the first, in its composition to the second. All members of the Cabinet are Privy Councillors, and (with the most temporary exceptions), they must be members of one or other House of Parliament. As Bagehot says, the Cabinet is 'a combining committee—a *hyphen* which joins, a *buckle* which fastens, the legislative part of the State to the executive part of the State'. He points out that 'the efficient secret of the English Constitution may be described as the close union and nearly complete fusion of the executive and legislative powers'. Sir W. Ivor Jennings confirms Bagehot's definition when he speaks of the Cabinet as 'the core of the British constitutional system. It is the supreme directing authority. It integrates what would otherwise be a heterogeneous collection of authorities exercising a vast variety of functions. It provides unity to the British system of government.'[1]

It is interesting to note the effect of the lack of such a buckle in the American Constitution. There, the Executive (the President and his Cabinet) *cannot* belong to the Legislature, and as a result the two branches of the Constitution can come into conflict with each other and remain in that condition, to the great disadvantage of the public business. If such a situation arises here, it is bound to be resolved. One or other body must give way, or the dispute is decided by the voters at a general election.

Another constitutional convention which is generally maintained is that the heads of the great Departments of State should be men of high general ability rather than technical experts. The First Lord of the Admiralty is not normally an admiral, nor the Chancellor of the Exchequer a financier, nor the Minister of Health a doctor; though all Ministers have at their disposal the best technical advice, to which they constantly refer. Once again common sense is the guiding principle, it being considered that the opinion of a Minister of vision and general experience, fortified with the best technical advice, will usually outweigh the narrower and possibly prejudiced views of an expert.

When the Prime Minister's chosen colleagues, having accepted office

[1] *Cabinet Government*, 3rd ed., 1959, p. 1.

at the Queen's hands, take over the responsibilities of the great Departments of State (the Treasury, Foreign Office, Home Office, Board of Trade, Ministry of Defence, of Health, etc.), their powers come to them from two very different sources. The first is Parliament, which, by means of statutes, has defined many of the powers and duties, particularly of the younger Ministries. The second is the *Prerogative*, which is the residue of the discretionary powers which used to belong to the Crown and which have not been taken over by Parliament. It means the few things which the Queen can still do, and the many which her Ministers can do, without an Act of Parliament. We have already noticed the Sovereign's own slender personal prerogatives. It may be useful to form some idea of what her Ministers (the Executive) can do in her name. Incidentally the doctrine that the 'Queen (or King) can do no wrong' originated long before the establishment of the constitutional Monarchy, under which the Sovereign has *nominal* but not *real* responsibility for the actions of his or her Ministers.

The following extract from Bagehot will illustrate just how substantial the prerogative powers still are, but if the passage alarms you, you must remember that the Ministers who alone could exercise these powers are the servants of Parliament, and so the real power comes round again to the House of Commons.

Although Bagehot was writing in 1872, when the Sovereign was, of course, Queen Victoria, the present position so far as the Prerogative is concerned has not altered.

> I said in this book that it would very much surprise people if they were only told how many things the Queen could do without consulting Parliament, and it certainly has so proved for when the Queen abolished purchase in the army by an act of prerogative (after the Lords had rejected the Bill for doing so), there was a great and general astonishment.
>
> But this is nothing to what the Queen can by law do without consulting Parliament. Not to mention other things, she could disband the army (by law she cannot engage more than a certain number of men, but she is not obliged to engage any men); she could dismiss all the officers, from the General commanding-in-chief downwards; she could dismiss all the sailors too; she could sell off all our ships-of-war and all our naval stores; she could make a peace by the sacrifice of Cornwall, and begin a war for the conquest of Brittany. She could make every citizen in the United Kingdom, male or female, a peer; she could make every parish in the United Kingdom a 'university'. She could dismiss most of the civil servants; she could pardon all

> offenders. In a word, the Queen could by prerogative upset all the action of civil government within the Government, could disgrace the nation by a bad war or peace, and could, by disbanding our forces, whether land or sea, leave us defenceless against foreign nations.[1]

No wonder that foreigners find difficulty in understanding our Constitution, if that passage is to be reconciled with the maxim that 'the King can do no wrong'.

The great authority, Professor Dicey, remarks that:

> If government by Parliament is ever transformed into government by the House of Commons, the transformation will, it may be conjectured, be effected by use of the prerogatives of the Crown.[2]

From whichever source their powers come, the members of the Cabinet are responsible individually to their leader and collectively to the whole House of Commons, before which some of them usually appear daily while it is in session. A government of any complexion must at all times command a majority of votes in the House of Commons, and the Cabinet depends entirely upon the support of the party or parties which form this majority.

THE HOUSE OF LORDS

The House of Lords is the oldest part of the Constitution with the exception of the Crown. Apart from its legal function as a final Court of Appeal, it has principally an important revising and, occasionally, delaying role, though its debates on general issues of policy are of the greatest interest and are often said to surpass in quality those of the Commons.

Despite the introduction in 1958 of the system of life peerages, the vast majority of peers still sit in the second Chamber by virtue of heredity alone. They form a perpetual Conservative majority, responsible to no one but themselves, and they do not command the support which belongs to an elected body. To overwhelm a thorough-going opposition in the House of Lords a Labour Government would have to advise the creation of enough new peers to give that House a membership of about 1,500. Moreover, the House of Lords escaped the reforms which invigorated the House of Commons from the period 1832 onwards.

[1] *The English Constitution*, World's Classics ed., 1958, pp. 283–4.

[2] *Law of the Constitution*, 10th ed., 1959, p. 469.

The inevitable clash occurred early in this century, when the Lords, under threat of the creation of 500 new peers, passed the Parliament Act of 1911, which broke their power to delay Money Bills for more than one month or any Bills for more than two years. Two notable limitations of the new powers thus granted to the Commons were that Bills for extending the duration of Parliament were exempted altogether and that the desire of the people for the disputed legislation must have been plainly indicated by its passage in three successive sessions (which it is important to note need not be in the same Parliament) during the minimum period of two years mentioned in the Act.

A Bill to clip still further the powers of the Upper House by reducing this period to two successive sessions during a minimum of one year was eventually passed in 1949 under the provisions of the Parliament Act of 1911, after being twice rejected by the Lords. It revived the whole question of reform of the House of Lords, which has simmered ever since and has recently been brought to a head by the Report of the Joint Committee on House of Lords Reform, 1962 (see pp. 151–153).

THE HOUSE OF COMMONS

The functions of the House of Commons and the relationship of its members to their constituents will be considered in a later chapter. For the moment it is enough to repeat that the Commons are ultimately the dominant power in the Constitution because they hold the power of the purse; that for the most part they criticize legislation prepared by the Executive, though they can originate it; and that, while not themselves the Executive, they produce, support, criticize, dismiss and generally control the Government.

In their turn the Members of the House of Commons are responsible to their constituents, before whom they must appear at the next general election which, except in war-time, will be within five years of the last, at a time selected by the Prime Minister, usually in agreement with his colleagues. Bagehot objected to the expression 'checks and balances' in the sense of characteristics supposed to be inherent in different forms of government and happily combined in our constitutional Monarchy, but it is a phrase which correctly describes the interdependent components of our system. We see the Sovereign, with little evident power but on occasion a decisive opportunity; the Prime

Minister, holding the greatest power in the State but answerable with his Cabinet to the House of Commons; the latter divided into at least two parties, each responsible to their constituents, but all conscious of the Prime Minister's power to request the Sovereign to dissolve Parliament, thus causing them to face the electorate. The gradual growth and incessant interplay of these diverse elements provide a fascinating study of constitutional development.

Chapter IV

THE FUNCTIONS OF PARLIAMENT

'What the greatest inquest of the nation has begun its highest tribunal will accomplish.'

Edmund Burke, *during the impeachment of Warren Hastings*, 1788.

The trial of Warren Hastings in Westminster Hall lasted on and off for seven years and ended in an acquittal. The process of impeachment has fallen into disuse, but the greatest inquest of the nation is still probably the best description for the House of Commons.

What does Parliament really *do*? As so often in our Constitution, there is quite a broad gap between what it *could* do and what it *does* do. De Lolme summed the matter up in the well-known maxim that Parliament can do everything but make a woman a man and a man a woman.

Sir William Anson remarks that although the most striking attribute of Parliament is its legislative sovereignty, Members of either House may also:

> Discuss all matters of national or imperial concern, and criticize the conduct of ministers; either House collectively may address the Crown on matters of general policy, may institute inquiries, in the public interest, into the conduct of persons or public bodies; while in the last resort Parliament may bring to justice a great political offender.[1]

[1] *Law and Custom of the Constitution*, 5th ed., 1922, Vol. I, p. 48.

It is usually convenient to separate these functions under the headings of legislation, finance and criticism.

LEGISLATION

Sir Edward Coke[1] described the power and jurisdiction of Parliament, in the lawyers' sense of Sovereign, Lords and Commons, acting together, as being 'so transcendent and absolute that it cannot be confined within any bounds'. Blackstone[2] remarked in a classic passage that Parliament

> hath sovereign and uncontrollable authority in the making, confirming, enlarging, restraining, abrogating, repealing, reviving and expounding of laws, concerning matters of all possible denominations, ecclesiastical or temporal, civil, military, maritime, or criminal: this being the place where that absolute despotic power, which must in all governments reside somewhere, is entrusted by the constitution of these Kingdoms. All mischiefs and grievances, operations and remedies, that transcend the ordinary course of the laws, are within the reach of this extraordinary tribunal. It can regulate or new-model the succession to the Crown; as was done in the reign of Henry VIII, and William III. It can alter the established religion of the land; as was done, in a variety of instances, in the reigns of King Henry VIII, and his three children. It can change and create afresh even the Constitution of the Kingdom and of Parliaments themselves; as was done by the Act of Union (with Scotland), and the several statutes for triennial and septennial elections. It can, in short, do everything that is not naturally impossible.

There are two necessary qualifications to these comprehensive assertions. The first is that Parliament only has a present power: it cannot bind itself or its successors not to make changes in the future. The second is, as we have seen, that the Parliament Acts of 1911 and 1949 varied the legislative powers of the two Chambers, leaving the House of Commons in a dominant position and able in exceptional circumstances to dispense with the concurrence of the House of Lords.

FINANCE

We have already seen how the Commons acquired their full and exclusive rights of taxation. During the Stuart period, the royal

[1] Lord Chief Justice of England, and one of the most famous of all English lawyers, 1552–1632.

[2] Sir William Blackstone, another English judge, and famous author of the *Commentaries*, 1723–80.

Executive was obliged to seek grants to meet exceptional liabilities of government from a reluctant House of Commons, who had the power to provide for the carrying out of a policy and little control over its formation. Under Charles II the Commons first made use of 'appropriation' to increase their control over the Executive. That is to say, they limited the use of the supplies they granted to stated purposes, and took care that their wishes in this respect were obeyed. But the system was not perfected until the setting up of the Public Accounts Committee in 1862 and the passing of the Exchequer and Audit Act in 1866 completed the new organization of control over the national accounts instituted by Mr. Gladstone and his colleagues.

The financial functions of Parliament may be said to date in their modern form from the Revolution. Prior to 1688 the Crown handled the national finance alone. If the country could be run on less than the proceeds of the Crown Lands and the taxes settled on the King for life, the balance went into his own pocket. If there was a deficiency the Sovereign was obliged to apply to the Commons. The beginning of a vital change came with the reign of William and Mary. Gradually the Sovereign was placed upon an allowance known as the Civil List, at first combining the charges for the Civil Departments and for the royal establishment but ultimately confined to the latter. The Commons were forced, in a period of frequent wars whose cost was far beyond the Sovereign's resources, to take over the handling of the naval and military expenditure, and they took to voting the necessary sums annually, thus acquiring a further great power to review and control the conduct of the King's Ministers.

The relative financial functions of the constituent powers of Parliament are still most tersely and accurately summed up by the words of Sir T. Erskine May:

> The Crown demands money, the Commons grant it, and the Lords assent to the grant; but the Commons do not vote money unless it be required by the Crown; nor impose or augment taxes, unless such taxation be necessary for the public service *as declared by the Crown through its Constitutional advisers.*

The Parliament Act of 1911 in effect only underlined the position by withdrawing the power of the Lords to do anything but assent to the supplies granted by the Commons to the Executive.

The financial functions of the House of Commons are therefore comprehensive. No tax is imposed and no expenditure sanctioned except by the authority of an Act of Parliament, which, in these respects, practically means the authority of the House of Commons. But only the Government may recommend the spending of public money—that rule is fundamental to the Constitution. They have to recommend the finding of the money as well as its spending. If Private Members (those not members of the Government) were once permitted, except in the most general sense, to make proposals which would financially benefit their constituencies or the 'interests' (see pp. 52–56) which they represent, the result might be a return to the 'jobs' and scandals of the eighteenth century, and the evils sometimes exposed in local government in present days.

The House first grappled with this problem in 1706, after a session during which a flood of petitions was presented from persons, such as officers claiming arrears of pay, whose demands 'being often promoted by Members who were friends to the parties, and carrying with them the appearance of justice or of charity, induced the rest of the House to wish well to, or at most to be indifferent to their success; and by this means large sums were granted to private persons improvidently, and sometimes without sufficient grounds'.[1]

CRITICISM

The remaining functions of Parliament, which we now class together under the general heading of 'criticism', were admirably described by Bagehot by means of a sub-division into four parts. The most important he gave as that of *electing* the Prime Minister, and he compared the Commons favourably in this respect with the American electoral college, since the Commons not only elected but also dismissed and remained in continuous relations with the Prime Minister, leading and being led, and forming a close link between him and the country.

Second in order of importance, he said the House of Commons had an *informing* function, a duty to present grievances, not so much to the Crown, as in old days, but to the nation who are the modern sovereign power. He found the English fair-minded but not quick of apprehension, and claimed that it was of immense importance to have in the country one assembly where the championship of a cause or opinion,

[1] Hatsell's *Precedents of Proceedings in the House of Commons*, 1818, Vol. III, pp. 241–2.

The impressive ceremonial part of Parliament: the Sovereign driving in state to open a session of Parliament

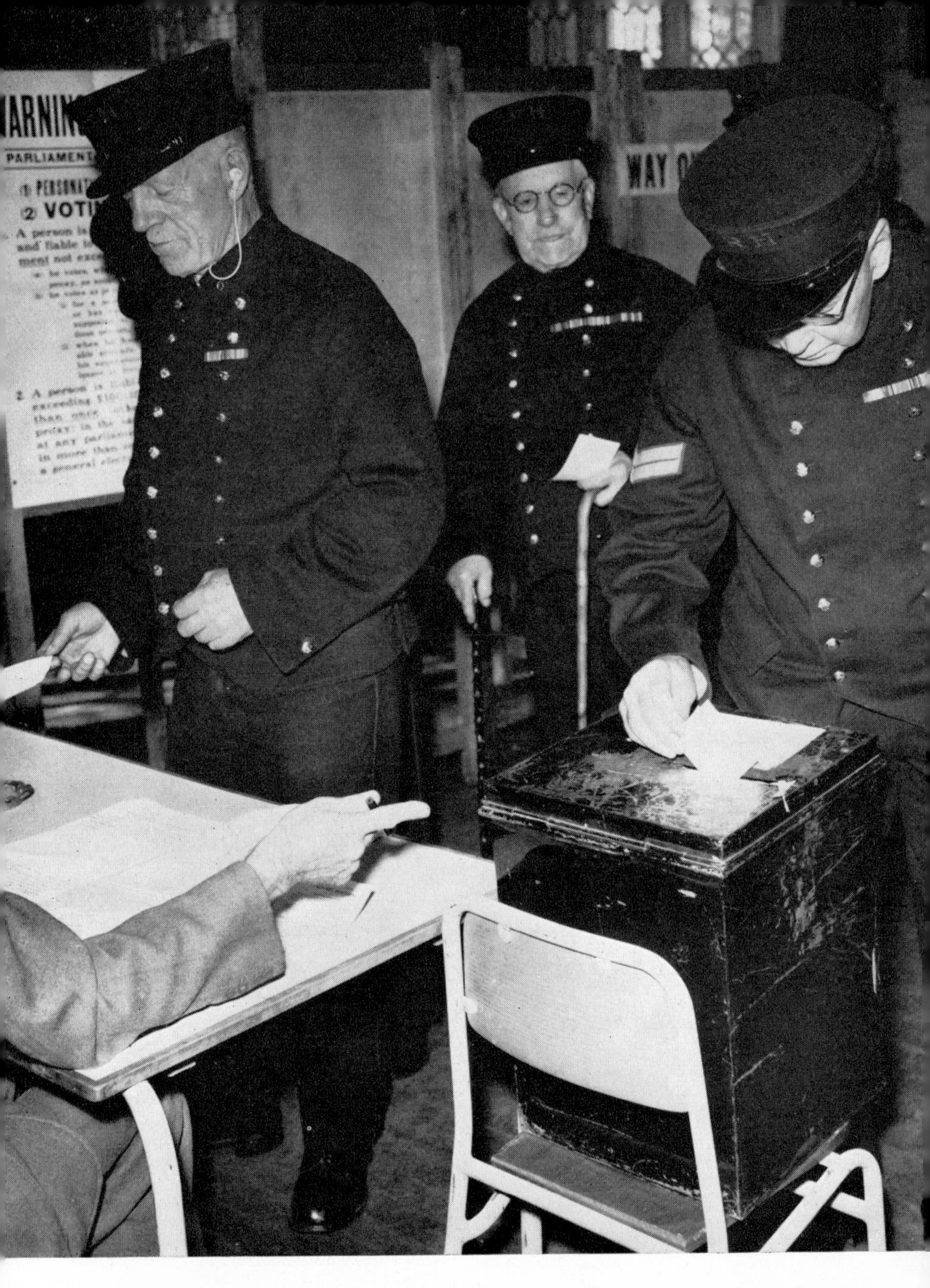

The essential foundation of Parliament: a polling station. The right of all the people to vote freely and secretly to elect their representatives to Parliament, in absolute safety from influence or interference, is the kernel of democracy, the envy of many foreigners and would have been unknown to our own ancestors. 'Freedom,' it has been said, 'is political power divided into small fragments.'

however unfamiliar or unpopular, by a certain number of Members, would at least secure to it consideration.

The third function he named *expressive*, the expression of the people's will, and this *lyrical* function as he called it, he claimed was well performed:

> On foreign matters, where we cannot legislate, whatever the English nation thinks, or thinks it thinks, as to the critical events of the world, whether in Denmark, in Italy, or America, and no matter whether it thinks wisely or unwisely, that same something, wise or unwise, will be thoroughly well said in Parliament. The lyrical function of Parliament, if I may use such a phrase, is well done; it pours out in characteristic words the characteristic heart of the nation.

The fourth, Bagehot called the *teaching* function:

> A great and open council of considerable men cannot be placed in the middle of a society without altering that society. It ought to alter it for the better.

He added, in words which are at least as true today:

> The greatest teacher of all in Parliament, the headmaster of the nation, the great elevator of the country—so far as Parliament elevates it—must be the Prime Minister: he has an influence, an authority, a facility in giving a great tone to discussion, or a mean tone, which no other man has.[1]

Let us now take one of the most up-to-date authoritative opinions to be published upon this important subject. Sir W. Ivor Jennings states that 'the true function of the House (of Commons) is to question and debate the policy of the Government', and he goes on to balance in the most interesting manner the two main influences which play upon the House during the discussion of each kind of business. On the one hand is the Government with its big stick of the threat of dissolution. On the other is the fact that government in this country is by the consent of the governed, and does eventually rest upon the public will.

> When the Government has a majority in both Houses, the 'transcendent and absolute' authority of Parliament is the authority of the Government. It is not really transcendent and absolute. Behind the Government and behind the House of Commons stands public opinion. . . . The fact that no Government

[1] *The English Constitution*, World's Classics ed., 1958, p. 149 *et seq.*

could secure powers to kill all blue-eyed babies is not due to any legal limitations in the power of Parliament but to the fact that both the Government and the House of Commons derive their authority from the people.[1]

Three notable occasions when the public made its opinion felt have been (1) in 1935, when widespread public criticism compelled the Government to denounce the Hoare-Laval agreement concerning Abyssinia; (2) in 1936 during the Abdication crisis, when Members dispersed to their constituencies in grave concern to gauge public opinion, and returned to assure the Government of overwhelming public assent to its conduct; and (3) in 1954 when public indignation at overbearing bureaucratic action by civil servants in the famous 'Crichel Down case' resulted in the resignation of the Minister of Agriculture, who felt himself ultimately responsible for what had happened. There have, of course, been several less spectacular occasions when the Government has given way to criticism expressed through Members of Parliament,[2] and infinitely more, especially during the Second World War, when public opinion supported and 'comforted' the Government's endeavours.

A case where the Government did *not* give way was the amendment to the Education Bill, carried in the House of Commons, giving equal pay for men and women teachers. But even here, in deference to public opinion, a Royal Commission was appointed in 1944.

The principal change since Bagehot's day has undoubtedly been a tendency for the Government's (and especially a strong Prime Minister's) power to increase at the expense of Parliament. There is more essential business and it is more complicated. Less time is left for the activities of Private Members. Therefore it would probably be fair to accept the above account of Parliament's functions with an emphasis upon the added strength of the Government which Sir W. Ivor Jennings describes. Parliament legislates, but it is largely the Government's legislative proposals and always the Government's financial proposals which are discussed. *Parliament does not govern*, because that is not its function. It incessantly questions and criticizes the Government's policy, and, in the process, it still has enormous influence upon the

[1] Sir W. Ivor Jennings, *Parliament*, 2nd ed., 1957, p. 8.

[2] Jennings gives as examples: the withdrawal by the Government of Unemployment Assistance Regulations (1934); of the Coal Mines Bill (1936); of proposals for a National Defence Contribution (1937); and the radical amendment of the Population Bill (1937).

choice of the Executive; it sometimes 'breaks' a Minister by exposing his incompetence; it is still the great forum of debate for thrashing out all questions and for the expression of the people's will; it is still the grand inquest of the nation for the raising of all grievances; it still perhaps—on occasion—teaches. This provides some answer to our first question—Why doesn't Parliament *do* more? Why does it only *talk*? Parliament's business is to talk; to focus the wishes of the nation quickly and closely upon Downing Street and Whitehall (this it does supremely well); to debate, and by its debating to procure the required action on the part of the Executive—the Government.

Chapter V

MEMBERS AND THEIR DUTIES

'So that it is a matter most essential to the liberties of this kingdom, that such members be delegated to this important trust, as are most eminent for their probity, their fortitude, and their knowledge; for it was a known apophthegm of the great lord treasurer Burleigh "that England could never be ruined but by a parliament".'

Sir William Blackstone (1723–80).

'But it is not only the antiquity of Parliament which cuts a man down in size. It is its terrible power to sum up character and detect fraud. Like a television camera, Parliament catches him at his weakest and most exposed.'

Nigel Nicolson, *People and Parliament.*

As soon as the Sovereign has by Proclamation dissolved one Parliament and summoned another to meet in its place, preparations are started for a general election. But not until Nomination Day will it be known whether the election in any particular constituency need be contested. On that day, not later than the eighth after the Proclamation, the Returning Officer, who is usually the Sheriff, Mayor or Chairman of the Urban Council, receives nominations from candidates, and, if more than one candidate is nominated, a contested election takes place nine days later. Nomination consists of handing in the candidate's name on a paper signed by a proposer, seconder and eight other electors of the constituency, and candidates are all obliged to make a deposit of £150, which is forfeited if they secure less than one-eighth of the votes polled in the constituency.

From this point most people are perfectly familiar with the course of a general election. Party committee rooms spring up newly painted in the streets, and the names and photographs of the candidates appear on every wall. Meanwhile, party programmes are published in the Press or in pamphlets, and the electioneering addresses of the candidates drop into the electors' letter-boxes. Canvassers call to explain and argue and persuade. Meetings are held in the open-air, or in halls or schoolrooms, and loudspeaker vans tour the streets and villages. At last comes polling-day, with cheering supporters wearing rosettes, and motor-cars, decked with ribbon and streamers of party colours, to carry voters to the poll. In an orderly polling-booth the all-important cross is marked in secret and the slip of paper dropped into the ballot-box.

All British subjects of either sex are eligible for membership, who are not minors, lunatics, bankrupts, traitors or felons serving sentence, Peers (except Irish Peers), clergymen of the Roman Catholic or the established Churches, judges, civil servants on the active list, and a few other categories of persons. Candidates need not (as they must for instance in the United States of America) inhabit their constituencies. This rule has, through the centuries, greatly benefited the country, since the acceptance of non-residents (or 'carpet-baggers' as they are called), often of outstanding quality, has given the House of Commons a more national outlook and a more distinguished membership than it would otherwise have commanded. Thus there is nothing whatever to prevent any reader of this book from himself standing for Parliament if he is not excluded under the above list and if he is prepared to produce or collect £150 and can persuade any ten electors in a constituency to nominate him to the Returning Officer. But in practice most serious candidates are party nominees.[1] Why this should be so and exactly how parliamentary candidates are selected are questions which lie outside the scope of this book. They have been fully dealt with recently by several authors, one of whom has spent ten years in studying the subject of parliamentary representation.[2] Two

[1] At the 1959 election there were 1,519 party candidates as against 17 independents.

[2] J. F. S. Ross: *Parliamentary Representation*, 2nd ed., 1948. See also McCallum and Readman: *The British General Election of 1945*; H. G. Nicholas: *The British General*

recent works are of especial interest since they deal respectively with the *British Political Elite*[1] and *Amateurs and Professionals in British Politics*.[2]

Who *are* the best men for Westminster? Frenchmen believe that human perfection is reached by '*une belle femme avec l'esprit d'un honnête homme*'. Obviously what is required for Parliament is variety, both of men and women, with more ability and less self-interest than the rest of us. Today, more than ever before, Parliament needs men and women from all walks of life who will pool their knowledge and experience in the national interest. Scientists, doctors, teachers, businessmen, lawyers, trade unionists, miners, farmers—all have a vital part to play at Westminster. But the most essential requisite is still the '*honnête homme*'. The institution of Parliament is often described as an intricate machine, superbly adapted to its varied tasks. It is all that and much else, yet it could be even more exquisitely contrived and still be worthless in the defence of our liberties if its Members lacked the necessary qualities. Facing page 37 of this book the ballot-box is given a place of honour, and indeed it is a vital part of the machinery of democracy—but only the machinery. Even the secret ballot can be circumvented. The real heroes of Parliament are those Members who, with or without exceptional ability, through its long history have fought for freedom and the general good with courage, energy and common sense, and who have been, above all, *men without any personal axe to grind*. The late Lord Campion, an expert and penetrating observer of Parliaments all over the world, found a specific basis for British parliamentary success. He believed that it was the *gentlemanly* qualities which were all-important; and it is sad that the book on the subject which he was contemplating during his last years was never written.

The formal parliamentary rules of courtesy are of course vital. Some years ago a Chief Whip of celebrated imperturbability was moved to surprising anger by some Members who jokingly prevented their opponents by force from entering the division lobby to vote. Doubtless dim memories of Pride's Purge and of earlier ructions in the history of

Election of 1950; D. E. Butler: *The British General Election of 1951*; D. E. Butler: *The British General Election of 1955*, and D. E. Butler and R. Rose: *The British General Election of 1959*.

[1] By W. L. Guttsman, 1963.

[2] By Philip W. Buck, 1963.

Parliament had made him apprehensive. Even the lesser rules of Parliament are important, such as the exact punctuality of the Speaker's procession; the meticulous discipline kept by the Serjeant at Arms in the Galleries; the promptitude of the publication of the Official Report of debates. The efficiency of Commonwealth and foreign legislatures is often seen to be in direct proportion to these observances.

But the national characteristics which Lord Campion had more in mind were above all those derived from our celebrated 'phlegm', which excites even among our enemies on the Continent a strong, though often begrudging, admiration. Aided no doubt by the delaying Channel moat, our nation has developed through the centuries a contemplative coolness of judgement, an aversion to hasty and extreme action, and an independent outlook which may have helped the democratic cause.

Lord Campion did not of course refer to qualities which are sometimes attributed to a single social class, or to rank and riches generally. He meant those qualities of tolerance, sincerity, and fair-mindedness which belong emphatically to individuals of every class, and which have produced that spirit of reasonable compromise which makes democracy work.

It is as notoriously difficult to define a gentleman as it is to define literary style, except perhaps in a negative sense. 'The only infallible rule we know,' said Surtees, 'is, that the man who is always talking about being a gentleman never is one.' It is probably true that in Britain the status of a true gentleman of any social class ranks, like the Victoria Cross, slightly above that of a peer of the realm. 'Somebody has said,' remarked Burke, 'that a king may make a nobleman but he cannot make a gentleman!' 'My state is well,' says one of Shakespeare's characters, 'I am a gentleman.'

Lord Campion was fond of remembering, too, the old observation that the wisdom of the whole House of Commons usually far exceeds that of any of its Members. He concluded that since the nation and its ideals are reflected in Parliament, and its finest qualities are tested there, this gentlemanly quality, which is so particularly necessary to Parliament, does in the main eventually prevail.

If, after all this, the reader asks to have the pattern of the perfect Member of Parliament pointed out to him, one is tempted to pass over a great many brilliant and interesting names and to alight instead upon a very undramatic person. It is the stout, simple figure of John Charles Spencer, later Earl Spencer, who, as Viscount Althorp, was a Member of the House of Commons from 1804 till 1834, and led the Whigs as Chancellor of the Exchequer under Earl Grey throughout the struggles for the great Reform Bill. He was a shy, tongue-tied man, without the least grain of ambition, devoted to country pursuits and detesting politics, who was only kept in public life by the almost physical persuasions of his friends. He was a notably poor speaker, with no brilliant qualities whatsoever, yet he became 'the very best leader of the House of Commons that any party ever had', and some claimed that the most important measure of the century would not have passed without him. 'It was Althorp carried the Bill; his fine temper did it.'[1]

How was all this achieved? The answer lies in Althorp's complete disinterestedness and integrity, which won eventually from friends and political enemies alike a confidence and regard which are perhaps unique in British politics. Lord Holland described him as 'a man who acts on all matters with a scrupulous, deliberate, and inflexible regard to his public duty and private conscience'. One likes to think of him standing at the box in the House of Commons, buttoned up to the chin 'even in the hottest weather, when other Members were within a few degrees of suffocation',[2] imperturbable and serene amid the din of political strife; or, much more happily, working all day in his shirt-sleeves at the Smithfield Club, to get the beasts into their stalls for the next day's show; but always the lovable, simple, yet effective English gentleman, representative of the best in any period and any rank of life. It is fortunate that few Parliaments—or Cabinets—have hitherto lacked men, universally trusted and respected, of a kind of whom Althorp was the perfect type.

Certain questions are often asked concerning the relations which ought to subsist between constituents and their Members:

> *Do Members represent all their constituents or only those who voted for them?*

The answer is that in so far as the minority have no one except the Member to represent them, he should (and does) serve them equally

[1] *Dictionary of National Biography*, 1937–38, Vol. XVIII, p. 772.

[2] *Random Recollections of the House of Commons*, 1830–35, by One of No Party, 1836, p. 174.

with his own supporters. Very often, of course, the Member remains unaware whether he received the votes of those who approach him, or how they will vote at the next election; but there seems little doubt that this duty of equal service to all constituents is honourably implemented. Nevertheless, under our present electoral system the political views of many constituents remain unrepresented.

Are Members of Parliament representatives or delegates, that is to say are they, once elected, free to use their own judgement (subject to any specific pledges they may have chosen to give) and to do their best for their constituents and the country generally, or are they restricted in voice and votes to act as the majority which elected them depute them to do?

Three authorities may be cited in reply to this question. Sir William Yonge, one of the most prominent politicians of his day, speaking of Members of the House of Commons, said in 1745:

> Every one knows that, by our Constitution, after a gentleman is chosen, he is the representative, or, if you please, the attorney of the people of England, and as such is at full freedom to act as he thinks best for the people of England in general. He may receive, he may ask, he may even follow the advice of his particular constituents; but he is not obliged, nor ought he, to follow their advice, if he thinks it inconsistent with the general interest of his country.

Secondly, Sir George Cornewall Lewis quotes perhaps the most useful definition, from David Hume, the Scottish philosopher, who was writing at about the same time as Yonge:

> Hume remarked long ago that this question [of instructions from or pledges to constituents], is in fact, one of *degree*; all admit, he says, that a member ought to attach some weight to the views of his constituents; all admit that he is not absolutely bound by their instructions. The difficulty is, to hit the right mean between these extremes. It cannot, indeed, be disputed that it is the duty of every representative to watch over the peculiar interests of that district which he more immediately represents and to which he is directly responsible; and to secure, so far as he is able, that a due regard be paid to its interest, in connexion with the general interests of the community. But he must not pursue that interest exclusively, or make it his paramount object, as if he belonged to a federal diet, in which each member is an ambassador from a sovereign and independent State treating with the other ambassadors according to his instructions.[1]

[1] Sir G. Cornewall Lewis, *Essay on the influence of Authority in matters of opinion*, 1849, p. 271.

Finally, the classic description of a Member's obligations is contained in Burke's address to the electors of Bristol in 1774. It is of sufficient importance to be quoted at length:

> Certainly, gentlemen, it ought to be the happiness and glory of a representative to live in the strictest union, the closest correspondence, and the most unreserved communication with his constituents. Their wishes ought to have great weight with him; their opinion high respect; their business unremitted attention. It is his duty to sacrifice his repose, his pleasures, his satisfactions, to theirs, and above all, ever, and in all cases, to prefer their interest to his own. But, his unbiased opinion, his mature judgment, his enlightened conscience, he ought not to sacrifice to you, to any man, or to any set of men living. These he does not derive from your pleasure; no, nor from the law and the Constitution. They are a trust from Providence, for the abuse of which he is deeply answerable. Your representative owes you, not his industry only, but his judgment; and he betrays, instead of serving you, if he sacrifices it to your opinion.
>
> My worthy colleague says his will ought to be subservient to yours. If that is all the thing is innocent: if government were a matter of will upon my side, yours, without question, ought to be superior. But government and legislation are matters of reason and judgment, and not of inclination; and what sort of reason is that, in which the determination precedes the discussion; in which one set of men deliberate, and another decide; and where those who form the conclusion are perhaps three hundred miles distant from those who hear the arguments?
>
> To deliver an opinion, is the right of all men; that of constituents is a weighty and respectable opinion, which a representative ought always to rejoice to hear; and which he ought always most seriously to consider. But authoritative instructions; mandates issued, which the member is bound blindly and implicitly to obey, to vote and to argue for, though contrary to the clearest conviction of his judgment and conscience—these are things utterly unknown to the laws of the land, and which arise from a fundamental mistake of the whole order and tenor of our Constitution.
>
> Parliament is not a congress of ambassadors from different and hostile interests; which interests each must maintain, as an agent, and advocate, against other agents and advocates; but Parliament is a deliberative assembly of one nation, with one interest, that of the whole; where, not local purposes, not local prejudices, ought to guide, but the general good, resulting from the general reason of the whole. You choose a member indeed: but when you have chosen him, he is not a member of Bristol, but he is a Member of Parliament. If the local constituent should have an interest, or should form a

hasty opinion, evidently opposite to the real good of the rest of the community, the member for that place ought to be as far as any other from any endeavour to give it effect.

It is over 200 years since Sir William Yonge's clear and forceful opinion was uttered, yet it and the others remain authoritative to this day. But what examples these early utterances must have provided to contemporary foreigners of the baffling and perhaps 'hypocritical' divergence between theory and practice in our Constitution! Yonge was George II's 'Stinking Yonge', of whom it was said that 'his name was proverbially used to express everything pitiful, corrupt and contemptible'. Burke was, of course, a very different character, but he lived in an age of notorious corruption, and a short digression may be useful to show how the character of Membership has improved during the last 150 years.

Before the Reform Act of 1832 reorganized the law, bribery and corruption unblushingly controlled elections, particularly in the boroughs. From two to twenty guineas per vote were figures commonly paid, and there are innumerable stories of how the contemporary laws against bribery were circumvented. A common attitude was for the voter to ask 'You will do what is usual after the election, Sir, I suppose?'; while *The Times* of 20th June, 1826, speaking of the general election in that year, remarks: 'At Sudbury, four cabbages sold for £10, and a plate of gooseberries fetched £25; the sellers where these articles were so dear being voters. At Great Marlow, on the contrary, things were cheap, and an elector during the election bought a sow and nine young pigs for a penny.'

Voters varied in numbers from a handful in the small boroughs up to thousands in Bristol, for instance, or the City of London; but constituencies of less than a score were common enough. Elections (with public voting) were usually orgies of drunkenness and gluttony, at the candidates' expense, and although they could sometimes be managed cheaply, where electors were few enough to be gathered round a dining-table, the cost was often enormous where they numbered thousands, and had to be carried to the poll from all parts of the country. In 1831 Lord Ashley (later Lord Shaftesbury, the great philanthropist) after winning Dorset as an anti-Reform candidate, was faced with bills for £15,600, of which £12,525 was paid to inns and public houses for refreshments for the people—at a time when most drinks were a penny or so a glass. In 1820 Mr. James spent £13,000 in *un*successfully contesting Carlisle. Payments of far greater sums are recorded. Liverpool cost Lord Penrhyn nearly £30,000 in 1790 and failed to elect him, while forty years later the vast sum of £80,000 was expended in the same constituency to bribe 2,060 freemen. The 'patrons' who thus procured the 'interest' of boroughs included the Treasury itself and members of the great landowning families. In 1816, out of 658 Members, it has been calculated that 300 were nominated by Peers and 187 by the Government and commoners, leaving only 171 to be returned independently. Boroughs were treated as property and advertised for sale in the papers. Between 1812 and 1832 £5,000 to £6,000 was the ordinary price of a seat purchased for a Parliament or £1,800 if rented for a year.[1]

Many of the men who bought or rented these seats aimed only, by voting or intriguing for the Government, at securing offices and appointments which would be a manifold recompense for their outlay on the road to Parliament. Thus, from the electors who regularly voted for 'Mr. Most', to the patron who paid them, and from the Member who bought his seat to the Government who finally bribed him with a sinecure, the edifice of corruption was complete. But although it was a corruption of system and habit rather than of character, and Ministries governed patriotically in spite of it, Parliaments before 1832 were inconceivably different from those of today.

With the rarest exceptions the personnel of the House consisted of aristocrats, landed gentlemen, rich bankers, merchants, brewers and traders, and East Indian Nabobs; manufacturers and their sons were only beginning to arrive. By contrast, the education and main occupations of the Members of the House of Commons elected in 1959 appear to have been as shown on the opposite page:

Plenty of corruption lingered on after 1832, but enormous strides have since been made in the direction of a free and fair Parliament. Secret voting by the electorate, which prevented intimidation by employers, came with the Ballot Act of 1872. New classes of male voters were added to the electorate in 1867, 1884 and 1918. Women aged thirty or more were admitted in 1918 and those aged twenty-one or more in 1928. The position today is that practically all men and women

[1] E. and A. G. Porritt: *The Unreformed House of Commons*, 1903, Vol. I, p. 358.

COMPOSITION OF THE HOUSE OF COMMONS, 1959

EDUCATION

	Conservative	*Labour*	*Liberal*	*Total*
Oxford	107	33	2	142
Cambridge	80	14	3	97
Other Universities[1]	31	64	1	96
Eton	73	3	2	78
Harrow	20	–	–	20
Other Public Schools	155	39	2	196
Service Colleges	37	1	–	38
Grammar, Secondary and Combination Schools	52	86	–	138
Elementary	5	54	–	59

[1] Includes Ruskin College and Labour and Co-operative Colleges.

MAIN OCCUPATIONS

	Conservative	*Labour*	*Liberal*	*Total*
Barristers	56	22	4	82
Solicitors	10	8	1	19
Journalists	10	22	–	32
Broadcasters	2	2	–	4
Directors	70	6	–	76
Manufacturers	3	2	1	6
Landowners and Farmers	30	4	–	34
Accountants	5	1	–	6
Publishers	4	–	–	4
Teachers and Lecturers	2	25	–	27
Engineers	3	9	–	12
Surveyors	3	–	–	3
Medicine and Dentistry	1	5	–	6
Brokers	12	1	–	13
Regular Forces	25	3	–	28
Diplomatic Service	3	–	–	3
Trade Union, etc., officials	–	40	–	40
Miners	–	23	–	23
Railwaymen	–	9	–	9
Secretaries	–	3	–	3

The above tables are taken from *The Times* of 19th October, 1959.

PRINCIPAL CHANGES IN THE ELECTORATE 1831–1951

'NINETY PER CENT. IN A HUNDRED YEARS'

Date	Title of Amending Act	Main Classes of population added	Electoral qualifications	Remarks	Date of a general election before and after the change	Statistics to show the effect of these changes[1]: Total Electorate	Population aged 20 years and over	Electorate as percentage of population over 20 years	
1831			Counties—40/– freeholders Boroughs—a medley of narrow and unequal franchises						
1832	Representation of the People Act, 1832, 2 & 3 Will. 4. c. 45 (known as the 'First Reform Act')	Small landowners, tenant farmers and shopkeepers	Counties: 40/– freeholders; £10 copyholders; £10 leaseholders; £50 tenants at will Boroughs—£10 householders	Similar Acts which were passed for Scotland and Ireland in 1832 differed in detail from the English Act	Before (1831)	509,391	10,207,000	5.0	
					After (1832)	720,784	10,207,000	7.1	
1867	Representation of the People Act, 1867 30 & 31 Vict. c. 102 (sometimes called the 'Second Reform Act')	Smaller agricultural owners and tenants; artizans and many town labourers	Counties: 40/– freeholders; £5 copyholders; £5 leaseholders; £12 tenants at will Boroughs: All occupiers of dwelling houses rated to poor rates, lodgers occupying £10 lodgings	Reform Bills were introduced in the Commons in 1852, 1854, 1859, 1860 and 1866.	Before (1864)	1,130,372	13,051,816	9.0	
				Similar Acts which were passed for Scotland and Ireland in 1868 differed in detail from the English Act	After (1868)	2,231,030	13,625,658	16.4	

1884	Representation of the People Act, 1884 48 & 49 Vict. c. 3 (sometimes called the 'Third Reform Act')	Agricultural and other labourers in country	Counties and Boroughs	A uniform householder and lodger franchise in effect giving a vote to every man over 21 who had a decent settled home	The Ballot Act was passed in 1872. No woman could yet vote	Before (1883)	2,955,190	16,426,233	18.0 
						After (1886)	4,965,618	17,394,014	28.5 
1918	Representation of the People Act, 1918 7 & 8 Geo. 5 c. 64 and Parliament (Qualification of Women) Act, 1918 8 & 9 Geo. 5 c. 47	Women of 30 and over	Counties and Boroughs	*Men* Final assimilation by abolition of property qualification in counties. Qualification now either six months' residence or occupation of £10 business premises *Women* Enfranchised at 30 and over	Plural voting by University graduates and holders of the business premises qualification was restricted to two votes, including one for residence	Before (1914)	7,483,165	24,969,241	30.0 
						After (1921)	19,984,037	26,846,785	74.0 
1928	Representation of the People (Equal Franchise) Act, 1928 18 & 19 Geo. 5. c. 12	Women 21 to 30	Women enfranchised at 21. In effect every man or woman of 21 and upwards thereafter entitled to vote		Male and female adult suffrage achieved	Before (1927)	21,895,347	29,654,721	74.0 
						After (1931)	29,175,608	30,096,135	96.9 
1948	Representation of the People Act, 1948 11 & 12 Geo. 6 c. 65 (Consolidated in 1949)		University constituencies and all plural voting abolished		'One man (or woman)—one vote'	After (1951)	34,915,112	(Dec. 1950) 36,078,000	96.7 

[1] These figures refer to Great Britain and Ireland until the separation of Eire: thereafter to Great Britain and Northern Ireland only.
The available statistics of population upon which the diagrams at the end of this Table are based relate to persons aged 20 years and over and not to those aged over 21. When the relevant allowance is made it will be seen that complete adult suffrage for both sexes has been achieved within a century.

who have reached the age of twenty-one have the right to vote; in 1959, the electorate was estimated at 99 per cent of the adult population.[1]

Our democracy has also steadily progressed towards the ideals of 'one man one vote' and 'one vote one value'. The Representation of the People Acts, 1948 and 1949 (see pp. 105–106), abolished plural voting and rearranged the constituencies to contain equal numbers of electors so far as is possible having regard to historic and local unities and geographical considerations. The *average* number of electors is about 57,000 out of a total electorate of just under 36 millions and a total population of 53 millions.

Should Members receive financial support from their parties or from outside individuals or bodies?

This question has been much discussed lately, inside and outside Parliament. All that can be done here is briefly to state the facts of the position.

In the Middle Ages, when a shilling was worth much more than the modern £, Members were paid at the daily rate of 4s. for Knights of the Shire, and 2s. for burgesses. At that date the relationship of a Member to his constituents was little more than that of a delegate. They paid him wages and often issued him with specific instructions as to his conduct in Parliament. The poet Marvell (1620–78) is considered to have been the last Member to receive wages, freely paid by his constituents.

Before the payment of Members was re-introduced in 1911, the membership of working men would have been impossible without outside financial support, and the support available at the time was from Trade Unions and not from parties. Furthermore, the expenditure of Union funds for this purpose was sanctioned by the Trade Union Act of 1913. At the present time many Members receive support from their parties. In addition, it is an open secret that, while on the one side the Trade Unions pay parliamentary allowances to the Members on their panels, on the other, great industrial concerns also subsidize Members to represent their interests, usually by the method of appointing them to directorships.[2] The alleged danger is, of course, that these interests

[1] For conditions governing the franchise and list of disqualifications, see Wade and Phillips: *Constitutional Law*, 6th ed., 1960, pp. 100–103.

[2] See *Parliamentary Representation* by J. F. S. Ross, 2nd ed., 1948, pp. 138, 163.

The Parliament of Henry VIII, probably the earliest authentic view of Parliament in session

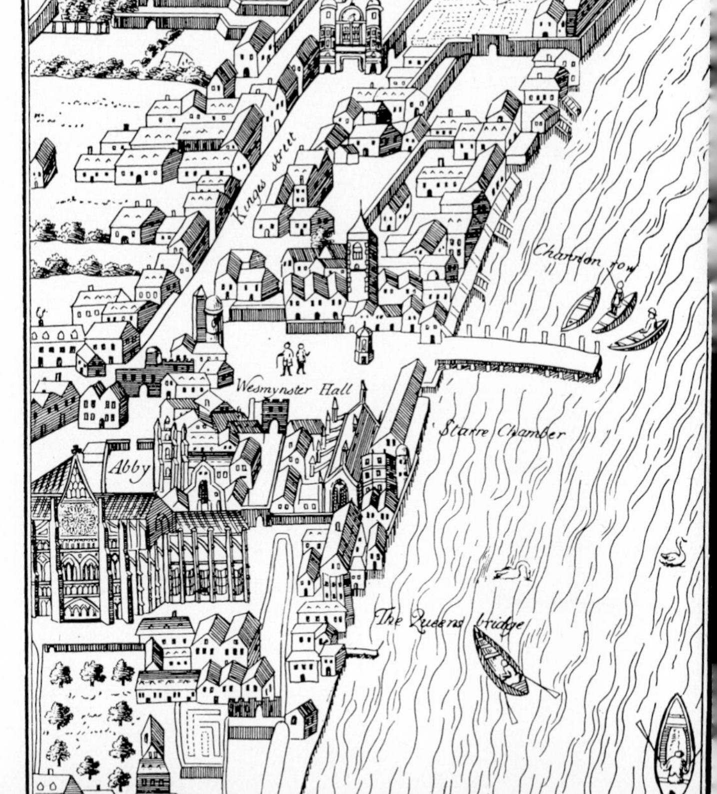

Bird's-eye view of the Palace of Westminster, taken from Aggas's sixteenth-century Map of Westminster

Guy Fawkes's lantern

Guy Fawkes's signature, before and after torture

might, on occasion, run counter to those of the Members' own constituents, or of the country as a whole, and that, at the worst, such Members might degenerate into the paid delegates of sectional interests and pressure groups. In any case it is a far cry to the free and independent membership of the ideal House of Commons described by Yonge and Burke.

Some critics only see harm in these payments where they are secret, and go so far as to recommend that the details of Members' incomes should be published. Others condemn the practice without reserve, and look forward to a date when it will be as inconceivable as the corrupt practices, so prevalent before 1832, are today.[1]

The salary of Members of Parliament was raised in 1937 from £400 to £600 a year, and they also enjoyed free rail, sea or air travel between their constituencies and homes and Westminster. Of this sum £100 was allowed free of income tax for secretarial assistance, postages, and other expenses; and if these could be shown to exceed £100, a further allowance was made, even up to the full figure of £600. It was still frequently pointed out that, under modern conditions, with probably two homes to maintain, heavy correspondence, and many calls on his purse both at Westminster and in his constituency, the most economical Member had difficulty in paying his way on under £1,000 a year, leaving a balance of £400 to be found from other sources. It was not always easy for him to find part-time work in another occupation, and hence the direct or indirect subsidies from 'interests' which find it useful to be represented in Parliament.

The difficulty was how to hit on a rate of salary for Members which was adequate for their legitimate expenses and yet not high enough to encourage a class of purely 'professional politicians' who would be quite alien to the spirit of our Constitution, since the assumption has always been that every Member is a private citizen, with his own profession, trade, or other means of livelihood behind him, from which he can bring useful experience to bear upon public affairs, and to which he can return if unseated. This 'representative' composition of the House of Commons has always been held to be essential to the health of the Constitution.

[1] Sir W. Ivor Jennings in his *Parliament* deals in detail with the 'interests' of Members; and there have been a number of recent books, including S. E. Finer's *Anonymous Empire* (1958), wholly devoted to this question.

These objections are not entirely theoretical, since in countries where professional politicians do exist, they are not always held in high repute: in France, and in America, where Members of Congress are paid a basic salary of £8,000 a year and can spend many thousands of pounds more on individual offices, staffs and expenses. It is whispered that Washington knows an undesirable element of rejected Cabinet Ministers, often lawyers, who become so identified with politics that, rather than retire to their practices, they prefer to remain near the seat of government, offering to make use of a boasted influence with the Government Departments.

A Select Committee was appointed in 1945 to consider the salaries, expenses and conditions of Members in respect of their parliamentary and official duties. In their unanimous report,[1] presented in March, 1946, they employed a memorable phrase which was used by the late Earl Lloyd George when he introduced payment of Members in 1911. They considered that a Member ought to receive, in addition to his expenses, a sum sufficient to maintain himself '*comfortably and honourably, but not luxuriously*' while a Member of the House. In their view it was desirable that a Member should remain free, as heretofore, to divide his time between his parliamentary duties and his private affairs as seemed to him best, but that he should not be paid a professional salary large enough to demand his full time in return. This sum they assessed at £500 a year. In addition they estimated the reasonable expenses 'wholly, necessarily and exclusively' incurred in the performance of his duties as a Member, at £500. Their main recommendation therefore was that the salaries of Members should be increased to £1,000 a year, of which £500 should be allowed as an expense allowance free of income tax. They did not recommend any general extension of the existing free travel, or any car allowance, or free postal, telegraph or secretarial services.

In May, 1946, the House agreed to these proposals with slight variations. As a result of the continuous rise in the cost of living another Select Committee soon recommended a further increase to £1,500 a year, but in face of criticism in the country the Government in July, 1954, proposed instead a subsistence allowance of £2 per day for expenses actually incurred, on every sitting day except Fridays. The long expected substantial rise was not granted until July, 1957, when the

[1] Report from the Select Committee on Members' Expenses, H.C. 93 (1945–46).

figure of £1,750 (including an expenses allowance of £750) was fixed. This is now the salary of a British Member of Parliament (1963), but there already exists amongst certain Members of all parties a strong feeling that this sum is inadequate.

The problem of remuneration which clearly only the House itself can solve, is perhaps more difficult, delicate and pressing today than ever before. The objection to a very high rate of pay which might encourage the purely 'professional politician' remains in force. Equally, however, it is accepted that the increasing volume and range of Parliament's business make tremendous demands on Members' time, and many find it impossible to combine an outside profession with the proper discharge of their duties in Parliament. A number of informed observers, including Professor Young in his recent book on *The British Parliament*,[1] are convinced that higher salaries are desirable, but it could well be that the House will once again be guided by public opinion in making its final decision.

It is not yet clear how far, if at all, such changes will affect the question of whether Members should receive financial support from outside bodies, which was indirectly raised by a case before the Committee of Privileges and the House of Commons. It concerned a dispute between a Member and his Trade Union to whom he was under contract for payment to deal, among other things, 'with all questions arising in the work [of the Union] which require Parliamentary or Political action', though it was also specifically stipulated that he should 'be entitled to engage in his political activities with complete freedom'.

The following extracts from the Committee's report (which was not unanimous) indicate the attitude of the majority to the problem:

> The relationship between a Member and an outside body with which he is in contractual relationship and from which he receives financial payments is, however, one of great difficulty and delicacy, in which there must often be a danger that the rules of privilege may be infringed. Thus it would certainly be improper for a Member to enter into any arrangement fettering his complete independence as a Member of Parliament by undertaking to press some particular point of view on behalf of an outside interest, whether for reward or not. . . .
>
> It has long been recognized, however, that there are Members who receive financial assistance from associations of constituents or other outside bodies,

[1] Roland Young, *The British Parliament*, 1962, p. 246.

and whilst those who enter into such arrangements must of course exercise great discretion to ensure that the arrangements do not involve the assertion or the exercise of any kind of control over the freedom of the Member concerned, Your Committee do not think that the making of such payments in itself involves any breach of privilege. . . .

When the subject was debated in the House on 15th July, 1947, the following motion was agreed to after a free vote:

That this House agrees with the Report of the Committee of Privileges, and in particular declares that it is inconsistent with the dignity of the House, with the duty of a Member to his constituents, and with the maintenance of the privilege of freedom of speech for any Member of this House to enter into any contractual agreement with an outside body, controlling or limiting the Member's complete independence and freedom of action in Parliament or stipulating that he shall act in any way as the representative of such outside body in regard to any matters to be transacted in Parliament; the duty of a Member being to his constituents and to the country as a whole, rather than to any particular section thereof.

So the matter stands at present, but the whole subject is a good example of a new constitutional problem which, though still in the fluid stage, is being solved, as so often before, in the clear light of public opinion. Students of Parliament should read the Report[1] and the debate,[2] and study the important distinctions and cross-currents of opinion with which both abound. They could not take a better lesson in the procedure of the House of Commons.

Finally, let us glance at the daily round of the Member of Parliament and try to judge whether he earns his pay or not. Here is one opinion:

As a result of seven years' experience, I am convinced that the average Member of Parliament works at greater pressure and for longer hours than nine-tenths of those who elected him, and that if the factory worker, miner, or engineer had the same strain put upon him, he would down tools within a month and demand better conditions of work.

Those are the words of the late Lord Snell, than whom no one, probably, of any party, could name a fairer witness. In his little book[3] he gives an interesting picture of the Member's daily business. Corre-

[1] Report from the Committee of Privileges, H.C. 118 (1946–47).
[2] Commons' *Hansard*, 15th July, 1947.
[3] H. Snell, *Daily Life in Parliament*, 1930.

spondence is a heavy job, because 'modern constituencies are great multitudes, who use their pens freely and expect replies'.[1] There are letters from constituents about Bills, pensions, rewards and jobs; a dozen daily appeals for money; invitations to open bazaars and to attend meetings and lunches; letters from tradesmen, moneylenders and madmen. Almost all have to be answered. 'Letter-writing,' says Lord Snell, 'is the greatest torment that a Member has to suffer, and, unless he is able to employ a secretary, it takes up a large proportion of his time.'

Members who are serving on morning committees have to be at the House by 10 a.m. to deal with their correspondence and papers before their committees meet—usually at 10.30 a.m. It is seldom realized outside what a vast amount of business Parliament transacts by means of committees, both official and unofficial, quite apart from the sittings of the House itself. From time to time efforts have been made to prevent committees from sitting simultaneously with the House. But then the press of business becomes too great, and the sittings are allowed to overlap, with the result that Members try to be in two places at once, which inevitably causes much strain and inconvenience—'business without work and idleness without rest', as Lord Morley called it.

The House now normally meets at 2.30 p.m. and continues nominally until 10.30 p.m., but in practice often far longer. The average annual number of hours *after* 11 p.m. which it sat during the years 1929 to 1939 was eighty-eight. The most usual hour of rising at present (1963) is about 11.30 p.m. You may at this point remind me that Members are not obliged to attend all day, or even at all, and that the House is often more than half empty. Where, then, is your Member? The answer is that he is upstairs, taking part in a select committee's investigation, moving an amendment in a standing committee, listening to the speeches of counsel for and against a Private Bill, attending a meeting of his party, or a 'private meeting' where he may keep abreast of events by hearing addresses from eminent persons—statesmen, travellers and experts, or discussing the parliamentary programme with any one of forty lobby correspondents. He may be in the Library with his correspondence, assembling the facts for a speech, or reading a report. Again, he may have been called into the outer lobby by means of a 'green card', to discuss 'urgent and important business' which

[1] Sir Courtenay Ilbert.

quite often turns out to be entirely frivolous. 'The lobbies are infested,' says Lord Snell, 'by the agents of a thousand causes, who seek him [the Member] out and try to induce him to put aside the nation's business in order to attend to theirs.'

It is unnecessary to labour the point. Indolent Members there are, of course, but that is too often the fault of the indolent voters who accepted them. Parliament reflects the nation, and its imperfections are the mirror of national imperfections. But it is perfectly obvious to any observer of the parliamentary scene that deficiencies in a Member's work for his constituents are due far more to overstrain than to inactivity.

Indeed, the reader may well ask at this point why so many persons of character and ability are willing to devote themselves to the hard work and pressing routine of their daily round. The answer is, of course, that there is another side to the picture. A former M.P., Mr. Nigel Nicolson, has vividly described the attractions of parliamentary life:

> Parliament is not dull. How can it be dull when almost every facet of the nation's life and work comes up sooner or later for debate, and when daily a Member associates with men who have immense power in their hands? There is no need for him to attend the debates which bore him. The libraries and dining-rooms are among the best-stocked and most comfortable in London, and if occasionally the House is a prison for an evening or a night, it is a prison from which no visitors are barred. The variety of business, the constant heightening and lowering of tension, the plotting, planning and grouping of men and women who have learned to tolerate the few of their colleagues whom they do not respect, dispel the weariness which is popularly supposed to overcome every Member in his sixth or seventh year.[1]

Another subject which is often raised is the length of the session. Why don't M.P.s work for more than about eight months in the year? The answer is that they do—but not at Westminster. Most Ministers undoubtedly look forward to the 'holidays', when they are free from parliamentary cares, as the periods when they can put their best work into their Departments. But for ordinary Members, too, reasonably long adjournments are a practical necessity. When a man has for many weeks been living a sort of double life, spending late nights at Westminster, speaking in his constituency at the week-ends, working in the

[1] *People and Parliament*, 1958, p. 64.

train in between, with his private affairs neglected and his nerves in shreds, it is surely right to allow him time to recuperate and think. Three hundred and seventy years ago the Lord Keeper was expressing the idea in almost lyrical Elizabethan style:

> The sessions [he said] cannot be long; by reason of the springtime, 'tis fit that gentlemen should repair to their countries; the justices of assize also to go to their circuits.
>
> So the good hours should not be lost in idle speeches, but the little time we have should be bestowed wholly on such businesses as are needful to be considered of.[1]

In 1931 Mr. Winston Churchill made the following observations to the Select Committee on Procedure on Public Business. Would it be easy to quote a witness with greater personal knowledge of the working of Parliament or of human capacity for work?

> If you wish to say what is wrong with Parliament . . . it is that it sits far too long in the year. I would lay down that except in times of war or great national emergency Parliament should not sit more than five months, with the ordinary short intervals, say, occupying six months of the year. That ought to be the maximum.[2]

And these remarks from his speech in the debate on the Address in 1944 show him to be still of the same mind:

> Do not . . . ever suppose that you can strengthen Parliament by wearying it, and by keeping it in almost continuous session. If you want to reduce the power of Parliament, let it sit every day in the year, one-fifth part filled, and then you will find it will be the laughing-stock of the nation, instead of being, as it continues to be, in spite of all the strains of modern life, the citadel as well as the cradle of Parliamentary institutions throughout the world; almost the only successful instance of a legislative body with plenary powers, elected on universal suffrage, which is capable of discharging, with restraint and with resolution, all the functions of peace and of war.[3]

[1] *Parliamentary History*, Vol. I, p. 859, 19th February, 1593.
[2] See Evidence given before the Select Committee, answer to question 1527.
[3] Commons' *Hansard*, 29th November, 1944, c. 26.

Chapter VI
THE PALACE OF WESTMINSTER

'It had been a Royal residence five hundred years before Catherine de Medicis laid the foundations of the Tuileries and the virile brain of Philip II of Spain conceived the grandiose idea of the Escurial.'

Wright and Smith, *Parliament Past and Present.*

Parliament 'sits' in the Palace of Westminster, to which it is summoned to perform its duties by Royal Proclamation. Since the Houses of Parliament buildings still form part of the Royal Palace, they are controlled by the Lord Great Chamberlain, a hereditary 'Great Officer of State'. For those who pass the place daily on their way to work, the structure must be something of a disappointment—eight acres of buildings four storeys high, with countless windows, and yet nothing ever to be seen on 364 days in the year except a trickle of legislators passing in and out. It would be more impressive if the actual 'Chambers' in which the Members and Peers meet were visible from the streets instead of being hidden in the centre of the building.

At the beginning of every session the House of Commons orders the Commissioner of Metropolitan Police to keep the passages through the streets leading to the House free and open for Members, and it is in pursuance of this Order that the police may regularly be seen holding up the traffic at the approaches to the Palace to permit Members to cross the roads.[1]

The area where Westminster Abbey and the Houses of Parliament now stand used to be a dank, unhealthy island in the Thames—'Thorney Island'—so called from a covering of dense undergrowth. Its earliest traditions were of religious settlements, but King Canute appears to have erected a royal residence on the site. Its ascertained history starts with Edward the Confessor, who rebuilt the palace while he was superintending the rebuilding of the church which was the germ of Westminster Abbey.

William the Conqueror adopted the Confessor's residence, and almost every succeeding monarch seems to have taken a hand in the work of improving the structure, until it ceased to be a royal residence in the reign of Henry VIII.

The history of the building is in one sense a melancholy catalogue of great fires. The first devastated it in 1298, in the reign of Edward I. The second destroyed a great part of the palace in 1512,[2] and sealed its fate as a royal home. Henry VIII moved to Whitehall, and after 1547 his son Edward VI made over the chapel of St. Stephen in the palace to the Commons for their use. It remained in this state until the fire of 1834 which, with the consequent demolitions, consumed everything save Westminster Hall, the crypt chapel and the cloisters. It seems rather extraordinary that a building of such importance and so fully manned should, time after time, succumb to the risks of fire. In the fourteenth century its twelve-and-a-half acres are said to have housed 20,000 persons, while after the fire of 1834, which was caused by gross carelessness in the burning of wooden Exchequer tally sticks, witnesses admitted that hours before the fire broke out the Chamber of the House of Lords was so full of smoke that the Throne was scarcely visible and visitors were feeling the heat of the stone floor through their boots.

Finally, in 1941, fire caused by a great German air-raid again totally destroyed the Commons Chamber and damaged the roof of Westminster Hall.

The entire structure now visible from outside, with the exception of

[1] For some interesting suggestions regarding the new House of Commons see the evidence given before the Joint Select Committee on Accommodation in the Palace of Westminster (H.C. 116–I of 1943–4 and H.C. 64–I of 1944–5).

[2] There is an illuminated model of the palace as it was in the time of Henry VIII in the Royal Gallery.

Westminster Hall, is the work of Sir Charles Barry, and was built between 1840 and 1852. It is in the Gothic style of the Tudor period and is everywhere profusely decorated with statues and symbolic ornamentation, designed by Pugin, of which full descriptions appear in the guide-books.[1] The present contents and past traditions of the building are, however, of far greater interest than the detail of the ornamentation.

A visitor who comes to hear a debate fortunately enters through St. Stephen's Hall, which is rebuilt on the exact site and to the exact size of the chapel of that name where the Commons sat after 1547 till 1834. Aided by the statues[2] of famous orators which line the hall on either side, he may soon feel the ghosts crowding thickly about him—from Burleigh and Walsingham to Palmerston and Gladstone. On the left, near Burke's statue, is the spot where the maniac Bellingham lurked, before pouncing out to murder Spencer Perceval, the Prime Minister, in 1812. This was the site of the House of Commons of the Tudors, the Stuarts, the first four Georges, and of William IV. 'Within those walls the battles of humanity have been fought, the privileges of freedom vindicated, and the liberties of England won.'[3]

Brass studs in the floor mark the former position of the Speaker's Chair and the Table of the House—where Charles I came when he burst in with armed men to arrest the five Members in 1642 and provoked Mr. Speaker Lenthall's historic reply: 'May it please your Majesty, I have neither eyes to see nor tongue to speak in this place, but as the House is pleased to direct me, whose servant I am here . . .'; where eleven years later Cromwell appeared in true dictatorial style to close down Parliament and to order the removal of the 'bauble' Mace; where Chatham, Pitt, Fox, Burke, Sheridan, all the brightest wits and greatest orators of the eighteenth century enjoyed their triumphs; where the struggle for the great Reform Bill was fought and won. To assist our memories, too, there are some colourful mural panels, notably those showing the secret reading of Wycliffe's Bible, and Queen Elizabeth commissioning Sir Walter Raleigh to discover new countries.

If you now walk forward into the Central Lobby (the huge, ornate,

[1] Many of these facts are taken from *The Houses of Parliament*, a short guide by Sir Bryan Fell, 9th ed., revised by K. R. Mackenzie, 1961.

[2] The spur on Lord Falkland's statue was broken when a suffragette chained herself to it in 1908.

[3] W. C. Townsend, *Memories of the House of Commons*, 1844, Vol. II, p. 464.

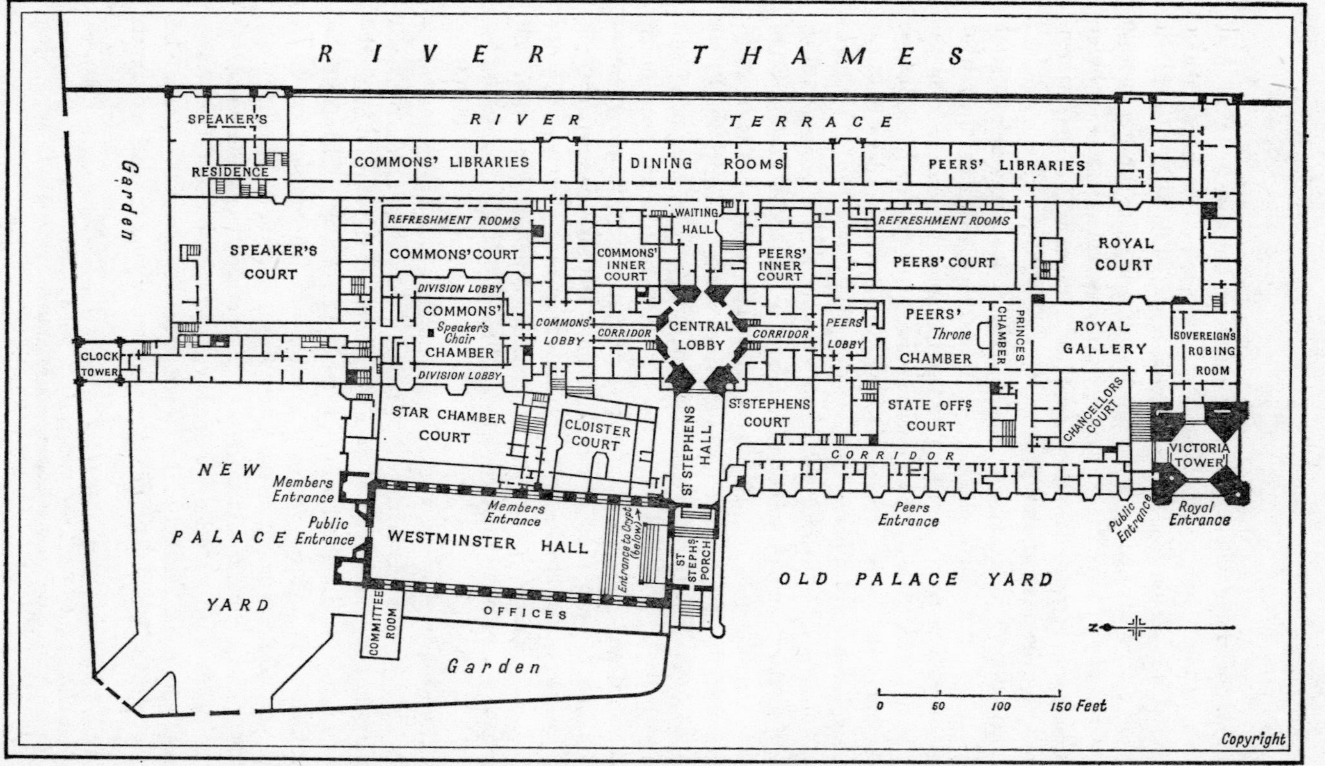

Plan of the Palace of Westminster (*by permission of Ward, Lock & Co. Ltd.*)

vaulted apartment where not only constituents but men and women of many nations come to interview Members), and stand in the centre, you will also be more or less in the exact centre of the Palace and at the hub of a cross formed by St. Stephen's Hall and three short corridors, on both sides of which are more panels of great interest. Ahead, overlooking the Terrace, lies a long series of libraries and dining-rooms, and above them committee rooms. Several of the latter contain interesting paintings, and one at least, the old No. 15, has a melancholy fame of its own. It was there, early in December, 1890, that Parnell wrestled day after day, amid scenes of indescribable bitterness, to keep the leadership of the Irish Party, until, at last, forty-five of his followers filed out of the candle-lit room, leaving him in stricken silence with his twenty-six faithful adherents.

I do not propose to drag you along the two miles of passages which the Palace contains, up and down the hundred staircases, nor into all of the eleven hundred rooms. Nor will I detain the reader with a discussion of the accommodation and various amenities which the Palace of Westminster offers (or does not offer) to its 630 Members. It is enough to say that this important domestic matter has been much examined and debated recently and certain major improvements—including the provision of extensive new accommodation *above* the existing structure and in Bridge Street—have been promised. Most of the present Bridge Street area is to be redeveloped, and part of it will form a Parliamentary precinct which will include individual rooms for many Members.[1]

With two exceptions, a straight line running due North and South through the spot where you are standing is the axis of all the principal apartments which we shall notice. To the right of the Central Lobby lie the Lords' Lobby, the Lords' Chamber, the Prince's Chamber, the Royal Gallery and the Queen's Robing Room. To your left, beyond a corresponding corridor, lie the Commons' Lobby and Chamber.

If you stand on this spot when both Houses are sitting, and supposing that all the doors between are open, you will see the Lord Chancellor (who acts as the Speaker of the House of Lords) on the Woolsack, and Mr. Speaker in his Chair, facing each other and exactly 425 feet apart.

[1] See, for example, the Reports of the 'Stokes' Committee on House of Commons Accommodation, etc. (H.C. 309, 1952–53; H.C. 184, 1953–54). There were debates on Accommodation in the House of Commons on 31st March, 1960 and on 1st August, 1963.

The apartments leading from the Queen's Robing Room to the House of Lords, being those through which the Sovereign passes to open Parliament, are all richly decorated in a style considered suitable in the middle of the last century. The Royal Gallery is of specially impressive proportions and contains two enormous paintings, 45 ft. by 12 ft., of Wellington meeting Blücher at Waterloo and of Nelson's death at Trafalgar. One of the sailors in the latter shows the mark of a shell splinter from an air-raid of the 1914–18 war.

The Chamber of the House of Lords measures 80 ft. by 45 ft. with a height of 45 ft., and the principal effect is of a wealth of colour and decoration. The gilt tracery and rails of the Throne (designed by Pugin), the stained-glass windows, the scarlet benches, the lofty ceiling, the dark, carved panelling—all combine to make a deep impression on the spectator, which is enormously enhanced on the occasion of the opening of Parliament. Then, hundreds of dimmed electric lights suddenly blaze up at the entry of the Queen, wearing her crown and royal robes, and accompanied by her Consort, and disclose the waiting Peers in their scarlet and ermine, the Peeresses in evening dress and jewels, the Bishops in their lawn, the wigged judges and the dazzling brilliance of the Diplomatic Corps, whose iridescent uniforms and sparkling decorations must indeed 'be seen to be believed'.

At the opposite end of the axis lies the new House of Commons. Barry's Chamber (the Chamber of Disraeli and Gladstone, Asquith and Lloyd George, Chamberlain and Churchill, I suppose it will be called) was destroyed, as we have said, by a night air-raid in 1941. Next morning nothing remained but a smoking pile of rubble and twisted iron girders. The Commons immediately moved across to their emergency Chamber in Church House, Dean's Yard, Westminster, where they sat from 13th May to 19th June, 1941. Both Houses had already sat there for short periods during the winter of 1940–41[1] and they returned there from 20th June to 3rd August, 1944, during the flying bomb attacks. But when the Commons found themselves homeless the Lords generously requested that their Chamber should be allocated by His late Majesty to the Commons and they themselves retired to the much smaller Robing Room, suitably fitted up, where it is said that their Lordships found themselves most comfortable. The

[1] They thus forsook the Palace of Westminster for the first time for 259 years, since Charles II summoned Parliament to meet at Oxford in 1681.

Commons continued to use the Lords' Chamber from 24th June, 1941, till 25th October, 1950, by which time the new House of Commons was ready.

No sooner had the Commons lost their Chamber than they set about rebuilding it. Barry's House seated only 346 Members on the floor and there were seats in narrow side galleries for ninety-one more. Here was the chance, thought many, to improve upon his conception. But that only illustrated the great difficulty of arriving at conclusions about Parliament without an intimate knowledge of its workings. Theoretically it would surely be advisable to build a Chamber large enough to provide every Member with a seat from which he could effectively speak—on the floor of the House. But that would mean a Chamber large enough to require a very different style of oratory from the 'formal conversations' preferred by modern generations. Moreover, large attendances at debates are exceptional, and a spacious Chamber would on most occasions be depressingly empty. Accordingly, after a debate in which Mr. Winston Churchill made a famous speech,[1] the Commons decided by an overwhelming majority to retain not only the rectangular shape of Chamber which is so congenial to the two- or three-party system, but also the restricted size which ensures intimacy of debate and on great parliamentary occasions a tense and exciting atmosphere.

These principles having been established, a Select Committee under the chairmanship of Earl Winterton, the then Father of the House of Commons, investigated the matter with the greatest care while flying bombs were falling all around, and made detailed proposals which were accepted by the House. It was found possible, while retaining the dimensions of Barry's Chamber, 86 ft. long by 45 ft. wide, to incorporate certain substantial improvements. All the galleries have been enlarged to provide more seats, each one with a good view, for Members, Press and public; and, since the most up-to-date system of heating and ventilation can now be housed in one storey below the Chamber, where in Victorian days it required three, the space saved has been devoted to rooms in which Ministers and Members may interview their constituents and secretaries—a notorious deficiency in the old House.

The new Chamber, built to the plans of the appointed architects, Sir Giles Gilbert Scott and his brother Mr. Adrian Gilbert Scott, was

[1] Commons' *Hansard*, 28th October, 1943, c. 404.

formally declared open on 26th October, 1950, immediately before a splendid ceremony which was attended by Their Majesties in Westminster Hall. Twenty-eight Speakers and Presiding Officers from the Parliaments of the Commonwealth and Empire marched in proud and solemn procession from the new Chamber, and the sincerity of the sentiments of loyalty and admiration which were everywhere expressed for the Sovereign and for the institutions of British parliamentary government made the occasion one of the most moving in our history.

The Dominions and Colonies vied with each other in offering gifts to furnish the new House, marvels of modern craftsmanship all brought into harmony by the skill of Sir Giles Gilbert Scott. Australia gave the Speaker's canopied Chair of black bean; Canada the great oaken Table of the House. The dispatch boxes which will be thumped by future generations of statesmen are of New Zealand purruri and the three Clerks' chairs of stinkwood from South Africa. The splendid oak doors of the House come from India and Pakistan. The bronze Bar (a long rod hidden in a tube from which it is pulled out when required to mark the technical boundary of the Chamber, some 15 ft. in front of the doors) came from Jamaica. Here, as in the olden days, persons will be called, to receive the thanks or censure of the House, and Members returned at by-elections stand while waiting to be introduced. Members may not speak from beyond the Bar, where they are technically outside the House. The chair of the Serjeant at Arms, just outside the Bar, was given by Ceylon, and the three Chamber clocks by Northern Ireland. Nigeria furnished one of the Division Lobbies in iroko wood and Uganda the other in mvule. It is through these 'Division Lobbies' on either side of the Chamber that Members pass to have their votes counted by the 'Tellers' and their names marked off for publication. Thus the list continues, beautiful and expensive tables and chairs; silver-gilt inkstands and ashtrays; bronze lamps and brackets for the Mace; magnificent steel firedogs. One of the most interesting items is a table in a small room behind the Speaker's Chair, inlaid with a specimen of wood from every part of the Commonwealth and Empire. It is a fit counterpart to the Woolsack at the other end of the building.

The declared intention of the architects was to lighten and enliven Barry's original late Gothic design by modifying the unrelieved richness of its decoration to two bands of ornament, one of oak carving around the Chamber below and the other of stone carving above. The result, whether seen by daylight through the latticed clerestory windows or by artificial daylight from the glass panels of the superbly shaped ceiling, seems to give general satisfaction.

The system of ventilating the new Chamber, which is in some respects untried anywhere else in the world, deserves a paragraph to itself. It is designed, by inducing gentle, lateral alternating movements of air, and by changing the whole air content as often as ten times an hour, to reproduce inside the House all the conditions of a warm spring day out of doors. Eight air conditioning plants are required for the Chamber and its ancillary premises. A typical plant 'consists of a white tiled concrete box, about 30 ft. long and 8 ft. square, which contains the following:

A super-silent fan.
An oil-coated filter for taking off large dirt particles.
An electro-static filter for removing fine particles.
Cooling coils for reducing temperature and humidity.
Eliminator plates for collecting the condensation.
Warming coils for warming the air.
Humidifying sprays for increasing the humidity.'[1]

The engineers, who regulate conditions accordingly, as the House and Lobbies fill or empty, watch the Chamber through a periscope 65 ft. long and hear the proceedings through loudspeakers. The general object of the system is to produce 'warm feet and cool heads' instead of—as was claimed for the old system of drawing air up into the Chamber through gratings in the usually filthy floor—'cold feet and hot heads'.

The acoustics, which depend upon hidden amplifiers, controlled and varied by watchful engineers, are excellent; partly perhaps because echoes escape through myriads of tiny holes in walls and ceiling, to be absorbed in glass wool beyond.

The 45 ft. square Members' Lobby outside the Chamber deserves a word. It is here that the privileged 'Lobby Correspondents' come, and so much informal political business and gossip takes place among Members that it is said on important occasions to wear a livelier appearance than the Chamber itself. By a happy thought the stone-

[1] From a description by the then Engineer, Dr. Oscar Faber.

Parliament in the reign of James I

Westminster Hall. Engraved from the picture by Thomas Sandby, R.A.

The interior of Westminster Hall

work of the main doorway into the Chamber has been carefully re-erected and is now known as 'the Churchill arch'. The combined effects of Nazi fire-bombs and of subsequent cleaning have given it an extraordinary appearance of weatherworn antiquity, so that, rather as a man's hair turns white in a night from shock, it seems to have grown older by several centuries since the night of 10th May, 1941. But without doubt it is serving its old purpose with an inestimable addition of dramatic memories.

No sketch of Parliament should omit mention of the clock tower. It is 320 ft. high and contains on the first floor the 'prisoners' ' room in which Members—and if need be, unruly visitors—are confined by order of the House. Charles Bradlaugh, the well-known free-thinker, was the last Member to be so imprisoned, in 1880. 'Big Ben' itself—probably named after Sir Benjamin Hall, the First Commissioner for Works at the time of the installation—must surely be the most famous clock in the world, and of all public clocks the most accurate. Apart from a few rare stoppages—once because a Member was pointing out its works with an umbrella, and quite recently (1963) because a hand-sweeping brush was left on a shaft—it has never been more than four seconds from Greenwich time. For weeks it runs to within one-tenth of a second per day—and that, with four minute-hands each fourteen feet long and weighing nearly two hundredweight to be operated!

But of all the buildings in the Palace, Westminster Hall is the most famous. It was built by William Rufus (New Palace Yard was 'new' in 1099), and remodelled between 1394 and 1399 by Richard II, who added the famous hammer-beam oak roof which is an artistic and architectural wonder.

The Hall has served many uses. It was the Great Hall of the old royal residence. For centuries the courts of law were held in or beside it. The special 'Parliaments' met there which forced Edward II to resign in 1327 and received Richard II's abdication in 1399. In Pepys's day it was a popular meeting-place and shopping market. It has been the scene of many notable State trials, including those of Sir William Wallace in 1305, Guy Fawkes in 1606, Lord Lovat in 1746 and Warren Hastings in 1788–95. Perhaps the most dramatic of them all was that of Charles I in 1649, during which the spirited royalist, Lady Fairfax, created a famous disturbance by interruptions and murmurings until 'sharp' measures were taken in the modern dictatorial manner, by a threatening order to the soldiers to fire into her box.[1] Revenge came twelve years later, when Cromwell's exhumed head stared from a pole on the roof of the Hall until 1684. The Hall has seen innumerable Coronation feasts, State ceremonies and in modern times the lyings-in-state of Kings. From first to last an endless pageant, dramatic and tragic, has wound its way through Westminster Hall and into British history.[2]

[1] Clarendon's *History of the Rebellion*, Bk. XI, 1706, p. 245.
[2] See H. St. G. Saunders, *Westminster Hall*, 1951.

Chapter VII

THE HOUSE OF COMMONS AT WORK (i): THE SPEAKER, OFFICIALS AND PARTIES

The Speaker and The Officials

'. . . his voice great, his carriage majestical, his nature haughty, and his purse plentiful.'

Mr. Speaker Yelverton, *describing the qualities necessary to a Speaker*, 1597.

'A Speaker's duty is to defend the rights, privileges, traditions and independence of this ancient Parliament. I love and venerate the House of Commons. But I know and I realize, and I believe every Member of this House realizes, that it is only with the assistance of the House of Commons that those objects can be attained.'

Captain FitzRoy, *on being elected Speaker, 20th June*, 1928.

The Speakership of the House of Commons is one of the most honourable, dignified and onerous offices in the world. The Speaker is elected by the House—very often unanimously[1]—for the duration of a Parliament, but in practice he is almost always re-elected for as long as he wishes to serve. He was by ancient custom the 'First Commoner in the Realm',[2] and he nowadays takes precedence behind the Prime Minister and the Lord President of the Council. He has a splendid residence in the Palace, a salary of £5,000 a year (plus £750 as a Member of Parliament), and he is usually granted a pension of £4,000. Upon his

[1] There was no contested election between 1895 and 1951.

[2] The position is also inferred in *I. William and Mary*, Chap. 21, s. 1 (1688).

SPEAKERS OF THE HOUSE OF COMMONS

1377 Hungerford, T.
1377 De la Mare
1378 Pickering
1380 Goldsbrough
1382 Waldegrave
1383 Pickering
1394 Bussy
1399 Cheney
1399 Dorewood
1401 Savage
1403 Redford
1404 Savage
1405 Esturmy
1405 Cheney
1406 Tiptoft
1407 Chaucer
1413 Stourton
1414 Hungerford, W.
1415 Chaucer
1415 Redmayne
1415 Beauchamp
1416 Flower
1420 Hunt
1421 Baynard
1422 Flower
1423 Russell
1425 Wauton
1426 Vernon
1428 Tyrrel
1429 Alington, W.
1431 Tyrrel
1432 Russell
1433 Hunt
1436 Bowes
1436 Tyrrel
1436 Burley
1439 Tresham, W.
1445 Burley
1447 Tresham, W.
1449 Say, J.
1450 Popham, J.
1451 Oldhall
1453 Thorpe
1453 Chalton, T.
1455 Wenlock
1459 Tresham, T.
1461 Green
1461 Strangewaies
1463 Say, J.
1472 Alington, W.
1482 Wode
1483 Catesby
1486 Lovell
1487 Mordaunt
1489 Fitzwilliams
1492 Empson
1496 Drury
1496 Bray
1505 Dudley
1509 Englefield
1510 Sheffield
1514 Neville
1523 More
1529 Audley
1533 Wingfield
1537 Rich
1540 Hare
1542 Moyle
1547 Baker
1553 Dyer
1553 Pollard
1554 Brooke
1554 Heigham
1555 Pollard
1558 Cordell
1558 Gargrave
1562 Williams, T.
1565 Onslow, R.
1571 Wray
1572 Bell
1577 Popham, J.
1585 Puckering
1589 Snagg
1592 Coke
1597 Yelverton
1601 Croke
1603 Phelips
1614 Crewe, R.
1620 Richardson
1623 Crewe, T.
1625 Finch, H.
1627 Finch, J.
1640 Glanville
1640 Lenthall
1653 Rous
1654 Lenthall
1656 Widdrington
1658 Chute
1658 Long
1659 Bamfylde
1659 Say, W.
1660 Grimstone
1661 Turnour
1672 Charlton, J.
1672 Seymour
1678 Sawyer
1678 (Seymour)
1678 Gregory
1681 Williams, W.
1685 Trevor
1689 Powle
1690 Trevor
1695 Foley
1698 Littleton
1701 Harley
1705 Smith
1708 Onslow, R.
1710 Bromley
1713 Hanmer
1714 Compton
1727 Onslow, A.
1761 Cust
1769 Norton
1780 Cornwall
1789 Grenville
1789 Addington
1801 Mitford
1802 Abbot
1817 Manners-Sutton
1835 Abercromby
1839 Lefevre
1857 Denison

1872 Brand	1905 Lowther	1943 Clifton Brown
1884 Peel	1921 Whitley	1951 Morrison
1895 Gully	1928 FitzRoy	1959 Hylton-Foster

Note: The spelling, and occasionally the chronological order, of early Speakers varies according to different authorities. The above list is that shown in gold letters on the walls of the Library of the House of Commons, where for simplicity titles have been omitted.

retirement he is offered a peerage. Alone among subjects he may hold 'levees', where the guests wear court dress. It is only when he is driven in his coach on certain great ceremonial occasions that his dignities may be thought to shade off a little. He is entitled to an escort of *one* Life Guardsman. His gilt carriage is very magnificent and older than the Royal State Coach or that of the Lord Mayor; but it has no brakes, and, since a century ago, when the then Speaker was connected with Messrs. Whitbread & Co., it has been drawn by horses provided by that firm.

The real authority so essential to the occupant of the Speaker's Chair (as FitzRoy's words in 1928, quoted above, show) is derived from the incomparable traditions of his office, and from the support of his colleagues who elected him—which in turn will inevitably rest upon qualities he has shown as a private Member. It is unnecessary to dwell on these qualities of good temper, common sense and scrupulous fairness, irrespective of the party to which he once belonged: for the evolution of the modern type of Speaker is one of the proudest achievements of the British Parliament. 'All Speakers become good Speakers,' observed Lord Rosebery, and there is far more truth than irony in the remark.

In addition to his duties during debates (in which he never now takes part)—regulating the discussion, keeping it to the matter in hand, and deciding points of order—the Speaker must be ready, upon request, to interpret the rules of the House, and to advise the humblest of his colleagues. Where no precedents exist he must minutely study the case and recommend the course most conformable to the traditions and convenience of the House. He must keep its honour and dignity ever in his mind. On formal occasions, principally in connexion with the Crown, he still exercises the function of spokesman for the whole House from which his name is derived.

He also executes the orders of the House, issues warrants for new writs, for the commitment of offenders and the attendance of witnesses, and administers reprimands. He exercises ultimate supervision and control over all the departments of the House. Finally, he takes the Chair at the rare 'Speaker's Conferences' of Members of both Houses which make recommendations concerning electoral reform and other matters.

It has been well remarked that such an office does not require brilliant or rare qualities so much as common qualities in a rare degree. It needs a practical man with a sound instinct for justice, who does his task honestly, firmly and good-humouredly.[1]

Speakers have not always been so satisfactory. Since the earliest days —the roll dates in an unbroken line from 1377—their election by the Commons probably always masked a strong element of royal nomination, and the growing importance of the lower Chamber caused Tudor and early Stuart sovereigns to ensure that the key position of Speaker should be filled by a compliant candidate of their own choosing, who in effect managed the royal business in the Commons and reported upon the attitude of Members. As a result the Commons became for a time suspicious and distrustful of their Speakers. The prestige of individual occupants of the Chair fell low and such incidents as these appear in the records:

> 16 July, 1610—Affirmed by Mr. Speaker, that Sir E. Herbert put not off his hat to him, but put out his tongue, and popped his mouth with his finger, in scorn;
>
> that Mr. T.T., in a loud and violent manner, and, contrary to the usage of Parliament, standing near the Speaker's Chair, cried 'Baw' in the Speaker's ear, to the great terror and affrightment of the Speaker and of the members of the House.

Nor has their personal character always been good. In particular the tortuous Sir John Trevor sounds the very antithesis of what a Speaker should be. He was expelled from the House in 1695 for taking a bribe of 1,000 guineas from the City of London for 'helping' a Bill through Parliament, and he suffered from such an atrocious squint that it is said two Members were habitually on their feet in different parts of the House, both under the impression that they had 'caught Mr. Speaker's eye'.

In the eighteenth century one of the greatest of all Speakers, Arthur

[1] Viscount Ullswater, *A Speaker's Commentaries*, 1925, Vol. II, p. 298.

Onslow (1691–1768), raised the office for a time to a high level of impartiality, but it was not until about 100 years later that such a standard became fully established. Nowadays a Speaker may be nominated by a party, but from the day of his election he is bound to avoid every suspicion of favour—even to the length of shunning all social contact with other Members in the dining-rooms and smoking-room.

In the Chamber Mr. Speaker does not always preside. The House often sits, for certain purposes, not as a House but 'in Committee', when debate is more informal and the Chair is occupied by the Chairman of Ways and Means, the Deputy Chairman or a temporary Chairman. The first two are party nominees, but while in office they act with the strictest impartiality; they can also relieve the Speaker in the Chair of the House, and they have other duties.

If the Speaker requires advice upon points of procedure, he can apply to the Clerk of the House—holder of an office dating back at least to 1388—or to his two Clerk-Assistants, who sit, wigged and gowned, at the Table of the House, and formally record its proceedings. Other Clerks have charge of the Bills which are under the consideration of the House, attend upon its committees and write its Journals. The Clerks must all bear constantly in mind that they are the servants of the House and not, as Civil Servants are, of the Executive.

Finally, the Speaker is assisted within and without the House by the Serjeant at Arms, who sits at the Bar in ceremonial court dress. His office has scarcely changed in five hundred years. He is still an officer of the Crown, lent to the Commons to assist in the preservation of order and in the last resort to enforce the orders of the Chair. He carries the Mace, which is the symbol of the authority of the House, and, through the House, of the Speaker. The Mace is decidedly one of the dignified and impressive accoutrements of Parliament.

The Parties and Their Whips

'A party is a body of men united for promoting, by their joint endeavours, the national interest upon some particular principle in which they are all agreed.'
Edmund Burke.

'I believe that without party, Parliamentary government is impossible.'
Benjamin Disraeli, *at Manchester*, 1872.

The answer to the question 'why have parties?' is simply—'for convenience'. There is nothing sacred about them, and although they existed in Athens in 600 B.C., the English Parliament functioned without them for hundreds of years. Parties in English politics, says Dr. Joseph Redlich, date from the division on 8th February, 1641, upon the question of the abolition of episcopacy.[1] They appear to suit the taste of the people, and, over a long term, the party system seems to be indispensable to the success of parliamentary government.

'But why,' you ask, 'set politicians against each other? Why not select the ablest among them and let them pool their talents and work out the best possible policy for the whole country? Why should we not all drive forward together with one tremendous surge of patriotic effort, to tackle the tasks ahead?' That is known as the 'Council of State argument' and, however attractive it may appear, it is in radical opposition to our political system.

For one of the fundamental assumptions of our Constitution is that men's opinions upon best possible policies do honestly differ, and should, indeed, be encouraged to differ. Another fundamental assumption is that the clash of these opinions shall be resolved in a general sense by the ordinary men and women of the country voting peacefully at the elections; and in greater detail by their representatives voting peacefully in the House of Commons. Now, obviously, the best brains can be collected in a 'Council of State'—that is exactly what happens in a desperate emergency like war, when the need for unity is paramount. Viscount Samuel has sagely remarked that 'it is a necessary part of the working of the Party system in this country for the Parties to know when to suspend Party controversy'.

Under the normal conditions of a free society, however, the best brains, when not united by any loyalty to a party or committed to any party programme, would constantly be disagreeing and getting at loggerheads, and so failing in their duties of government. For two or three hundred years, therefore, the active political elements in the country have found it increasingly convenient to group themselves together according to the general trend of their political feelings and desires. Cavaliers or Roundheads, Whigs or Tories, Unionists or Liberals, Socialists or Conservatives—the list is certainly not complete.

Under a Council of State system there is only one party, in peace as

[1] *The Procedure of the House of Commons*, 1908, Vol. I, p. 39.

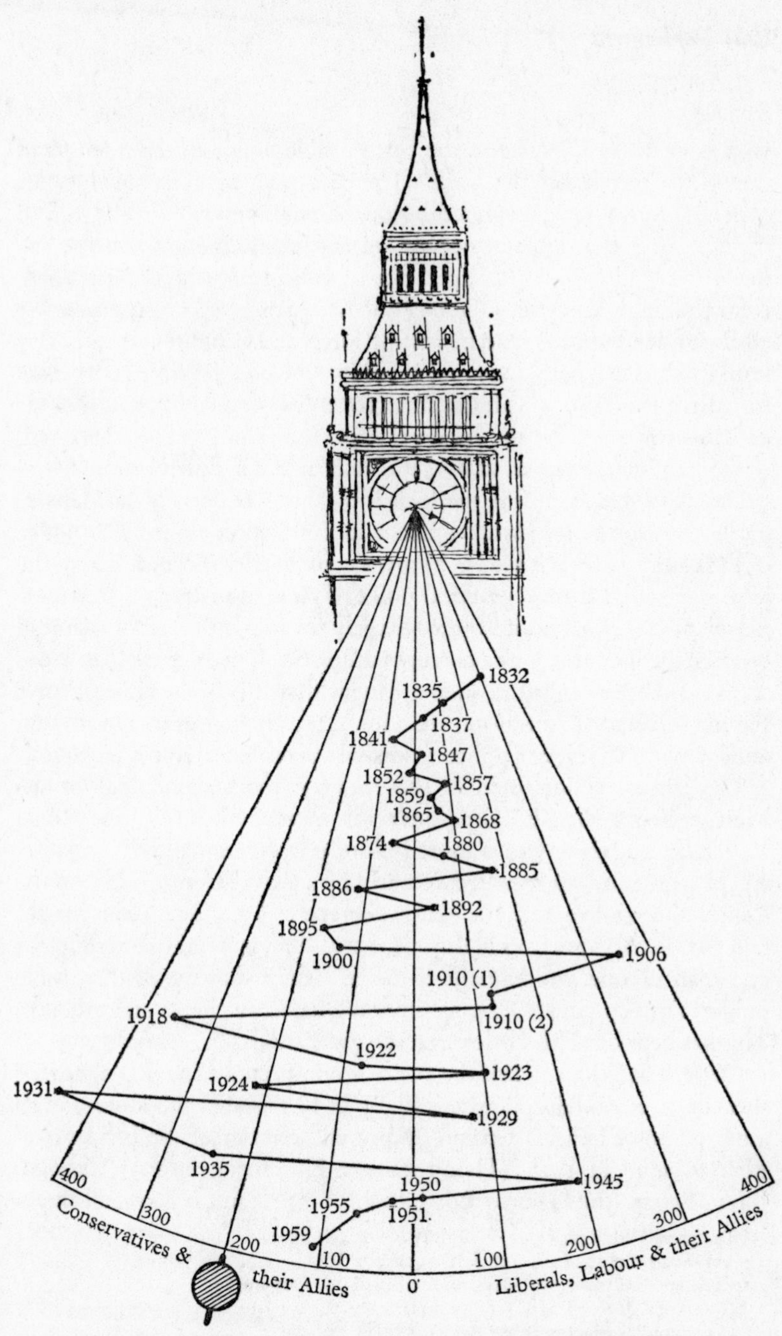

The Pendulum of Politics (*from Sir W. I. Jennings's* British Constitution, *by permission of the Cambridge University Press*).

well as in war, to decide on the best possible policy in the interests of the whole people or 'the State'. The principles of unity and of 'the general interest' (as interpreted by the party in power) are allowed to triumph over the rights of opposition parties and individuals, and the inevitable tendency, especially in face of difficulties at home or abroad, is for the single party in power to discountenance and crush dissenting parties and individuals with increasing force, and to tighten its authority until it achieves a permanent dictatorship. The only possible instrument for such a process is a widespread secret police, and concerning the use of that instrument by the modern police states of Europe, there will remain, so long as any of us live, the most agonizing memories.

Has the average elector the least idea, one wonders, of his debt to Parliament for its incessant vigilance in this respect alone? The police of the country are split into 157 separate forces. However attractive the idea may sound from a practical point of view, no party at Westminster wants a *national* police force—largely for fear lest one day it should become the instrument of a corrupt authority. All parties are so anxious to avoid the possibility of such a danger that it is often difficult for a Home Secretary to persuade the House to sanction even the modest amalgamations of lesser police forces which are essential for efficiency.

The largest police force in the country, the 20,000 men[1] of the Metropolitan Police, is indeed under the direct authority of the Home Secretary; but no power is more jealously watched than his.

The principle was re-stated recently by a Royal Commission on the Police, and confirmed by a Home Secretary. 'I am quite convinced,' said Mr. R. A. Butler on 26th June, 1962, 'that it would be wrong for one man or one government to be in charge directly of the whole police of this country. Our constitution is based on checks and balances. This has kept our liberty through the generations.'[2]

On rare occasions, when the police are suspected of having exceeded their duty, a searching debate is likely to be raised in the House, in an atmosphere of unusual tension. Many will remember the incidents of Miss Savidge in 1928,[3] Flying Officer Fitzpatrick in 1933,[4] and of John Waters (the 'Thurso Boy') in 1958–59.[5] Faint echoes still linger

[1] The present strength (1963) is slightly below this figure.
[2] *The Times* report of a speech at Torquay.
[3] Commons' *Hansard*, 7th May, 1928, *cc.* 1216–20, 1303–39.
[4] Commons' *Hansard*, 26th July, 1933, *cc.* 2589–90, 2719–39.
[5] Commons' *Hansard*, 17th February, 1959, *cc.* 204–28.

down the years since 1887, when an entirely respectable young woman called Miss Cass was arrested for soliciting in Regent Street, and, at the conclusion of a series of heated debates on the subject of her arrest, the Government were defeated.[1] The absence of fear which the police inspire in our hearts today is due to the incessant vigilance of Parliament. Such vigilance is a small price to pay for a priceless security.

Experience has shown that if an authoritarian state rises, no Parliament such as ours can possibly survive, composed as it is of independent men and women holding different political opinions and attached to several parties, but free to change their views and allegiances. Conversely, no dictatorship could establish itself in face of such a Parliament.

But dictatorship is not the British choice. Under that system there are no alternative parties and none of the restraints which the watchful eyes of an Opposition inspire. 'All power tends to corrupt,' said Lord Acton, 'and absolute power corrupts absolutely.' The British cherish their minorities, and even the individuals out on the fringes beyond. They remember their only dictator of three centuries ago, and they cling steadfastly to their beloved right *to change their own rulers*.

It is outside the scope of this book to describe what modern parties stand for, except perhaps to say that all parties tend naturally either towards the 'Right' or towards the 'Left', those extreme ways of thinking which Macaulay described so well, and the distinction between which had, he said, always existed and always must exist:

> For it has its origin in diversities of temper, of understanding, and of interest, which are found in all societies. . . . Everywhere there is a class of men who cling with fondness to whatever is ancient, and who, even when convinced by overpowering reasons that innovation would be beneficial, consent to it with many misgivings and forebodings. We find also everywhere another class of men sanguine in hope, bold in speculation, always pressing forward, quick to discern the imperfections of whatever exists, disposed to think lightly of the risks and inconveniences which attend improvements, and disposed to give every change credit for being an improvement. In the sentiments of both classes there is something to approve. But of both the best specimens will be found not far from the common frontier. The extreme section of one class consists of bigoted dotards: the extreme section of the other consists of shallow and reckless empirics.[2]

[1] Commons' *Hansard*, 1st and 4th July, 1887, *cc.* 1491, 1796.

[2] *History of England*, 1849, Vol. I, pp. 98–9. For modern views on parties see I. Bulmer-Thomas, *The Party System in Great Britain*, 1953; R. T. Mackenzie, *British Political*

Many people are apt to condemn what they call the 'incessantly obstructive attitude' of a major party (if it happens to be in opposition to their own), without perhaps realizing that they are thereby striking at the whole basis of party parliamentary government. It is as much the duty of an Opposition to criticize as it is of a Government to govern. For once a Minister has decided upon a plan—especially if it has given him a lot of trouble and he happens to be overworked—human nature ensures that he should easily overlook its deficiencies, and continue to swear (and perhaps to believe) that it is the best plan that ever was made. Party solidarity and the doctrine of Cabinet responsibility will also probably cause his colleagues to rally to his support in the House and in the country.

The criticism of a well-organized Opposition is exactly what is required to control this fault. It will be well-informed criticism, since some of the critics will have held office and will be in a position accurately to appraise the plan and its probable results: it will be responsible criticism because if it turns out to be sufficiently justified the critics will change places with their victims and themselves shoulder the Government. In fact the day to day arguments of the Opposition and of minorities in their own party, and even of individuals, do modify the Government's action, though certainly not always to the extent desired by the arguers. Concessions of detail are often made; it is by no means a case of 'ploughing the sands'.

The Opposition have thus in normal times come to be accepted as a sort of reserve government—almost a branch of the Government itself. The term 'His Majesty's Opposition' was first used, half jokingly, by John Cam Hobhouse early in the last century. It has been said that no Government can be long secure without a formidable Opposition, and it was in recognition of the value of these arrangements that the 'Leader of the Opposition', and therefore alternative Prime Minister, was in 1937 granted an official salary of £2,000 a year (increased to £3,750 in 1957). It must be yet another strange experience for the foreign observer to discover that the British Government pays its principal critic handsomely for his criticism! Further proof of the importance and respect accorded to the post of 'Leader of the Opposition' was recently given when, on the sudden and premature death of Mr. Hugh Gaitskell in January, 1963, the House of Commons created

Parties, 1955; and Sir W. Ivor Jennings, *Party Politics*, 3 vols., 1960–2.

a precedent by adjourning for twenty-four hours after paying generous tributes to his achievements. Mr. John Strachey, writing in the *Sunday Times* on 20th January, 1963, claimed that Mr. Gaitskell's work on the Opposition front bench was no less important than that of a Minister of the Crown.

It is in this clash of criticism, Opposition versus Government, resulting eventually in an exchange of places, that the success of our parliamentary institutions chiefly depends. Even in this country, a single party or coalition continuing for very long in office might become as hard to dislodge as a continental dictatorship. When Mr. Quintin Hogg, M.P. (recently Viscount Hailsham) wrote that 'The truth is that Party is as vital a political institution in this country as Parliament: without Party, Parliament would wither and decline into a debating club without responsibility, or a *Reichstag*, whose business it would be to register approval of the decisions of a dictator or a bureaucracy', he was re-stating in modern terms what Disraeli emphasized a hundred years ago: 'I say you can have no parliamentary government if you have no party government; and therefore, when gentlemen denounce party government, they strike at that scheme of government which in my opinion, has made this country great, and which, I hope, will keep it great.'

Another line of attack upon party government is that it encourages a type of Member who is nothing but a voting robot—the sort of whom W. S. Gilbert wrote:

> I always voted at my party's call,
> And I never thought of thinking for myself at all;

the sort who adheres to Disraeli's alleged advice: 'Damn your principles; stick to your party.' But, as has already been explained, the volume and complication of modern political business make it quite impossible for Members to inform themselves about every question they vote upon.

Nor must it be supposed that an Opposition is *always* opposing—that it is a sort of pull-devil, pull-baker arrangement, with the Government incessantly harassed and obstructed. Some of the business is quite uncontentious and the Opposition are glad to see it go through. Moreover, political opponents are often sincere friends both inside and outside Parliament.

Lord Balfour pointed out many years ago that our party system could only be worked under the best conditions if the differences between the parties were real, without being of such a revolutionary character as to divide the classes of society or sections of opinion 'in hopeless alienation one from another'. If differences scarcely exist, as in the eighteenth century, politics are not much more than a football match—or worse, a sordid game for the prizes of office. On the other hand, if the differences are too fundamental, as often upon the Continent, then the system is apt to break down into disorder and civil war. 'It is because,' he said, 'there seems to be some natural moderation in our British blood which enables us to be political enemies without attributing every infamous motive to those to whom we are opposed in politics—it is because we are capable, and can judge calmly, relatively calmly, and criticize charitably, relatively charitably, that we have made the British Constitution the great success it is.'[1]

Certainly for many years past, the main parties have had much common ground in the political objects they desired—defence, employment, trade, and the welfare of all the peoples of the Commonwealth and Empire. The differences have concerned method and approach rather than principle.

From past experience, more particularly of the last hundred years, it would clearly seem that the British Constitution works best upon the two-party system, or something near it, and, fortunately, that is the position which general elections have most often produced—that is to say, two powerful parties facing one another in the House, with not too great a disparity of support in the country. The party in power is then able to govern in the confidence that it is sustained by substantial backing in the country, while their opponents are encouraged to a healthy and vigorous criticism by the knowledge that no great distance separates them from the opportunity to test their own policies.

There have, of course, never been two well-defined parties and two alone. Lesser parties, 'splinter' groups and independent Members are always present; but so long as one party has an absolute majority—and can therefore always command more votes than all its opponents together—the principle of the two-party system is not disturbed. When no party has an absolute majority, however, the position is not nearly so satisfactory. None can enjoy the confidence which only a clear majority in the country (but not necessarily an absolute majority

[1] *Daily Chronicle*, 22nd September, 1902.

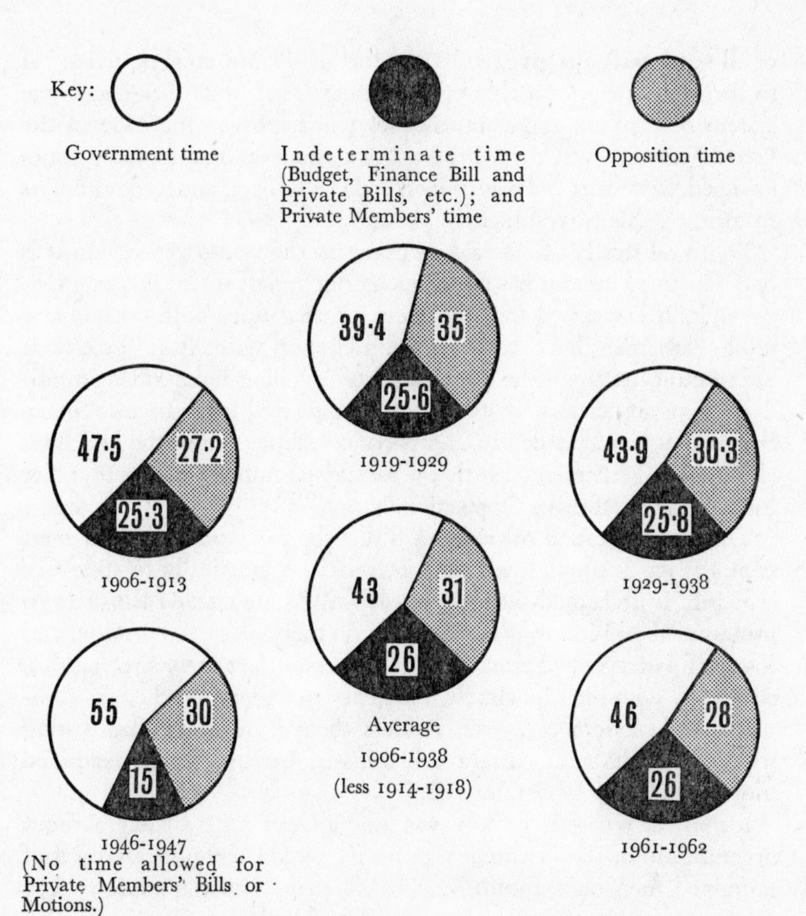

THE CAKE WHICH MUST ALWAYS BE SHARED

OPPOSITION VERSUS GOVERNMENT

It is vital for the proper working of a democracy that the Government should not monopolize the time of the House of Commons. The above diagram shows that, excluding the two war periods, the official Opposition has been granted a reasonable share of debating opportunities by Governments of all complexions. The above percentages, based partly on Reports of the Select Committee on Procedure, and partly on the evidence of *Hansard*, are an approximate guide only, since it is not always easy in practice to distinguish between 'Government' and 'Opposition' time (*cf.* e.g. Third Report from Select Committee on Procedure, H.C. Paper 189–I of 1945–46, p. xxx).

of all votes cast) can give, and some sort of alliance must be arrived at to form a majority capable of governing. That in its turn entails the system of bargains and compromises which proved the bane of the French pre-war system, where a great number of minority parties grouped, flew apart and re-grouped, in kaleidoscopic and futile attempts to form a stable Government.

When all this has been said in praise of the two-party system it is only fair to add that it has been much criticized of recent years on two grounds. It is claimed that the party organizations both outside and inside Parliament have become strong enough virtually to force their own candidates upon the electorate by excluding independent candidates from any chance of success. It is considered by some that Members who act independently of a party constitute one of the healthiest elements in Parliament and that a substantial number might together form a highly effective Opposition.

The second ground of criticism is that the party organizations exert such a strict discipline over their members as practically to stifle free criticism. It is claimed that present-day M.P.s are already half-way to professional politicians, too dependent on their salary and position and too fearful of a general election to dare to resist their party and that this, combined with their inevitable incapacity to understand the vast complexity of modern measures, renders them little more than voting robots. The different current criticisms of Parliament are examined more thoroughly in chapter XII.

It must be recognized, however, that a Government party without organization in the House of Commons would resemble a crowd of untrained men on a football field. No matter how numerous they might be, their trained opponents would almost invariably outmanœuvre and defeat them.

It is interesting to see how clearly Jeremy Bentham put the case 170 years ago. But his claim that the party system was essential for an efficient procedure, and that those of the same party ought to possess every facility for concerting their operations, applies nowadays with much greater force to the Government than to the Opposition side:

> Without this concert it is impossible that the arguments should be presented in the most suitable order, and placed in the most advantageous light. It is only by a continual correspondence among the members themselves that they

The night of Saturday, 10th May, 1941, showing what an incendiary bomb did to Barry's House of Commons

The Speaker's Procession

can prevent a multitude of useless operations, delays, contradictions, repetitions, inconsistencies, and other incidents, of which the common tendency is to interrupt that unity of plan which is necessary in conducting business to its termination. In this respect, party interests are the same as those of the public. It is necessary for the public good that each party should plead its cause with all its force—should employ all its resources; since truth only has everything to gain in the concussion.

The force of competition and the development of the complex modern State has converted the loose and lax party managements of Bentham's age into the comparatively iron control of today.

We need only glance at the structure of a party outside Parliament. There are local organizations in the constituencies, part of whose function is to carry on the work of their originators, the Registration Societies, who secured the registration of the new voters added by the Reform Act of 1832. There are central organizations (dating from between 1867 and 1877) for purposes of control, co-ordination and research. There are also funds for political education—'party is organized opinion', it has been said—for the financing of candidates and for many other purposes.

But the party organization inside the House concerns us closely. It is carried out by officials called Whips, who are all Members, and who, on the Government side, hold more or less nominal posts (some unpaid) either at the Treasury or in the Royal Household. The Chief Whip—also known as the Patronage Secretary—acts as a sort of Chief of Staff to the Prime Minister (and to the Leader of the House, if the two Offices are not jointly held) with whom he is in close and constant touch. With his assistants he is responsible for planning the Government's business in the House for months ahead, so that it shall fit in with certain fixed dates (relating particularly to the financial year), with the convenience of the House and of Ministers and with the time available. The negotiations which are carried on between the Whips of the different parties (usually in the most cordial manner) are said to take place 'through the usual channels'. The common description of the Whips' duties—'to make a House, to keep a House and to cheer the Minister' is a serious understatement. Besides ensuring that sufficient Members of their party are in the Chamber or in the precincts to carry the Question for a Closure Motion (at least one hundred on the majority side) and to outvote the Opposition in any impending division, their chief duty is to act as efficient and tactful liaison officers between the Government and Private Members, explaining procedure, reporting complaints and keeping themselves accurately informed of all trends of political feeling.

The term 'whip' is also used for the weekly circular of forthcoming business which is issued to Members by their party, and the withdrawal of which is the rare sanction which signifies a Member's excommunication from his party. The relative urgency of the items is intimated by a system of underlinings—'a two (or three) line whip'. (See opposite page for specimen.) Whips, underscored by as many as six lines, were sent to the King's friends in the House of Commons as early as 1621.[1]

[1] E. and A. G. Porritt, *The Unreformed House of Commons*, 1903, Vol. I, p. 509.

SECRET

ON MONDAY, 27th February, 1961, the House will meet at 2.30 p.m.

A Debate will take place on Defence on a Government Motion and an Opposition Amendment. (1st Day)

A good attendance throughout this debate is particularly requested

Mr Proudfoot's Motion to refer his Petition to the Select Committee on the Covent Garden Market Bill.

Opposition Prayer to annul the Chancery of Lancaster Rules, 1961(S.I. No. 3). (EXEMPTED BUSINESS)

A Division may take place and your attendance at 10 p.m.

and until the Prayer is concluded, is particularly requested,

unless you have obtained a pair.

ON TUESDAY, 28th February, the House will meet at 2.30 p.m.

Conclusion of the Debate on Defence.

There will be most important Divisions and your attendance

at 9.30 p.m. is essential.

Consideration of the Motion to approve Double Taxation Relief (Taxes on Income)(Faroe Islands)Order (EXEMPTED BUSINESS)

Opposition Prayers to annul the Skimmed Milk with Non-Milk Fat Regulations, 1960(S.I. No.2331) and the Skimmed Milk with Non-Milk Fat(Scotland)Regulations,1960(S.I. No.2437) (EXEMPTED BUSINESS)

Divisions may take place and your continued attendance

until the Business is concluded is particularly requested,

unless you have obtained a pair.

A WHIP

Part of the actual Whip for the week beginning Monday, 27th February, 1961. The meaning of the expression 'three-line Whip' is obvious.

Chapter VIII

THE HOUSE OF COMMONS AT WORK (ii): THE ESSENTIALS OF PROCEDURE[1]

'In this bye-corner, an observing eye may trace the original seed-plot of English liberty; it is in this hitherto neglected spot that the seeds of that invaluable production have germinated and grown up to their present maturity, scarce noticed by the husbandman, and unsuspected by the destroyer.'

Bentham, *on British parliamentary procedure.*

'The man in the street, from all classes, is surprisingly ignorant of all parliamentary procedure, and has never given it any serious consideration at all.'

Mr. Speaker FitzRoy, *to the Select Committee on Procedure,* 1931.

Are rules of procedure necessary? The word procedure is derived from the Latin 'procedere', *to go forward,* and the question scarcely requires an answer. A handful of friends called together to discuss the simplest project will at once vote someone into the Chair, and that someone will immediately find himself in trouble, trying to keep the garrulous and irrelevant in check and to bring the group to a decision. If in doubt as to the truth of this assertion, the reader may recognize the justice of Jeremy Bentham's description of the abortive discussions constantly to

[1] The standard work on current practice and procedure is Sir T. Erskine May, *A Treatise on the Law, Privileges, Proceedings and Usage of Parliament,* 16th ed., 1957. See also Lord Campion, *An Introduction to the Procedure of the House of Commons,* 3rd ed., 1958; and the current edition of the official House of Commons' *Manual of Procedure in the Public Business.*

be heard at any meeting where the speakers are unfettered by the Chair. After the real subject of debate has been raised,

> somebody catches or pretends to catch the idea of something else more proper to be done. The next speaker takes this for his theme. Affections grow warm; and crowding about this second subject the first is insensibly departed from and forgotten. And so on, till men's minds are effectually confused, and their whole stock of time and patience gone.[1]

Without some recognized code of rules, then, no handful of parish councillors can settle the least piece of contentious business. How much the more essential is such a code to regulate the debates of over 600 individuals of radically different beliefs and interests who decide the vast and vital affairs of a great nation!

Granted that procedure is necessary to enable the House of Commons to do its work, what fundamental principles ought to determine its nature? The standard authority on the *history* of procedure (Sir T. Erskine May's book was intended purely as a treatise on *practice*) is still the work of the late Dr. Joseph Redlich, an Austrian scholar who undertook the drudgery of ransacking a long series of technical reports in a foreign language to produce his invaluable book in 1908.[2] He gave the opinion—which is still valid today—that the technical requirements for the formation of the will of a legislative assembly and for the state actions of such a body are 'expressed to perfection' in Jeremy Bentham's *Essay on Political Tactics*, written towards the close of the eighteenth century. Let us see what these rules are, and, very shortly, how far modern procedure conforms to them.

Bentham names *publicity* as the essential foundation for a satisfactory procedure. It constrains Members to perform their duty, secures the people's confidence, and with it their assent to laws; the electors learn to act from knowledge, and the governors to know the wishes of the governed. By this Bentham means the fullest publicity, both external and internal, for everything which is to happen, is happening or has happened in Parliament, unless such publication should favour the projects of an enemy or result in injustice to individuals. It follows that Members should receive due notice of the hours of sitting and the business to be taken; that all questions in the House should be clearly

[1] Abridged from *Essay on Political Tactics*, in *Works*, 11 vols., 1843: Vol. II, p. 342.
[2] *The Procedure of the House of Commons: a Study of its History and Present Form.*

stated; and that all debates, divisions, decisions and reports should be punctually published.

The House for long forbade the publication of its debates (see pp. 130–132), but the principle of publicity in peace-time is, of course, now firmly established; and even in time of war Parliament still holds as few secret sessions as possible (thirty-seven in five-and-a-half years of the last war, apart from those dealing only with the dates and times of sittings of the House).

The arrangements to ensure efficient 'internal' publicity are comprehensive. The *Votes and Proceedings* have been printed with but brief interruptions since 1680. They form a record of business transacted by the House and are circulated to Members on the morning after the day to which they relate. The *Notice Paper* (delivered in the morning) details the current day's business. The *Journal* records the proceedings of the House permanently—in formal language, stereotyped since the eighteenth century. The printed *Journals* date back to 1547, and history speaks from many pages. (In the margin of the *Journal* of 18th December, 1621, is written, in a different hand, 'King James, in Council, with his own hand rent out this Protestation.' The Protestation concerned the privileges of the House. The *Journal* of 4th December, 1660, contains the following resolution: 'Resolved, That the carcasses of Oliver Cromwell, Henry Ireton, John Bradshaw and Thomas Pride, whether buried in Westminster Abbey or elsewhere, be with all expedition taken up and drawn upon a hurdle to Tiburne and there hanged up in their coffins for some time, and after that buried under the said gallows.') A glance at the electric annunciator in various parts of the Parliament buildings informs Members of the item in progress and of the speaker who is on his feet. Reports, Bills and Papers are either delivered to Members or available in the 'Vote Office' in the Commons Lobby.

So anxious was Bentham that every Member should be correctly informed while speaking, that he advocated a large frame above the Speaker's Chair with hooks similar to a cricket scoreboard, upon which attendants would hang the words of the motion under consideration, with similar frames for amendments and rules of procedure.

We may mention, in passing, Bentham's insistence upon the necessity for the full attendance of Members, and upon the canon of the absolute *equality* of Members. The power and authority of men must needs vary in practice by reason of their different abilities, but all Members are still held to be theoretically equals—a principle which might on occasion prove invaluable in helping to check individual ambitions.

The second great principle of his theory of procedure is that of the *absolute impartiality of the president*, and no better sense has ever been written on the subject. After laying down that there should be only one president, chosen for a long period of time but with a substitute always available, he explains that the president's (that is to say, the Speaker's)

No. 78 **VOTES AND PROCEEDINGS OF THE HOUSE OF COMMONS** **291**

Friday 15th March 1963

1. FIRE Services,—Copy *presented,*—of Regulations, dated 5th March 1963, entitled the Fire Services (Appointments and Promotion) (Scotland) Regulations 1963 (S.I., 1963, No. 441) [by Act] ; to lie upon the Table.

2. London Traffic,—Copy *presented,*—of Order, dated 7th March 1963, entitled the Parking Places (St. Marylebone) (No. 1, 1961) (Amendment) Order 1963 (S.I., 1963, No. 454) [by Act] ; to lie upon the Table.

3. Local Government,—Copy *presented,*—of Order, dated 11th March 1963, entitled the Northumberland (Advance Payments for Street Works) Order 1963 (S.I., 1963, No. 462) [by Act]; to lie upon the Table.

4. Parliamentary Reform,—*Resolved,* That this House resolves to maintain Parliament as the paramount forum of the nation and to bring its practices and procedures into harmony with this end and in accord with the needs of 1963.—(*Mr. Charles Pannell.*)

5. Adjournment,—*Resolved,* That this House do now adjourn.—(*Mr. Martin McLaren.*)

Adjourned accordingly at one minute to Four o'clock,

Harry Hylton-Foster
Speaker

MEMORANDUM

Mr. Speaker will take the Chair at half-past Two o'clock upon *Monday* next.

The daily issues of the *Votes and Proceedings* (see page 90) vary greatly in size and complexity. The above example is shorter than the average 'Vote', which may contain more than a dozen items.

functions are of two kinds. He is a judge as between the individual Members and an agent of the whole assembly. From his actions as a judge there ought to be an ultimate appeal to the whole assembly. As an agent he should be subject to the immediate control of the assembly. In neither capacity ought he to possess any power, the effect of which would be to give him any control over the will of the assembly. For:

> it is for the sake of the assembly and for their use alone, that the institution of this office is either necessary or proper. . . . It is only in as far as it may be conformable to the will of the assembly, that the will of this officer can, as such, have any claim to regard.

The idea which the Commons have shaped out for themselves about their president, as a past Clerk of the House has remarked, 'is to keep, to the fullest extent, the power in their own hands, while extending as much respect as possible to the occupants of the chair'.[1]

Finally, to enable the president to act with complete impartiality, he should be excluded from all partisan activity. The description still closely fits the modern type of Speaker, in spite of the statutory and other duties since laid upon him.

One of the main duties of a parliamentary body is to ascertain its own will in regard to innumerable matters; but as the ideal goal of unanimity can seldom be obtained, it is customary to attribute to the united will of the majority the same effect as to that of the whole body. Bentham accepts this *principle of the majority* as part of the theoretical basis of parliamentary government without argument. 'How far so ever the will of the simple majority may be from the really universal will, it is nearer to it than the contrary will.' In early times unanimity was aimed at. In the seventeenth century the House went through a sort of ceremony on important occasions to show that the minority accepted the decision of the majority. Sir G. Cornewall Lewis describes the earliest decision by a majority of votes recorded in authentic history as follows: 'Before the battle of Marathon the ten strategi were equally divided in opinion. The polemarch archon . . . gave his vote in favour of fighting, and decided the question, upon which the minority acquiesced. (Herod., VI, 109.)'[2]

Bentham insists as his fourth principle upon certain vital points of

[1] Sir R. Palgrave, *The House of Commons*, 1878 ed., p. 68. See also *Report from Select Committee on Parliamentary Elections* (*Mr. Speaker's Seat*), H.C. 98 of 1938–9.

[2] *An Essay on the Influence of Authority in Matters of Opinion*, 1849, p. 244.

designed to bring hostilities between Israel and Egypt to an end and to safeguard vital international and national interests, and pledges its full support for all steps necessary to secure these ends"—(The Prime Minister),—instead thereof.

And the Question being put, That the words proposed to be left out stand part of the Question;

The House divided.

The Yeas to the Right;

The Noes to the Left.

Tellers for the Yeas, Mr. *Bowden*, Mr. *Pearson*: 255.
Tellers for the Noes, Mr. *Heath*, Mr. *Galbraith*: 324.

So it passed in the Negative.

And the Question being put, That the proposed words be added after the word "House" in the Main Question;

The House divided.

The Yeas to the Right;

The Noes to the Left.

Tellers for the Yeas, Mr. *Heath*, Mr. *Galbraith*: 323.
Tellers for the Noes, Mr. *Bowden*, Mr. *Pearson*: 255.

So it was resolved in the Affirmative.

And the Main Question, so amended, being put;

The House divided.

The Yeas to the Right;

The Noes to the Left.

Tellers for the Yeas, Mr. *Heath*, Mr. *Galbraith*: 320.
Tellers for the Noes, Mr. *Bowden*, Mr. *Pearson*: 253.

So it was resolved in the Affirmative.

Resolved, That this House approves of the prompt action taken by Her Majesty's Government designed to bring hostilities between Israel and Egypt to an end and to safeguard vital international and national interests, and pledges its full support for all steps necessary to secure these ends.

Adjournment. *Resolved*, That this House do now adjourn.—(Lieutenant-Commander *Thompson*.)

And accordingly the House, having continued to sit till eight minutes before Eleven of the clock, adjourned till to-morrow.

[No. 217.]

Friday, 2nd November, 1956.

The House met at Eleven of the clock.

PRAYERS.

Estimates. ORDERED, That the Minutes of the Evidence taken before Sub-Committees D, E, and F, appointed by the Select Committee on Estimates, and not yet reported by that Committee, together with Appendices, be laid before this House.—(Captain *Waterhouse*.)

House of Commons Accommodation, &c. *Ordered*, That the Minutes of the Proceedings of the Select Committee on House of Commons Accommodation, &c., be laid before this House.—(Captain *Waterhouse*.)

Civil Aviation. *Resolved*, That this House, in reviewing the progress of Civil Aviation, takes note of the Reports and Accounts of the British Overseas Airways Corporation and the British European Airways Corporation for the year ended the 31st day of March 1956.—(Mr. *Watkinson*.)

Sittings of the House. A Motion was made, and the Question being proposed, That this House do meet to-morrow at Twelve of the clock and that Mr. Speaker at Three of the clock do adjourn the House without putting any Question—(Mr. *Richard Butler*):—And a Debate arising thereupon;

Mr. *Heath* rose in his place and claimed to move, That the Question be now put.

Question put pursuant to S.O. (Closure of Debate). And the Question being put, That the Question be now put:—It was resolved in the Affirmative.

And the Question being accordingly put;

Resolved, That this House do meet to-morrow at Twelve of the clock and that Mr. Speaker at Three of the clock do adjourn the House without putting any Question.

Adjournment. *Resolved*, That this House do now adjourn.—(Mr. *Galbraith*.)

And accordingly the House, having continued to sit till four minutes before Four of the clock, adjourned till to-morrow.

[No. 218.]

Saturday, 3rd November, 1956.

The House met at Twelve of the clock.

PRAYERS.

Adjournment. A Motion was made, and the Question being proposed, That this House do now adjourn—(Mr. *Heath*):—And a Debate arising thereupon;

Closure claimed. Assent withheld. Mr. *Smith* rose in his place and claimed to move, That the Question be now put; but Mr. Speaker withheld his assent and declined then to put that Question:—Then the House resumed the Debate.

And it being Three of the clock, Mr. Speaker adjourned the House, without a Question first put, pursuant to the Resolution of the House yesterday, till Monday next.

THE *JOURNAL*

A page of the *Journal* during the Suez crisis. In the exceptional circumstances the House of Commons met on a Saturday.

procedure. A logical order of stages must be strictly observed in the formation of the will of the assembly, and a precise separation maintained between them. Proposition, debate and voting must not mingle, as they were allowed to do in French eighteenth-century provincial assemblies with disastrous results. Above all, only one question should be debated at a time.

Modern practice in this connexion dates from a few simple rules of the House laid down near the beginning of the seventeenth century:

> 1. 'Ordered, That nothing do pass by order of the House without a Question; and that no order without a Question Affirmative and Negative.'
> 2. 'When a Motion hath been made, the same may not be put to the Question until it be debated, or at least have been seconded or prosecuted by one or more persons standing up in their places.'
> 3. 'When a Motion hath been made, that matter must receive determination by a Question, or be laid aside by the general sense of the House before another be entertained.'
> 4. 'A Question, being once made, and carried in the Affirmative, or Negative, cannot be questioned again, but must stand as a Judgment of the House.'

They show the House of Commons in its most business-like shape. It was by solving such technical problems as these that the early House proved itself to be an efficient body and survived, while many of its fellows in Europe, then and since, failed and disappeared. Although it now seems obvious to decide a matter by putting it to the vote, and accepting the decision of the majority, it took Western civilization many generations to evolve this seemingly simple procedure.

The process of debate nowadays passes through four stages. First, a Motion is proposed by a Member in such form that, if carried, it can stand as a Resolution or Order of the House. Resolutions express the opinion of the House; Orders express its instructions: both must originate as Motions.

Next, the Speaker proposes the question in the same form. Debate ensues. It must be relevant to the question, but amendments may be moved to alter the latter, or attempts made to shelve it (*e.g.*, 'Previous Question', see Glossary). At the end of the debate all Members vote simultaneously and the decision of the majority is accepted as the decision of the House.

Bentham's final principle—that of complete *freedom of speech* to the extent of each Member speaking as often as he wishes—is the only one which has had to be modified to fit modern conditions. Together with the *Protection of the minority* (it is the same thing with an alteration of emphasis) this question of how far complete freedom of speech has to be curtailed forms, of course, one of the crucial problems of all Parliaments.

It was the first of the great Speakers, Arthur Onslow (he occupied the Chair throughout the reign of George II), who insisted upon a strict adherence to the forms of procedure, since only by this means could the weaker party 'be protected from those irregularities and abuses which these forms were intended to check, and which the wantonness of power is but too apt to suggest to large and successful majorities'. That principle has been cherished ever since, and the instinct to 'hear the other side' exists nowadays in the marrow of all good Englishmen.

There are two reasons why the ideal of complete freedom of speech advocated by Bentham has had to be modified—the development of systematic obstruction and the ever-increasing press of business.

Obstruction in the House of Commons has hitherto assumed one of three forms. It has been a sudden explosion of protest directed against a single measure or against the apparently overbearing conduct of the Government or the majority. Such action has always been understood and sympathetically treated by the House. Or, secondly, it has taken the form of protracting debate beyond the furthest reasonable limits of the most detailed arguments, by means of dilatory motions, repetition by relays of speakers and irrelevancies—all with the sole object of delaying an unpopular measure. The legitimacy of such obstruction is much in dispute today. The third form of obstruction consists in the intensification of all the others with the tacit or avowed object of making the work of Parliament impossible. Throughout the eighteenth and the first half of the nineteenth centuries political feeling in England never reached such extreme bitterness as to threaten the allegiance of Members to the State. Hitherto, with all their failings, they had been good parliamentarians. They had debated and disputed through the ages under the overriding assumption that Parliament could and should function. That was taken for granted. A convention existed that, after every reasonable opportunity had been taken by the Opposition to oppose within the rules, the Government's business should be allowed to go through. There was also the notion that no question should be decided while there remained any Member who still wished to speak upon it. Human nature being what it is, the notion was often obscured. In the eighteenth century the practice called 'rubbing out' obtained—'accursed hawking, and spitting, and shuffling of the feet, at any Member the House does not like to hear speak'.[1] Just prior to 1832 this had become a shouting down or laughing down of tedious speakers, and towards the end of the evening, when the Speaker saw that the House was ready to come to a decision, he chose the chief protagonists for the concluding speeches and by a sort of general consent any smaller men who sought to speak would be drowned in clamour until the division was called. The modern form of this mild closure is a talking down, sometimes combined with a steady chant of 'vide-divide-divide'.

But in the 70's and 80's of the last century the Irish Home Rule Party, inspired by Parnell, created an entirely new position. Their political feelings became so embittered against a Parliament which was not prepared to attend to the Irish question that they determined to try to wreck the whole business of government by impeding the work of the House *within its rules*. In the session of 1881, which lasted for 154 days, fourteen Irish Members between them delivered 3,828 speeches—a daily average of almost twenty-five speeches from that group alone. In the same session, questions were multiplied several times over, so that *Hansard* required nine volumes for the complete debates of the year, compared with four or five in former years. Such obstruction is in effect nothing less than a repudiation of the existing Constitution of the country.

The attempt was bound to fail, and, at 9.30 a.m. on Wednesday, 2nd February, 1881, after a sitting of forty-one hours, and the most patient consideration extending over months, Mr. Speaker Brand delivered his celebrated *coup d'état*. He put the question while Irish Members still wished to continue the debate and thus instituted the 'closure'. Once accepted, the retention of the closure was necessitated as much by the increasing flood of parliamentary business as by a fear of the recurrence of systematic obstruction, and the procedure was hastily adapted to enforce the authority of the Government over a recalcitrant Opposition.

Four other points should be made before we can attempt a summing-up of the essential characteristics of procedure. The first is its com-

[1] Pearson's *Political Dictionary*, 1792, p. 50.

plexity. A suspicion seems to lurk that procedure has in the past been unnecessarily elaborated into a kind of 'nonsense on stilts', serving only to confuse Members and to delay beneficent legislation. The only basis for this belief is that, in the eighteenth century, the rules and stages of debate were multiplied with the object of decreasing the opportunities for surprise.

In the nineteenth century the history of procedural reform consisted largely in the safeguarding of the Order of Business by stripping off these and many other forms, and the framing of fresh methods to restrict debate and to facilitate the Government's business.

Let us take one example of the inevitable increase and intricacy of modern procedure—the well-known and valuable 'parliamentary Question'. The inside of an hour is all that can be spared for oral Questions, and in that time only about sixty (often far fewer) can secure the sought-after publicity of an oral reply. There are some twenty Government Departments to be questioned and only four question days in the week, so that a highly intricate system has to be worked out to try to give Members the fairest chance of questioning the Departments in turn and in some proportion to the importance of the latter. But that is not nearly all. Question time is far too valuable to be wasted, so that questions of the following types, to take only a few examples, are ruled out:

The identical question repeated daily or at short intervals;

Advertisement of some person or article masquerading as a question;

Abuse of an individual disguised as a question;

The giving of information or the continuation of a previous argument disguised as a question.

Many other complicated rules, on the subject of Questions alone, have to be administered with the most meticulous fairness, apart from rules governing the other sections of parliamentary business—such as Bills, Committees, the scope of debate, divisions and ballots. That is the answer to those who click their tongues and toss their heads against 'a lot of red tape' and wonder why 'a dozen simple straightforward rules' would not suffice.

Secondly, it cannot be stated too plainly that the House of Commons is entirely free at any time to adapt and alter its rules as it thinks fit, and as it has repeatedly done throughout its history. That would seem to supply the complete answer to all those critics within the House of Commons who point to its detailed procedure as the obstacle to efficiency. Nor does the House's reverence for tradition prevent it from sweeping away old forms if it finds them unsuitable. The ancient system of using Latin dates (still in vogue in the House of Lords), which obliges those of us with no Latin and a little French to come round by way of the latter, was exchanged for English by unanimous consent, as the first act of the first House of Commons which Mr. Gladstone led in 1866.[1] More recently, the House passed a Bill to amend and modernize the numbering and citation of Acts of Parliament.

The third notable consideration is that the question of reform has for many years been treated from the point of view of the interest of the State, and not in any party spirit. Remembering that the Opposition of today may be the Government of tomorrow, Members have regarded the rules of the House as machinery common to all parties, and if they have opposed the rearrangement of the rules to the advantage of the Government it has been because they believed that political responsibility is laid on all Members alike and that the lessening of this responsibility is prejudicial to the interests of the State. Such an attitude greatly cements the parliamentary system.

Fourthly, it should be noted how powerfully the House has defended the principle of minority rights in its attitude to the reform of procedure. The regular succession of events before one of the Select Committees which has customarily considered the subject over the last hundred years has been for witnesses to propose a series of much-needed reforms. The Committee in their recommendations would prune down this list and diminish the severity of its effect upon the Private Member, to whom the House would still further temper the wind by adopting a mere fraction of the original proposals—usually by Sessional Order for a trial period only. Soon the Government's difficulties would become clamant once more and the whole process would start anew, from a point a little in advance of the last investigation. But the tendency has always been the same—the higher the authority the more reluctant it has proved to countenance any reduction in the rules which protect the minority. That is perhaps one of the healthiest aspects of the British Parliament, and one of its greatest difficulties. As Sir George

[1] Sir G. O. Trevelyan, *The Early History of Charles James Fox*, 1880, p. 382.

Cornewall Lewis pointed out in 1875, the procedure is almost *too* fair: 'The forms of the English House of Commons are avowedly contrived for the protection of minorities; and they are so effectual for their purpose, as frequently to defeat the will of the great body of the House, and to enable a few members to resist, at least for a time, a measure desired by the majority.'[1] The trouble is that opinions vary on how long that time ought to be.

Earl (then Mr.) Attlee, in almost his first speech as Prime Minister in the House of Commons, on 16th August, 1945, clearly stated the position as follows:

> I have sat too long on the Opposition benches not to be sensitive of the rights of the Opposition and of the rights of private Members. It is the right and duty of the Opposition to criticize the administration and to oppose and seek to amend the legislation of the Government, but it is none the less the right and duty of the Government to govern and to pass into law the programme which it has been elected to carry out. The successful working of our Parliamentary institutions depends on harmonizing these conflicting rights and duties. It will be the object of the Government to preserve the rights of minorities as an essential feature of democracy while, at the same time, ensuring that democratic institutions are not wrecked by a failure to carry out and implement the will of the majority.

The other real obstacle to the reform of procedure lies in its growing volume and complexity. Parliament, during its long history, has coped with a multitude of varied situations, the records of which may, at any moment, be required to meet similar cases. Procedure, therefore, like freedom, 'slowly broadens down from precedent to precedent', until it now demands years of study and experience to span its vast extent. Exceptions and qualifications necessarily abound, and we may glance back with admiration at Elsynge, the Clerk, who sat below poor timid and confused Speaker Lenthall in the Long Parliament and was much commended as 'so great a help to the Speaker and to the House in helping to state the question and draw the orders *free from exceptions*, that it much conduced to the despatch of business and the service of Parliament'.[2]

[1] *An Essay on the Influence of Authority in Matters of Opinion*, 1849, p. 219.

[2] Whitelock's '*Memorials*' ii, p. 364, ed. 1832. (The present writer has feelingly italicized three words.) See also *The Officials of the House of Commons*, 1909, by O. C. Williams.

The House alone can alter its own procedure and few Members can find the time to master all its complications (which have vastly increased since Elsynge's time) and to prune away what dead-wood there may be. However, Select Committees still periodically investigate this vital matter, and these reports and evidence provide a rich education in Commons procedure.

I do not propose to trace in any detail the history of procedural reform, a subject which would merit a book in itself and which has in any case been considered at length in the Hansard Society's recent work on *Parliamentary Reform*.[1] But procedure affects Members exceedingly closely. It rules their lives and may enable them to realize life-long ambitions. The Report of the most recent Select Committee set up to examine the whole question of Procedure[2] was debated with animation in the House of Commons on 8th February, 1960. As usually happens, not all the Committee's proposals were adopted by the Government or accepted by the House. For instance, a recommendation that an experienced officer (or officers) should be appointed to help Private Members to draft Bills and amendments to Bills was rejected on a division. But the Government and the House did accept certain other suggestions: Money Resolutions were made 'exempted business' for three-quarters of an hour; the time allowed for a 'Count' was increased from two to four minutes, and the method of balloting for the daily half-hour Adjournment Motions was altered.[3]

The above are but a random few of the procedural suggestions which the House has discussed recently. But they show that procedure *continues to develop*. As Mr. R. A. Butler pointed out to his fellow Members: 'If . . . we cannot adapt our procedure to get the best people into the House, it will be our fault.'[4]

To sum up, we find that the procedure of the House of Commons is, in its essentials, very old, very complicated and always evolving. Procedure was originally a shelter and defence against the Crown and the Executive, but the forms used for this purpose were subsequently adapted for the protection of minorities. It may at any time be altered by the House, but such alterations are only carried out after full

[1] Published by Cassell for the Hansard Society, 1961.
[2] H.C. 92–I of 1958–9.
[3] Commons' *Hansard*, 16th December, 1959, cc. 1462–6; 8th February, 1960, cc. 34–5.
[4] Commons' *Hansard*, 13th July, 1959, c. 168.

discussion (and often by common consent, which is the best security for maintaining procedure) and with the strictest attention to the rights of minorities. Just as Bentham's words quoted at the head of the chapter point to the close relation between the history of procedure and of our liberties, so Dr. Redlich shows the connexion which it has with the Constitution. He calls the working of Parliament:

> A political pressure gauge, indicating the tension in the parliamentary machine and thence in the whole organism of the state.
>
> An attack upon any of the great fundamental principles which we have learnt to recognize as the theoretical bases of procedure is a danger signal. If equality among members, or publicity of the proceedings, or freedom of speech, or the majority principle is consciously challenged by one of the constituents of parliamentary life, we have an indication of the existence of some serious internal defect in the life of the State.

Or, as Sir Kenneth Pickthorn more recently and more succinctly said: 'Procedure is all the Constitution the poor Briton has.'[1]

[1] Commons' *Hansard*, 8th February, 1960, c. 70.

Chapter IX

THE HOUSE OF COMMONS AT WORK (iii): THE DETAILS OF PROCEDURE

'Members exhibit, in their collective demeanour, the peculiarities of our national disposition; and those very qualities which make the Empire what it is—simple straightforwardness of action, deference to the will of the majority, and reverence for ancient usage—symbolize the express genius of Parliament.'

Sir R. Palgrave, *The House of Commons*, 1878.

'The facility for compromise, which is all that the British "genius for government" means . . .'

Sir W. Ivor Jennings, *Parliament*.

There is no secret about the detailed procedure of the House of Commons. It is divided into three parts of very unequal size. The smallest consists of procedure which must be observed because it is the law prescribed by Act of Parliament, of which much the most important item is procedure under the Parliament Acts, regulating the powers of the two Houses in respect of disputed Bills. The next part consists of more than a hundred Standing Orders (apart from those regulating Private Business, whose fundamental object, it should be observed, is to give to all affected parties due notice and opportunity to protect their interests) and a few Sessional Orders. Only three Standing Orders date back before 1832. The remainder have been necessitated by the busy conditions of modern Parliaments. The third and by far the largest part is composed of a huge mass of traditions and precedents collected in the *Journals* and in certain textbooks, and in the experience of Members of Parliament and of the officials of the House. Because the Standing Orders are so much less in extent and so much more easily accessible to Members than the practice as interpreted from lengthy textbooks and scattered precedents, the relation of the one to the other has been likened by a former Clerk of the House to an iceberg—a tiny visible fraction giving warning of a huge invisible mass looming below.

The precedents which form the basis of so much of Parliament's procedure are, as the dictionary says, 'previous cases taken as examples for subsequent cases, or as a justification'.

'The House conducts both its business and its manners,' says Sir Reginald Palgrave,[1] 'according to chance remarks, or casual rules, recorded in the *Journals* of about three centuries ago; which rules were in their turn founded upon custom and usage of immemorial antiquity.' And through the ages those rules have been pored over, discussed, used and refined until they form what has been called 'the distilled common sense of centuries'. It is as hard to argue effectively against a sensible and well-used precedent of procedure as against an established classic in literature.

Let us take three examples of precedents, one old and two new. Readers may have been puzzled on occasion to hear that some Member has been 'named' for disorderly conduct in the House—a process which in Parliament is as effective as 'shooting the ringleader' in a less civilized community. A precedent of 9th June, 1641 supplies the answer. On that day Mr. Speaker Lenthall, having tried in vain to silence 'divers members who were talking at the lower end of the House, in the west corner under the gallery, at last called on Sir W. Carnabie, by name, to desist'.[2] The picture immediately springs to life: Mr. Speaker endeavouring to obtain silence by the usual method of calling 'Order! Order!' without singling out individuals, then clearing his throat and glancing with increasing irritation at the offenders, until at last by calling out the name he breaks an old convention and makes a new one. For long the naming of a Member was the Speaker's ultimate sanction. Under Standing Orders Nos. 23 and 24 the process now almost automatically entails the suspension of the Member.

New precedents are constantly being formed. On Friday, 13th April,

[1] *The House of Commons*, 1878, p. 9.
[2] Ibid., p. 11.

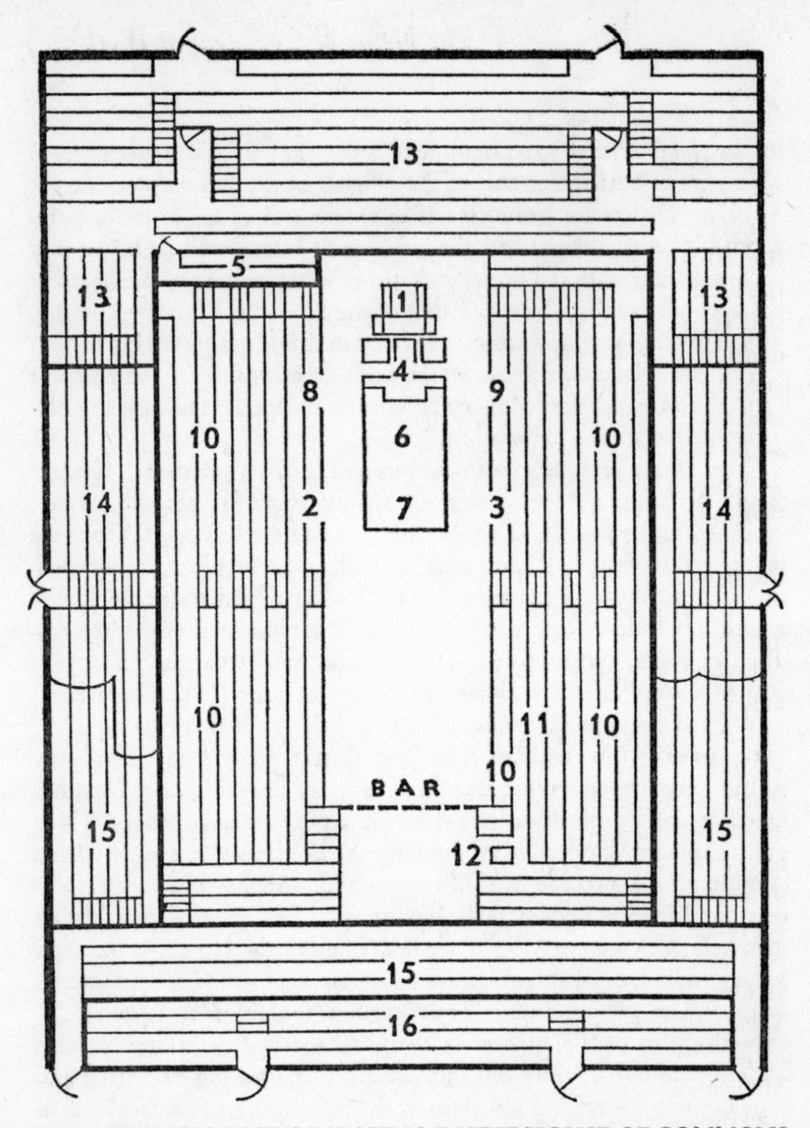

THE ARRANGEMENT OF SEATING IN THE HOUSE OF COMMONS

1 The Speaker
2 Prime Minister or Government spokesman
3 Leader of the Opposition or Opposition spokesman
4 Clerks at the Table
5 Civil Servants in attendance
6 The Table
7 The Mace
8 Government front bench, occupied by Ministers
9 Opposition front bench
10 Back benches
11 Other opposition parties
12 Serjeant at Arms
13 *Hansard* and press gallery
14 Members' side galleries
15 Special galleries, including Peers', 'Distinguished Strangers', Diplomatic and Commonwealth galleries
16 The public gallery

1945, the House decided to adjourn out of respect for the late President Roosevelt. Never before had an adjournment taken place upon the death of the head of a foreign State, and the incident has gone to swell the mass of parliamentary traditions which may be called into use in the future.[1] More recently a Member asked Mr. Speaker for guidance concerning the correct method of raising a point of order during a division. It had been traditional, at least since 1785, for the Member concerned to remain seated and covered. But the passage of time had seen hats almost entirely disappear from male heads in the Chamber, while lady Members had meanwhile arrived. This led on occasion to ludicrous scenes which need not be described, and the Member asked that in future a decent 'property' hat be kept at hand by the Serjeant at Arms. After discussion 'through the usual channels' the adoption of this new precedent was agreed to.

QUESTION TIME

Emphasis was laid in the preceding section on the *fairness* of procedure; let us now try to judge how *efficient* it is by watching the House of Commons at work.

Since so much of the proceedings may easily be missed during a first visit, let us make a strictly practical approach. It is well worth arriving in plenty of time (that is to say before 2.30 p.m.) in order to have a close view of the Speaker with his officers marching in dignified procession behind the Mace to the Chamber. Once we are installed in the public gallery a glance down will prove, I hope, that the threads of previous chapters are all drawing together to form an intelligible picture. We recognize the Speaker in his Chair and the Clerks at the Table before him. The Mace will be lying *on* the Table and the Serjeant at Arms seated at the Bar. We shall recognize the principal Members of the Government—perhaps from caricatures or from their television appearances—on the 'Treasury Bench' to the Speaker's right, with their supporters behind them. Facing them are the Opposition benches, occupied by lively critics of the Government. Minor Opposition parties occupy the seats on the Speaker's left, but below the gangway. (See illustration facing page 133 and the diagram on page 104.)

In 1945 the House of Commons was temporarily increased from

[1] The precedent was called into use all too soon, when the House of Commons adjourned on Monday, 25th November, 1963, after the assassination of President Kennedy.

615 Members to 640, to deal with certain overgrown electoral areas, while Boundary Commissions were recasting the whole country into single-member constituencies.[1] The Representation of the People Act, 1948, accepted their recommendations that there should be several new constituencies for England and one for Wales. In pursuit of the ideal of 'one man one vote', however, it reversed the findings of the Speaker's Conference of 1944 by abolishing the twelve University seats and the separate representation of the City of London. As a result of these changes and of others made in 1955 the House of Commons now consists of 630 Members, 511 returned from England, 71 from Scotland, 36 from Wales and 12 from Northern Ireland. The above Act (which incidentally repealed the famous Reform Act of 1832) and the consolidating Act of the following year, 1949, also brought the electoral law up to date by a host of amendments relating to such subjects as the registration of electors, the conduct of elections and expenses of candidates. In a matter so vital to democracy as the election of its representatives no detail is unimportant. The presiding officer at a polling station must know how to deal with an elector who arrives drunk, or has no hands, or is deaf, dumb *and* illiterate, or marks his voting paper with half a cross, or simply with the word 'Nap'.

How many Members will be present at any particular time depends upon the interest and importance of the business in hand; but Question Time, which begins not later than 2.45 p.m. on the first four days of the week, generally produces a good attendance.

The first few minutes may be occupied with 'Private Business', which usually means the stages of a special class of Bills dealing with some local or personal matter which requires the sanction of Parliament —the extension of the powers of a local authority, a railway, gas or water company, for instance, or the regulation of a private estate. (Bills of this kind, even when opposed, do not occupy more than a few hours of the House's time, but for their Committee stage they are formed into 'Groups', and four Members, sitting in a semi-judicial capacity, hear the case for or against them argued by Counsel. It is an example of essential but unostentatious work required of Members.)

During these few moments, while Private Business is going on amid a low hum of conversation, it is advisable to glance through the

[1] See initial Reports of the four Boundary Commissions, 1946–7 (Cmd. 7231); 1947–8 (Cmd. 7260), (Cmd. 7270) and (Cmd. 7274), all well garnished with maps.

'Notice Paper' (secured from a gallery attendant) and to mark any of the 'Questions' which are of personal interest to the visitor. There are Questions to suit every taste. They relate as often to personal grievances as to matters of wide interest, and they cover every conceivable subject. On 23rd January, 1963, the following typical examples of questions were answered in the House of Commons:

Mr. Lipton asked the Minister of Agriculture, Fisheries and Food what action he is taking to recover the cost of helicopter services provided to farmers owning livestock on Dartmoor.
The Minister of Agriculture, Fisheries and Food (Mr. Soames): 'The Government have decided that the Exchequer should bear the cost of the helicopter and aircraft flights requested by my Department for the supply of fodder to farms, on Dartmoor and elsewhere in England and Wales, which are in urgent need and have been isolated by the recent blizzards. I shall be asking the House to approve a Supplementary Vote for this purpose when the final cost is known. The cost of the fodder delivered will be paid by the farmer to his supplier in the normal way.'

Mr. Frank Allaun asked the Minister of Defence if he will state the expenditure on new works completed in the Cyprus Sovereign Base areas since the new Defence Plan was published; and what is the proposed further expenditure there.
The Minister of Defence (Mr. Peter Thorneycroft): '£13.5 million, plus £4 million on new works approved to date.'
Mr. Allaun: 'If, as is well known, the number of British troops is diminishing there, why are the Government spending millions on new military works? Secondly, would the Minister give the House an assurance that there is no connection with a nuclear or rocket base on the island?'
Mr. Thorneycroft: 'The money is being spent to build accommodation for troops either there or planned to be there.'

Commander Courtney asked the Minister of Defence whether, in view of the considerable operational and technical training problems which will require solution before the first British Polaris submarine joins the fleet, he will approach the United States Secretary of Defence with a view to a loan by the United States Navy to the Royal Navy of one American Mark I Polaris submarine equipped with dummy warheads and provided with adequate United States instructional personnel.
Mr. Thorneycroft: 'The problem of operational and technical training of crews for British Polaris submarines is among those being discussed with the United States naval authorities. Her Majesty's Government will take whatever steps

are necessary in the light of those discussions, but I cannot anticipate their outcome.'

Mr. Woodburn asked the Secretary of State for Scotland what information he has about the large shoals of small herring coming into the Forth and the numbers being destroyed in the Kincardine Power Station cooling system; and what steps he is taking to safeguard the possibilities of a return of the herring to the Forth.
The Under-Secretary of State for Scotland (*Mr. Brooman-White*): 'There are very few small herring in the Forth at present, but sprats have increased substantially this winter. Recently exceptional numbers of sprats penetrated the protecting screens at the cooling system intake and were destroyed. Over a period, however, losses at the intake have been only a very small percentage of catches of herring and sprats in the Forth and it does not seem that they will materially affect the fishery prospects.'

By the end of Question Time (normally lasting about an hour) the visitor will have guessed that many Questions have a past history of differences between Members and Departments, and that they are as often designed to press for action in remedying some grievance as to obtain information. He will also have some appreciation of the vast field covered by Parliament. During this time it will have been exercising its *critical* function, and Ministers of the Crown will be the best witnesses as to its efficiency: the Treasury Bench is not always a comfortable seat at this hour. Questions are a comparatively recent development of procedure. The earliest instance was in 1721, but the first printed Questions did not appear on the Order Paper until 1835 and a fixed time was not given up to them until 1869.[1] Originally their place was taken by numerous other opportunities for debate and by petitions, laboriously prepared, often with thousands and even millions of signatures. The saving of time and trouble resulting from the substitution for a petition of a Question concerning helicopter services, nuclear rocket bases or small herrings, may be imagined. In years gone by a Member could ask daily as many Questions as he wished, but pressure of time has compelled a restriction first to eight, next to four, then to three, and finally to two. All Questions which are 'in order' are placed on the Notice Paper, any in excess of a Member's daily allowance being put down for a later date.

[1] See P. Howarth, *Questions in the House*, 1956; and D. N. Chester & N. Bowring, *Questions in Parliament*, 1962.

A NEW MEMBER

Although the next item on your Notice Paper is '*Fort William Pulp and Paper Mills Bill; Second Reading*', several proceedings may intervene. Let us imagine two of them. A new Member, elected at a by-election, is standing at the Bar between his two sponsors. At the Speaker's invitation they walk up the centre of the House, stopping three times to bow, and Mr. —— then takes the oath, signs the Test Roll and is introduced to Mr. Speaker. Yesterday he was an ordinary citizen; today he is a Member of Parliament.

The resolution of the House requiring Members elected at by-elections to be introduced by sponsors 'so that they may be the better known to the House' was passed in 1688. On 17th April, 1945, a newly elected Member refused to accept sponsors, on the ground that there were none of his party in the House. It was decided upon a division not to dispense with the rule, and on the following day the Member accepted two sponsors and was introduced in the usual fashion.

PRIVILEGE

A sudden buzz of interest causes you to lean forward. A back-bench Member, the Chairman of a Private Bill Committee, is on his feet to raise a point of 'Privilege'. He has a newspaper cutting in his hand and is claiming that a provincial editor has questioned his fairness in the conduct of the Committee. The 'privileges' of the House form a special sort of law—its own law, interpreted and administered by itself within the walls of Parliament, but acknowledged and recognized everywhere as part of the law of England—which has grown up through the ages for the express purpose of maintaining the dignity and independence of the House and of its Members. The privileges of Members include freedom of speech, freedom from arrest (except on a criminal charge) and protection against assaults and indignities. Privilege must not, however, be thought of as some special favour which enables Members to ignore the ordinary law. It is a very necessary protection, without which a Member could not defend the electors' own interests. The privilege of Members is therefore to be regarded as the privilege of every citizen. No new privileges may be created and the present practice of the House seems to be to insist upon no more than the bare minimum of its rights necessary to uphold its proper dignity and efficiency. If necessary, a complaint of breach of privilege is referred to the Committee of Privileges—the most authoritative of all Committees—and after they have reported, if the offender is punished at all, a majority of the House must first agree and decide what sanctions are to be imposed.

LEGISLATION

The House will next proceed to the 'Orders of the Day'. On pages 112–14 is a copy of the Public Bill in question, in case the reader has never seen one. The principal point to observe is that certain words—those imposing a financial charge on the country—are printed in italics, as a reminder of the special procedure required for this part of the Bill. As we have seen (p. 36) only 'the Crown' (*i.e.* the Government) can propose such a charge, and the Financial (or Money) Resolution, which is said to 'cover' it, is printed on page 116. But, in order to allow Members some latitude, the Resolution should be drawn more widely than the wording in the Bill, so that alterations of the incidence of the charge, *and even increases in its amount*, may be proposed, so long as they are within the Resolution. This Resolution has to be agreed to both in Committee of the Whole House and in the House itself, before the particular clause can be proceeded with in the Committee on the Bill. If for any reason the Government wish *themselves* to increase the charge beyond the original Money Resolution they are bound either to withdraw it and introduce another, or to introduce a supplementary Resolution covering the extra charge.

The purpose of these additional stages (which some critics of parliamentary procedure consider superfluous[1]) remains what it was when they were adopted almost 300 years ago by the House of Commons 'in the exercise of that great and most important privilege, "the sole and exclusive right of granting aids and supplies to the Crown": in order (as it is their duty, when they are imposing burthens upon their fellow subjects, to give every opportunity for free and frequent discussions) that they may not, by sudden and hasty votes, incur expenses, or be induced to approve of measures, which might entail heavy and lasting burthens upon themselves and their posterity.'[2]

[1] A recent move in the Australian House of Representatives drastically to simplify financial procedure on Bills was described in *The Times* of 13th November, 1962.

[2] J. Hatsell, *Precedents of Proceedings in the House of Commons*, new ed., 1818, Vol. III, p. 176.

The following three pages show what a short Public Bill looks like. The London Government Bill of 1962 *ran to* 205 *pages and the Income Tax Bill* [*Lords*] *of* 1952 *to* 511 *pages. The corresponding Financial (or Money) Resolution, as it appeared in the 'Vote', is reproduced on page* 116.

Fort William Pulp and Paper Mills Bill

EXPLANATORY AND FINANCIAL MEMORANDUM

This Bill empowers the Board of Trade to make loans to Wiggins, Teape & Co. Limited for the purpose of building and equipping a pulp mill and associated paper mills at Fort William, Inverness-shire, Scotland. The Bill places a limit on the total amount of such loans and the period during which they may be made and provides that interest shall be charged at 5½ per cent. per annum.

The Bill further provides for grants to be made to the Company equivalent to the amount of interest payable in respect of the period ending 31st December 1966, and authorises the Board of Trade to make an agreement or agreements with the Company defining the other terms and conditions of the loan, including the repayment conditions. Copies of such agreements are to be laid before both Houses of Parliament.

Financial Effect of the Bill

The amount of the charge on public funds which the Bill authorises in respect of loans is £10 million. It is intended that not more than £8 million of this total will be advanced during the period ending 31st December 1966. The total of the grants which the Bill authorises the Board of Trade to make in respect of interest payments falling due during this period must not exceed £1·3 million. The Bill provides that all the sums required are to be paid out of monies voted by Parliament, and that any sums received by the Board as interest or repayment of loans are to be paid into the Exchequer.

[*Note:*—This Bill was presented under Standing Order No. 80]

A

BILL

TO

Authorise the Board of Trade to make advances to Wiggins, Teape & Co. Limited in connection with the construction and equipment of pulp and paper mills in the neighbourhood of Fort William, and to make grants to that company in respect of interest on such advances.

A.D. 1963.

BE IT ENACTED by the Queen's most Excellent Majesty, by and with the advice and consent of the Lords Spiritual and Temporal, and Commons, in the present Parliament assembled, and by the authority of the same, as follows:—

Power of Board to make advances, and grants in respect of interest on advances.

5 **1.**—(1) *The Board of Trade may from time to time advance by way of loan to Wiggins, Teape & Co. Limited* (*in this Act referred to as the Company*) *sums not exceeding* £10 *million in all for the purpose of the construction and equipment of pulp and paper mills in the neighbourhood of Fort William in the* 10 *county of Inverness.*

(2) Sums advanced under subsection (1) above shall carry interest at 5½ per cent. per annum, and subject thereto shall be advanced at such times, and on such terms as to repayment and otherwise, as may be agreed upon between the Board and the 15 Company; but no sums shall be advanced under that subsection after 31st December 1972.

(3) *The Board of Trade may from time to time make grants to the Company in respect of the liability of the Company for interest on sums advanced under subsection* (1) *above, being interest* 20 *accruing before* 1*st January* 1967, *of such amounts not exceeding* £1·3 *million in all as may be agreed upon as aforesaid.*

(4) A copy of any agreement made between the Board and the Company with respect to the making of advances or grants under this section shall be laid before each House of Parliament.

(5) There shall be paid out of moneys provided by Parliament all sums required by the Board of Trade for making advances or grants under this section; and all sums received by the Board by way of interest on or repayment of advances under this section shall be paid into the Exchequer. 5

(6) Section 24 of the Local Employment Act 1960 (powers of Board of Trade) shall apply for the purposes of this section.

Short title. **2.** This Act may be cited as the Fort William Pulp and Paper Mills Act 1963.

Fort William Pulp and Paper Mills

A
BILL

To authorise the Board of Trade to make advances to Wiggins, Teape & Co. Limited in connection with the construction and equipment of pulp and paper mills in the neighbourhood of Fort William, and to make grants to that company in respect of interest on such advances.

Presented by Mr. Erroll
supported by
Mr. Chancellor of the Exchequer,
Mr. Secretary Noble and Mr. David Price

Ordered, by The House of Commons, *to be Printed, 4 April 1963*

LONDON
PRINTED AND PUBLISHED BY
HER MAJESTY'S STATIONERY OFFICE
Price 5*d.* net
(37051)

[Bill 94] 42/4

This Bill has been selected because, though not of particular importance, it is short, basically uncontentious, and includes a Financial Memorandum and an italicized 'Money' clause.

It is difficult for the uninitiated to realize the amount of work which goes into a Bill before its appearance in the House. Even such a slight Bill as this one will have been thoroughly thought out and discussed in all its bearings, and in the case of an important and complicated measure such as an Education Bill or a Coal Mines Bill the labour is enormous. It is said that Mr. Gladstone originated the system of preliminary consultations with affected interests, and this procedure saves much time. In addition, there will be thorough discussion with the Treasury and other Departments, and numerous drafts may have to be prepared before approval for the introduction of the Bill is finally secured from the Cabinet Committee on Legislation.

The expert barristers who put the required ideas into proper legal form are called 'Government draftsmen'. 'One might fairly say of these draftsmen,' writes Sir Cecil Carr, a recent Counsel to Mr. Speaker, 'that they are, in fact and of necessity, the key men of Whitehall, the hardest-worked, the most severely tried. Having no politics themselves, they have to know . . . every move in the political game. They could—but you may be sure they will not—tell you the truth about many a famous Minister, his strength and his weakness. . . . Their knowledge of law must be extensive and accurate. Their responsibility is grave.'[1]

In spite of the care taken in the preparation of Bills, many emerge as Acts whose interpretation puzzles the shrewdest judges in the country. To the man in the street they are often almost unintelligible. The following extract is taken at random from the Local Government Bill, 1947:

> (4) There shall be paid out of moneys provided by Parliament to the council of each such county or large burgh as aforesaid such sum as bears to the excess of the amount estimated under subsection (2) of this section in relation to the county or large burgh over the amount estimated under sub-section (3) of this section in relation thereto the like proportion as the number of days in the part of the year 1948–49 which precedes the appointed day for the purposes of Part II of the National Health Service (Scotland) Act, 1947, bears to the number of days in the whole of that year.

Further confusion results from legislation by reference back and amendment of previous Acts, of which the following, taken from sub-

[1] *Concerning English Administrative Law*, 1941, p. 171.

21. Fort William Pulp and Paper Mills [Money] (Queen's *Recommendation* signified),—*considered* in Committee under Standing Order No. 84 (Money Committees) :—

(In the Committee)

Resolved, That, for the purposes of any Act of the present Session to authorise the Board of Trade to make advances to Wiggins, Teape & Co. Limited in connection with the construction and equipment of pulp and paper mills in the neighbourhood of Fort William, and to make grants to that company in respect of interest on such advances, it is expedient to authorise the provision out of moneys provided by Parliament—

(*a*) of sums not exceeding £10 million in all to be advanced by the Board of Trade to the said company by way of loan;

(*b*) of sums not exceeding £1·3 million in all required by the Board of Trade for making grants to the said company in respect of the company's liability for interest accruing before 1st January 1967 on sums advanced by way of loan under the said Act;

and the payment into the Exchequer of sums received by the Board of Trade by way of interest on or repayment of such advances by way of loan.—(*Mr. Secretary Noble.*)

Resolution to be reported.

Report to be received *To-morrow.*

A FINANCIAL (OR MONEY) RESOLUTION

Extract from the *Votes and Proceedings* of 10th April, 1963, showing the Financial Resolution which must be agreed to, first in Committee of the Whole House and then (on Report) in the House itself, before the part of the Bill which imposes a charge on the public revenue can be considered (see page 110).

The House of Commons in 1742. The best-known view of St. Stephen's in the eighteenth century. Mr. Speaker Onslow is in the Chair and Sir Robert Walpole is addressing the House. *From a print by John Pine*

William Pitt addressing the House of Commons, 1793. Among the Members present are Canning, Wilberforce, Sheridan, Erskine and Charles James Fox

section (5) of section 21 of the Finance Act 1936, is a terrible example:

> Sub-sections (2) and (3) of Section twenty of the Finance Act, 1922, shall have effect as if references to paragraph (c) of sub-section (1) of that section included references to the foregoing provisions of this section, as if references to a disposition included references to a settlement, and as if the reference to the making of a disposition included a reference to the making of or entering into a settlement, and sub-section (4) of that section shall have effect as if the reference to that section included a reference to the said provisions of this section.

Where the matter of a previous Act which it is desired to amend is short it is sometimes printed as a schedule to the new Bill with the amendments shown by typographical devices, but this attempt at clarification can only be used in certain cases.

The explanation given by the draftsmen is that an involved style is often unavoidable owing to the extreme complexity and wide range of modern legislation; the desire of Parliament to control its effect as closely as possible; and the necessity of avoiding difficulties of interpretation in the Courts. They add that legislation by reference is often a convenient and economical method, since the alternative to amending old Acts is to repeal them and to enact whole new measures, which involves much extra printing and throws the entire new measures open to discussion and amendment by Parliament, instead of only the matters requiring alteration.

But the making of laws seems fated to be a thankless task. In 1825, for instance, the Treasury had but a single specialist draftsman at their disposal and many Bills were drawn in a very defective manner, 'so abounding in errors of grammar even, that the very printer puts *sic* in the margin'.[1] The 'highest legal authorities' were as dissatisfied then as they are today, but they found the legislation unintelligible for an opposite reason—the Acts were 'so loosely worded that no proceedings could be instituted upon them' and they were 'passed in ignorance of the practice they tried to improve'. The effect upon the unfortunate citizen at both periods appears to be identical: 'Any attempt of the unlearned public to understand the statutes is like an endeavour to interpret a Runic inscription.' Perhaps some committee of lawyers and men of letters and other sensible speakers of the Queen's English may one day

[1] W. Wickens, *An Argument for more of the Division of Labour in Civil Life in this Country, Part I*, 1829, p. 22.

examine this matter which so nearly affects the work of Parliament. They might enjoy the task of selecting monstrous specimens and first calling critical experts to suggest alternatives, and then the draftsmen to defend their drafting and to criticize the critics. Together they might all hammer out some recipes for more intelligible laws; but even if they found that *no* improvement was possible, that in itself would be a comfort and a reassurance to the man in the street.

It is unnecessary to follow in full every detail of procedure on a Bill. Everyone has heard of its three 'Readings'—dating back, of course, to days before printing. The First Reading stage has for long been formal. It is merely a signal that such a Bill is on its way. Between First and Second Readings the Bill is printed and circulated to Members. Upon the Second Reading the *principle* of the Bill is discussed and a wide debate may take place; in Committee its *details* are examined, line by line and word by word. Then follows the Consideration (or Report) stage, in the House, with further opportunities for amending the Bill. Finally, on the Third Reading, debate may be raised on the Bill as it stands. If the Bill has passed all these stages without the House voting for its rejection at any stage, it is then sent to the Lords. The endorsements on Bills passing between the Houses are still made in Norman French—in this case 'Soit baillé aux Seigneurs' (let it be forwarded to the Lords). The whole process is repeated in the second Chamber. The Lords either agree to the Bill as it stands or return it with Amendments, and in the latter case it continues to pass between the Houses until either an accommodation is reached and it becomes an Act by receiving the Royal Assent (from a Commission representing the Sovereign) with the words 'La Reine le veult', or neither side will give way and the Bill is lost. No Government Bill had been rejected by the Lords since 1914 (when two were forced through by the Parliament Act) until they threw out the amending Parliament Bill in June, 1948. Disagreements over Amendments are rarely pushed to extremes. Although in 1930, after repeated Messages had passed between the two Houses, a deadlock seemed inevitable, in the case of the Unemployment Insurance (No. 2) Bill, the Commons gave way, and in the case of the Coal Mines Bill the Lords did so. Private Members' Bills and Private Bills, however, often pass through one House only to be rejected or shelved in the second.

In the case before us the Bill is simple and uncontentious, a short chapter to be added to the great body of existing law. Nevertheless the brief debate (lasting about ninety minutes) upon the Second Reading is taken very seriously. An Under-Secretary explains the measure; two or three interested Members raise queries; these are answered by the Minister, and the House is satisfied and allows the Second Reading. Some days then elapse before the Committee stage, according to the usual practice. But let us suppose instead that it is necessary for the Bill to pass at once. The Serjeant at Arms will put the Mace below the Table top and the Speaker and Clerk will leave their chairs for a few moments while the Chairman of Ways and Means, from the Clerk's place, conducts the Bill through its Committee stage. A few small Amendments may be incorporated or withdrawn in face of an explanation from the Minister in charge of the Bill. Then, after the Speaker and Clerk have resumed their places and the Mace has reappeared, the Bill, if amended in Committee, is considered; then the Third Reading is taken and the Bill is passed. (These details are inserted to explain the actions and pauses during the proceedings which visitors must often find rather baffling.)

The process is exactly the same, though much longer, for more important measures. The Second Reading, for example, may occupy two or even three days, and the Committee stage (which is now generally taken upstairs, in a Standing Committee) several weeks.

A Second Reading can be opposed either by voting against the question 'That the Bill be now read a Second Time' or, more usually, by moving an Amendment in one of the two forms: (1) to substitute the words 'This day six months' (or three months, if moved after Whitsun) for 'now', which, if successful, is accepted as a definite rejection of the Bill or (2) a 'reasoned Amendment', setting out the grounds on which the Bill should be refused a Second Reading. Again, if carried, the Amendment will almost certainly be fatal to the Bill. To comply with the principle of 'publicity', notice of the great majority of parliamentary proceedings is required before they come on in the House.

In Committee both the supporters and opponents of a Bill may attempt to secure its alteration in detail by proposing Amendments to it. Since the possible number of such Amendments is unlimited, certain steps have had to be taken to prevent an indefinite hold-up of business. (1) The Chairman and his Deputy have been granted a permanent power to select Amendments, known as 'the Kangaroo', since the choice leaps over some Amendments to descend upon others—those not selected being ignored. In this selection they have the advice of various experts and endeavour to treat all Members with scrupulous fairness, by selecting those Amendments which cover the widest ground. (2) Various forms of closure have been instituted (see Glossary). Of these the old form of demanding 'That the question be now put', after each Amendment has been under discussion for a reasonable time, is not effective enough in its action, and, in the case of long and controversial Bills, has been largely superseded by the 'Guillotine' system. This is a Motion proposed by the Government, which, if agreed to by the House, allots fixed periods of debating time for the stages of a Bill or for its detailed parts during one stage. But in recent years a voluntary agreement for this purpose has sometimes proved equally effective.

These are the means by which Parliament exercises its *legislative* function. That it can work fast in an emergency was proved once again at the outbreak of war in 1939, when forty-nine Bills passed through both Houses in three weeks; a great deal of preparatory work had, of course, been done by the Departments in anticipation of the crisis.

Before leaving the subject of legislation a word should be said about White Papers, when they take the form of explanatory statements of Government policy on a particular subject. Of late years the custom has grown up of testing opinion by a Motion such as:

> That this House approves the Proposals of Her Majesty's Government for Civil Aviation contained in Command Paper No. 6712,

before introducing the relevant legislation. This saves time by clarifying the views of the House and of the country at an early stage, and presents the subject to the public in a form more intelligible than that of a Bill. The procedure of discussion by White Paper was followed during 1944 in the cases of some of the great projects of our time, the establishment of a National Health Service, Social Insurance and Industrial Injuries Insurance.

THE MAIN DEBATE

By this time the House is packed to the doors if, as we shall suppose, you have been very lucky and the main business of the day is a great debate upon, say, foreign affairs. Since the House will not in all probability wish to come to any particular Resolution upon such an occasion, and since some question should always be before the House,[1] the debate will proceed upon the Motion 'That this House do now adjourn'. After the Chief Whip has formally moved this Motion, the Prime Minister opens the debate with a general statement upon the trend of events and the Government's policy. And it is on such an occasion that you are most likely to come under the spell of the House of Commons. You will feel the excitement of the crowded and traditional setting, the exhilaration of fresh news (for the House likes well to be first informed), the jests sparking like electricity across the Floor, sudden sallies of laughter, the cheers and counter cheers, above all a sense of being really at grips with the subject. There is some ill-informed and misinformed talk in the House—but not so much as outside. After listening to a House of Commons debate it is difficult not to feel that one is at any rate nearer *a chance* of arriving at the truth. That is the advantage of listening to the Grand Inquest of the nation at work.

After the Prime Minister's opening speech, Member after Member will be selected to speak from the number who rise in all parts of the House. You will soon have a just suspicion that 'catching the Speaker's eye' is not the pure hazard which it sounds. Members with special authority or qualification to speak, diplomatists, service Members or economic experts, will have previously informed the Speaker of their desire to take part, and he will have these names in mind during the debate. This is another instance of a rule of absolute fairness tempered by common sense. The element of chance still remains and on the whole the arrangements work to the advantage and satisfaction of the House.

Later in the debate specific and relevant matters or grievances may be raised, such as the merits of certain disputes, or conditions affecting British subjects in different parts of the world. You may perhaps be surprised by the simple, almost conversational style of speaking. That has been the trend for at least the last hundred years. In the eighteenth century a handful of aristocratic protagonists on each side delivered

[1] There are exceptions to the rule demanding that a question shall always be before the House, such as 'Questions' themselves, statements by Ministers and personal explanations; but exceptions and less common proceedings have had to be ignored in this sketch, to try to give the reader a view of the wood without smothering him among the branches of the trees.

speeches of several hours' duration, in the grand style, modelled on the orators of the ancient world and packed with classical quotations, while the masses of country squires sat by, applauded, and scarcely spoke at all themselves. The main change came with the new type of Member in 1832 and since then there has been a steady tendency towards shorter and simpler speaking. 'If I were asked to supply in three words the clue to good parliamentary speaking at the present time, those words would be *clearness*, *simplicity*, *restraint*,' says Lord Snell in his *Daily Life in Parliament*. The House hates hollow declamations and false sentiment—but above all it hates bores. As early as 1819 Sir T. Buxton remarked that 'The House loves good sense and joking, and nothing else,' and more lately a writer has cruelly called the House of Commons 'a body without any principles or prejudices, except against bores'.

THE ADJOURNMENT

Unless a motion to extend the usual hour of sitting has been moved by the Government and agreed to by the House (a frequent practice nowadays) or unless 'exempted business' (see Glossary) is under discussion, the House at present concludes its main business of the day at 10 p.m. The remaining half-hour before the House finally rises is eagerly sought after by Members to raise small debates on a Motion for the Adjournment. Formerly this period used often to be seriously diminished by certain formalities, but as some indemnification for the loss of practically all Private Members' debating time during and immediately after the war, they are now assured of a full half-hour for this purpose. It is a useful and popular opportunity to raise topics and grievances of a somewhat urgent character, often arising out of 'Questions'. For example, a Member was much disturbed some years ago to find a 'wounded soldier' on crutches begging in the rain outside an American Service Club, who told him that he had been discharged by an ungrateful country without a sufficient pension. The Member raised the matter first with the Minister of Pensions and then on the evening Adjournment, when the man was shown to be an impostor.

Two other types of Adjournment Motion should be mentioned: motions moved upon the eve of the parliamentary vacations, which provide opportunities for general debates, and the rare Adjournment under Standing Order No. 9, to discuss 'a definite matter of urgent public importance'. The latter requires the Speaker's assent as to its definiteness and urgency, and its public importance is to some extent ensured by the stipulation that at least a quorum of the House must support it. A debate was successfully claimed under this Standing Order on 6th March, 1958, to discuss the deportation from Great Britain of a young Spanish sailor, and resulted in securing a delay in the deportation proceedings.

COMMITTEES OF THE WHOLE HOUSE ON BILLS OR RESOLUTIONS

A Committee of the Whole House is composed of all the Members of the House sitting under the presidency of a Chairman instead of the Speaker, and with the Mace below the Table. Members are free to speak more than once on the same question, no seconders are required, and the whole atmosphere of debate is more informal. The ordinary 'Committee of the Whole House' deals with the Committee stage of Bills which are either of constitutional importance, or in other respects too important or too urgent (and this sometimes includes small uncontroversial Bills) to send to Standing Committees. Committees of the Whole House also deal with Resolutions authorizing the grant of public money, mainly for the purposes of legislation (see p. 110).

STANDING COMMITTEES

The majority of Bills go upstairs for their Committee stage to Standing Committees. These are microcosms of the House itself, each usually composed of up to about fifty Members, in party proportions corresponding to those in the House. The Scottish Standing Committee, for example, consists of about thirty Members from Scottish constituencies, with the addition of not more than twenty other 'nominated' Members.[1] Nominations are made by the Committee of Selection, and the Chairman is appointed by the Speaker from a special panel of experienced Members. The quorum of a Standing Committee is seventeen, or one-third of the number of its members, excluding the Chairman, whichever is the lesser.

SELECT COMMITTEES

Under an ancient procedure dating back more than three hundred years, the House regularly sets up Select Committees to examine

[1] The Scottish *Grand* Committee consists of all 71 Scottish Members, with from 10 to 15 non-Scottish Members added.

special matters on its behalf. These Committees, so-called because their members are 'selected' by the House, are usually fairly small in size. Often, they have powers to send for persons and papers, and their Reports, when presented to the House, may form the subject of important, animated debates.

Among the *regular* Select Committees which the House sets up are the Committee of Privileges (see pp. 109–110), and the Estimates Committee and the Public Accounts Committee (see p. 125).

THE COMMITTEE OF WAYS AND MEANS

Two other 'Committees of the Whole House', apart from those on Bills and Resolutions mentioned above, exercise the principal financial functions of the House. On Budget day, when the Chancellor of the Exchequer makes his comprehensive review of the national accounts, the necessary changes in taxation are proposed in 'Committee of Ways and Means'. They must later be reported to the House itself and agreed to, and subsequently embodied in the annual Finance Bill which has to pass through all the usual stages within certain limits of time. (For other functions of this Committee, see Glossary.)

THE COMMITTEE OF SUPPLY

Certain expenses of government (such as the Civil List and the salaries of Mr. Speaker, the judges and the Comptroller and Auditor General) are charged directly upon the 'Consolidated Fund', which is the public purse, with the express object of avoiding the necessity for them to be annually voted and reviewed. The remainder, almost 70% of the total, are provided for out of 'moneys provided by Parliament' in the form of 'Estimates'[1] which, after the most careful preparation in the Departments, and scrutiny by the Treasury, and, if necessary, the Cabinet, are presented to the House and voted in 'Committee of Supply', which is another Committee of the Whole House.

The Committee of Supply, therefore, grants the money which is later found by the Committee of Ways and Means. But there is one final step. It would be no use, for instance, voting an Estimate of millions of pounds for all the branches of the Army if the War Office chose to spend it all on pay for the men or for the officers. One of the Consolidated Fund Bills (known as the Appropriation Bill) therefore

[1] See pages 126–7.

closely 'appropriates' the money to its intended objects, and it is later the duty of a small committee of the House, the Public Accounts Committee, and one of its officers, the Comptroller and Auditor General, to ensure the strictest adherence to this measure.

Twenty-six days are occupied by the Commons in considering the estimates in the Committee of Supply; but, as these estimates cover all the vast field of the Government's activities, it is rarely possible to examine the details of financial administration, and the debates are usually concerned with questions of policy. However, pursuing the ideal of fairness, as ever, it is the practice to allow the Opposition or Oppositions a free choice of subject on these days, and they may plunge in their dip or sampler and bring up any item they wish for discussion. Moreover, the relic of a practice still exists which dates back to the earliest Parliaments, when the Commons were only called together to vote sums to the Sovereign, and it was their right first to have their grievances discussed—the old doctrine of 'grievances before supply'. This practice is as follows: upon first going into Committee of Supply (see p. 124) on the Civil Estimates a question is put 'that Mr. Speaker do now leave the Chair', and by moving Amendments to this question attention can be drawn to relevant grievances or subjects. Apart from this one occasion, when Members ballot for precedence in moving Amendments, the choice of subject for debate lies with the Opposition. Thus by this slender thread a very ancient tradition of the Constitution survives.

Two Select Committees help the House to maintain control of expenditure. The Public Accounts Committee, as already mentioned, are largely concerned with the appropriation of sums voted for the past year; and they may also make recommendations for improving the form and method of the national accounts. The Estimates Committee in normal times examine the current Estimates and report what, if any, economies, *consistent with policy*, may be effected in them. During the war, the place of the Estimates Committee was taken by the National Expenditure Committee, who covered a wide field of investigation into possible economies in war expenditure, both by personal visits to factories, etc., and by calling thousands of witnesses before them.

That, briefly, is how the House of Commons exercises its *financial* functions. It raises all taxes and grants their proceeds for specific purposes to the Crown. It is only the *initiation* of financial policy which

(2)

BRITISH MUSEUM (NATURAL HISTORY)

I. ESTIMATE of the amount required in the year ending 31 March 1964 for the salaries and expenses of the British Museum (Natural History), including a purchase grant in aid.

Six hundred and fifty-seven thousand pounds

(£657,000)

II. Subheads under which this Vote will be accounted for by the Trustees of the British Museum, and additional detail.

1962–63		1963–64	
£		£	£
558,000	A. SALARIES, &c.		603,000
	The number of staff provided for is 504 at 1 April 1963 increasing to 527 by 31 March 1964 (502 with provision for a further 2 in 1962–63). *See* Appendix.		
27,490	B. GENERAL ADMINISTRATIVE EXPENSES (Provision adjusted for rounding)		32,990
10,500	C. PURCHASES (GRANT IN AID)		14,500
8,000	(1) Annual grant	12,000	
2,500	(2) Special grant	2,500	
	Expenditure will be accounted for in detail to the Comptroller and Auditor General. Any unexpended balance of the sums issued will not be liable to surrender to the Exchequer.		
28,000	D. MUSEUM TECHNICAL EXPENSES		28,500
22,750	(1) Materials, apparatus, &c., for preparing and preserving specimens	23,000	
5,250	(2) Book binding	5,500	
10	E. PUBLICATIONS DEPARTMENT (NET)		10
4,400	(1) Salaries, &c. (6 staff)	5,000	
18,110	(2) Printing, &c.	20,010	
22,510		25,010	
	Less:		
14,500	(3) Receipts from sales	15,000	
8,000	(4) Cost price of publications given in exchange or for services rendered (charged to Subhead B.)	10,000	
624,000	Gross Total		679,000
	Deduct:		
21,000	Z. APPROPRIATIONS IN AID		22,000
	(1) Contributions from donors with specific interests:		
400	(*a*) Rothschild Trust (Siphonaptera)	400	
	(*b*) Department of Technical Co-operation—		
10,100	(i) Overseas Geological Surveys	11,270	
1,150	(ii) Research grant	600	
7,850	(*c*) U.S. Public Health Service—		
	(i) Schistosomiasis research	5,230	
	(ii) Acarological research	3,000	
500	(2) Receipts from sale of photographs	500	
1,000	(3) Miscellaneous receipts	1,000	
603,000	Net Total		657,000

Increase £54,000

These two pages show the Estimate for the Natural History Museum

Additional expenditure in connection with the service is estimated at:

1962–63		1963–64
£		£
151,800	(1) Maintenance, furniture, fuel, light, &c. (Class IX, 1 and 2)	139,000
20,000	(2) Rates (Class IX, 11)	23,000
59,000	(3) Superannuation (Class IX, 16)	73,000
9,093	(4) Miscellaneous	11,000
239,893	TOTAL	246,000

NOTE

The provision of free accommodation and services at the Museum to certain bodies receiving assistance from public funds is noted on the respective Estimates. In addition free accommodation and services (estimated at £540 per annum) are provided to the Zoological Society of London and limited accommodation (estimated annual rental value £1,621) is provided to other organisations whose work is of immediate value to the Museum.

NATIONAL ACCOUNTS CLASSIFICATION

The whole Vote is classified as current expenditure on goods and services.

APPENDIX

TABLE I: SENIOR STAFF

1962–63		1963–64
Nos.		Nos.
1	Director (£4,050)	1
3	Deputy Chief Scientific Officers (£3,125–£3,450)	3
12	Senior Principal Scientific Officers (£2,650–£3,000)	13

TABLE II: PROFESSIONAL STAFF

1962–63		1963–64
Nos.		Nos.
85	Scientific Officer Class	85

Whether a Member wishes to have an Estimate decreased or increased his method of criticism is to move for a reduction. For example, if he wished to procure either an increase or a decrease in the amount of money spent out of the public purse for purchases of exhibits for the Natural History Museum he might put down the following motion:

Mr. ——, — On Civil Estimates, Class VIII, Vote 2: to move to reduce Sub-head C by £100.

belongs to the Executive, and that policy must at every step be authorized by the House.

The Commons exercise this control over policy and administration by means of debates on the main Estimates in Committee of Supply. Detailed control, so far as it exists, comes through discussions on the Supplementary Estimates and through the work of the Public Accounts and the Estimates Committees.

Chapter X

HOW THE PROCEEDINGS REACH THE PEOPLE

'It is not natural, nor rational, that the people who sent us hither should be not informed of our actions.'

Sir Francis Winnington, M.P., 1681.

The attitude of the House of Commons towards the publication of its proceedings and debates must, until recent years, have appeared vacillating, parsimonious and unhappy. But it should be remembered that Members had, at different times, sound reasons to fear the vengeance of an overbearing Sovereign or of the capricious London mob.

In early times Acts of Parliament were promulgated in the county courts, and, at any rate from the beginning of Elizabeth I's reign until about 1641, all the other proceedings of the House of Commons were supposed to be secret. 'Every person of the Parliament,' said a contemporary Member,[1] 'ought to keep secret . . . the things done and spoken in the Parliament House to any manner of person, unless he be one of the same House, upon pain to be sequestered out of the House . . .' It should be remembered, however, that at all periods private diaries and notes kept by Members and others in the House have leaked out to a greater or lesser extent.

[1] Hooker, in Lord Mountmorres, *The History of the Principal Transactions of the Irish Parliament from the Year 1634 to 1666*, 1792, Vol. I, pp. 143–4.

By a series of orders made from 1641 onwards, for printing specific Votes and Resolutions, the House showed its desire that the public should be made aware of its proceedings, *but only through its own action and through official channels.* In 1680 the supervision of the printing of the Votes was confided to the Speaker and the order has since been repeated on the first day of every session. The more formal records of the House's proceedings comprised by the *Journals*—which are almost continuous since 1547—are on sale to the public, and copies are sent to various libraries and Government Departments, at home and abroad. The Votes and Proceedings were originally printed, by Order of the House, with the intention of providing an accurate record of its actions, available within a few days, in place of the often inaccurate reports which appeared in news-letters. The *Journal*, being the full record of its proceedings, took a long time to prepare and was not published. Gradually, however, the Votes also became tardy and voluminous, and a Select Committee in 1817 recommended that they should be converted into the concise record of transactions, available on the following morning, which they have ever since remained. Specimen copies of a page of the Votes and Proceedings and of the *Journal* are reproduced on pages 91 and 93.

Division lists were published for the first time, unofficially, as electioneering literature, in 1689. It is interesting to note that in 1696 the Commons declared that the printing of the names of a minority was a breach of Privilege, as destructive of the freedom and liberties of Parliament;[1] but again it should be remembered that the House has always held that all its members are bound by the decision of the majority. In 1770 Burke advocated the official publication of the lists, but it was not until 1836 that the present practice was adopted of officially publishing the votes of every Member day by day. The Official Report of Debates also records the full list of names for each Division.

There only remains to trace the somewhat unhappy history of the publication of the debates themselves. In the reign of James I, if a stranger found his way into the House he had to swear at the Bar not to disclose what he had heard in the Chamber. This practice and the frequent nervousness shown by the House when its proceedings were published without leave were of course due at this time to a fear of the

[1] E. & A. G. Porritt, *The Unreformed House of Commons*, 1903, Vol. I, p. 587.

Sovereign's displeasure and, as Macaulay says, were inseparably associated with constitutional freedom. The Commons even ordered their own Clerk Assistant, Rushworth, 'not to take any notes here without the precedent directions and commands of the House, but only of the orders and reports made in this House'. Nevertheless, Members and others continued to take notes, which found their way into the coffee-houses and news-letters of the day. News-letters were both the precursors of modern newspapers and the pioneers of parliamentary reports. They were distributed in manuscript, for a payment of two or three guineas a year, to subscribers who were mainly members of the county families. For over a hundred years the policy of the House vacillated. Between the Restoration and the Revolution much latitude was allowed to the news-writers, who plied their business in the lobby as freely as correspondents do today. But in 1694 a writer called Dyer was reprimanded kneeling at the Bar, 'for his great presumption' in reporting the proceedings of the House, and news-writers were forbidden henceforth to meddle in the debates. There was, however, an increasing public demand for parliamentary news, and other writers followed Dyer to the Bar.

When news-letters gradually gave place to printed magazines and newspapers the conflict was transferred to them and it became clear that what the House principally feared was misrepresentation, though it was also urged that to print speeches tended to make Members accountable outside the Chamber for what they said within, which, it was felt, would conflict with their dignity and privileges. In 1738 the House declared it 'a high indignity and notorious breach of Privilege' to print accounts of debates or proceedings in letters or papers and, in 1762, it further threatened 'to proceed with the utmost severity against offenders'. The newspapers had at first disguised the names of speakers and adopted other evasions, but by 1771, at the instigation of Wilkes and encouraged by the popular clamour for news, they boldly printed debates with the names of the speakers attached. The House promptly took action by summoning the printers of the papers to the Bar, and there ensued the unseemly contest which ended in the defeat of the House. The printers failed to attend and their servants insulted the Serjeant at Arms who was sent to apprehend them. The Corporation of the City of London, headed by the Mayor and an Alderman, both Members, and inspired by Wilkes, championed the printers' cause. As a result the House committed the Mayor and Alderman to the Tower. There they were so overwhelmed with visits, compliments and presents, that their imprisonment became one long ovation. There was no doubt on which side the public sympathy lay. After six weeks' confinement the Prorogation released the prisoners, and a year later the sheriffs were able to boast with justification that the House of Commons had 'tacitly acquiesced in the claim made by London citizens on behalf of the public at large that the constituents had a right to be informed of the proceedings of their servants in Parliament'.[1]

The great constitutional contest was over and the public had won. The House, however, refused to acknowledge their defeat; the publication of debates was still declared to be a breach of Privilege, though the offence was committed with impunity. Reporters had still to crowd into the gallery with other strangers and it was not till 1803, after a memorable occasion when they failed to get in and no report of a debate on the war with France appeared anywhere, that their right to the back bench was acknowledged by the Speaker and the Serjeant at Arms. After the fire of 1834, a separate reporters' gallery was, for the first time, provided in the temporary Chamber and in 1845 the presence of the reporters was recognized in an Order of the House. The permanent accommodation allotted to reporters in Barry's Chamber had several times to be enlarged, but ample and commodious space has been provided in the entire gallery allotted to the Press in the new House. Thus has grown the importance of what Carlyle called 'the Fourth Estate'.

BROADCASTING AND TELEVISING OF DEBATES

One wonders whether the Fourth Estate may not soon be joined by a Fifth (Broadcasting) and even a Sixth (Television). The opening of Parliament by the Queen at the beginning of the session has already been shown on television. No debate in either House of Parliament has yet been broadcast or televised in this country; but the subject has often been discussed, and a Motion which stood on the Order Paper in 1962 in the names of twenty-eight Members, suggested a Speaker's Conference to consider the matter. In New Zealand the proceedings of Parliament have been on the air since 1936 and listening to them is a popular and well-established national habit. In Australia (since 1946) it

[1] E. & A. G. Porritt, *The Unreformed House of Commons*, 1903, Vol. I, p. 594.

The House of Commons, 7th May 1940, during the debate which led to Mr. Chamberlain's resignation. Mr. Chamberlain, Sir John Simon and Mr. Churchill can be seen on the Government front bench, and Mr. Attlee and Mr. Lloyd George among the Opposition. From a painting by John Worsley

The present House of Commons

is hardly less so. Judging from the substantial popularity of the daily and weekly descriptive broadcasts of parliamentary news and of staged debates between politicians, and in view of the tremendous influence of political broadcasting and television at general elections, it seems likely that the broadcasting and even the televising of actual debates would be well received. There are, however, sound arguments against the practice, and hitherto many of our leading parliamentarians have been antagonistic to the idea. Although the Leader of the House of Commons, during the debate on Parliamentary Reform on 15th March, 1963, said that he personally favoured the edited televising of debates, the prevailing view is at present that circumstances do not justify 'so radical a departure from our traditions'.[1]

HANSARD

Since the debates were for so long reported unofficially and under conditions of the greatest discomfort, it is not surprising that they were also incomplete and inaccurate. Readers may recall the story of how Dr. Johnson (a staunch Tory), who had reported for the *Gentleman's Magazine* about 1740 by composing splendid speeches which he put into the mouths of politicians, was asked whether he had treated the parties fairly. 'Yes,' he replied, 'but I took care that the Whig dogs should not have the best of it.'

Another famous reporter was William ('Memory') Woodfall, whose astonishing powers of memorizing speeches won him a great reputation at the end of the eighteenth century. Charles Dickens was also a reporter for a few years in his youth, and readers may remember the vivid account of Bellamy's Kitchen and a brilliant description of the expulsion of an intruder from the House in *Sketches by Boz*.

Shorthand reporters were at work in the gallery by 1786, but it was not until nearly a hundred years later, in 1878, that a special corps was officially engaged, and not till 1909 that it became part of the staff of the House. It consists today of an editor, a deputy-editor, two assistant-editors and twenty reporters; these last-named take regular 'turns' in the gallery. The turns vary from fifteen minutes by day down to five minutes late in the evening, and one man is generally sufficient to take the 'note', with another sitting by, ready to relieve him or to help in a difficulty. At Question Time, when several Members are apt to speak

[1] Mr. Harold Macmillan, in a statement to the House of Commons on 1st March, 1960 Sir Alec Douglas-Home confirmed this view on 5th December, 1963.

simultaneously, a full 'check note' is always taken. Later the note has to be transcribed, corrected and printed, and it is a remarkable achievement in normal times that, day after day, the full report, from the time the House meets until about 10.30 p.m., is delivered to Members early on the following morning.

The doctrine of absolute fairness affects the verbatim report by rigidly excluding such enlivening and descriptive touches as 'laughter' and 'loud cheers' which used to be freely entered but which were sometimes unfairly attributed. The only expression permitted is a strictly neutral one—[interruption], except that [laughter] is printed if required to explain the context of a speech, and, for the same reason [Hon. Members: 'Hear, hear']. The Press Gallery is also open to a large number of newspaper correspondents, who take reports, verbatim or condensed, write parliamentary sketches, or act as political correspondents. A number of rooms are available for their amenities and the affairs of the gallery are managed by a committee, elected annually from among all the reporters, sketch writers, and holders of Lobby tickets. The Lobby Correspondents also elect their own committee to regulate their own affairs, as distinct from those of the gallery as a whole.

The name 'Hansard' is the name of the most famous family in the history of reporting parliamentary debates. In 1812, T. Curson Hansard, son of Luke Hansard, the printer of the *Journals*, took over publication of a report of the debates started in 1803 by William Cobbett, the celebrated parliamentary journalist and reformer. The enterprise continued without public subvention until 1855, when the Treasury subscribed for a hundred sets to T. C. Hansard, junior, grandson of Luke. Thereafter a history of ever-changing and always insufficient subsidies from the Treasury ended in the sale of the enterprise by Mr. Hansard in 1890 to the 'Hansard Publishing Union', which undertook to carry it on without a subsidy and promptly went bankrupt. It was followed by various printers who failed to extract a sufficient grant from the Treasury even to cover their expenses, and it was not until 1909 that the Government shouldered its rightful burden and placed the production of the debates in the hands of the Stationery Office, but under the direction of Mr. Speaker. The name 'Hansard' had disappeared from the title page in 1890, but in view of its close associations with the debates of Parliament and in response to

Volume 669
No. 35

Monday
17th December, 1962

PARLIAMENTARY DEBATES

(HANSARD)

HOUSE OF COMMONS

OFFICIAL REPORT

CONTENTS

LONDON
HER MAJESTY'S STATIONERY OFFICE
PRICE 1*s.* 6*d.* NET

The title-page of a copy of *Hansard*

representations inaugurated by the Hansard Society it was replaced by order of the Speaker in 1943.

Copies of *Hansard* (Lords and Commons Debates) may be purchased by the public from H.M. Stationery Office, price 1s. 6d. They are delivered free to Members.

It should be remembered that every time a Member speaks in the House of Commons he is liable to affect any one of his various reputations. If he is a member of the Government his speech may modify his prestige (1) in the Cabinet; (2) abroad; and (3) in his Department. Since he is certainly a Member of Parliament and probably of a party his words may alter his reputation (4) inside the House; (5) within his constituency and the country; and (6) at his party Headquarters. Nor does success in one role preclude disaster in another. A man may stand up and endear himself for life to the House of Commons, even as his speech, faithfully reported by *Hansard* or embellished by the Press, is speeding out to spoil his popularity in his constituency or his party. Such are the checks and balances—and the hazards—of politics.

William Cobbett (1763–1835), a pugnacious and homespun John Bull character, whose able parliamentary journalism predominated among many pursuits, originally conceived the idea of compiling a *Parliamentary History of England from the Norman Conquest in 1066 to 1803*, by sifting the *Journals* of both Houses, constitutional and general histories, the diaries of Peers and Commoners, memoirs, manuscripts, and the meagre reports of news-letters, magazines and newspapers. With the help of a man called John Wright,[1] whose name deserves to be placed beside that of Hansard, this was accomplished, and, together with *Cobbett's Parliamentary Debates* and later *Hansards*, forms a continuous, though extremely patchy, record.

A somewhat similar scheme was originated in 1933 by the late Lord Wedgwood, a true 'Parliament man', and is now (1963) controlled by a Trust of eminent members and officials of both Houses. For the next nine years a grant will be made from public funds for compiling a *History of Parliament* which will contain biographies of the Members of both Lords and Commons from 1264 to 1918, an outline of the principal transactions in each recorded session and a survey of the development of Parliament through the centuries and its place as an integral part of the British Constitution. When completed it should

[1] Michael MacDonagh, *Parliament, Its Romance, Its Comedy, Its Pathos*, 1902, p. 346.

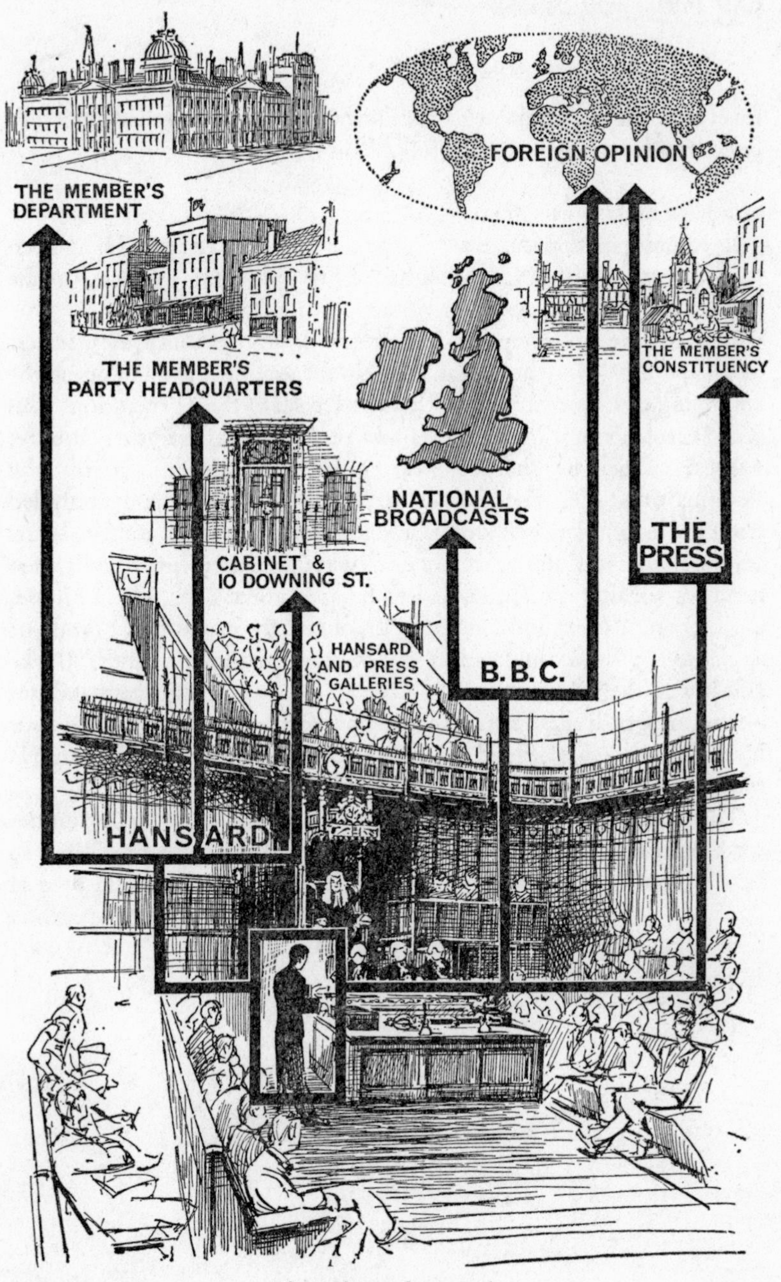

The Effects of a Speech

form a worthy monument to the institution which is perhaps Britain's finest contribution to world civilization.

THE BEST SPEECH IN PARLIAMENT

It is only in comparatively recent years that debates have been reported verbatim, and if, for instance, we indulge in a search for 'the best speech of all' the results are disappointing.

It is manifestly impossible to name with any certainty the greatest of all speeches, but there was little doubt among those living at the beginning of last century as to the best speech of their generation. This was Sheridan's oration in the House of Commons on 7th February, 1787, in which he charged Warren Hastings with plundering the Begums of Oude. The *Hansard* report is unexciting and compiled from the incomplete versions of listeners. Sheridan spoke for five hours and forty minutes, and so tremendous was the excitement created when he sat down that the House had to be adjourned. 'The whole House, the members, peers and strangers, involuntarily joined in a tumult of applause . . . loudly and repeatedly clapping with their hands.' Burke said it was 'the most astonishing effort of eloquence, argument and wit united, of which there is any record or tradition'. Within twenty-four hours Sheridan was offered £1,000 for the copyright of the speech. He refused—because, it is said, he was too indolent to re-write it.

There are no Sheridans in Parliament today, and no opportunities for orations in that style. But some of those who were privileged to hear a certain address in the House of Commons in the fateful June of 1940 will remember to the end of their lives the most famous speech of their time: 'We shall fight on the beaches. . . .'[1]

[1] Commons' *Hansard*, 4th June, 1940, c. 796.

Chapter XI
THE HOUSE OF LORDS AT WORK

'The order of nobility is of great use, too. . . in what it prevents. It prevents the rule of wealth—the religion of gold.'

Bagehot, *The English Constitution.*

We have seen that the House of Lords descends directly from the Great Councils of feudal landowners and notables of the Norman Kings, and even from the earlier Witenagemots. But the element of family continuity which it contains should not be exaggerated. The present House of Lords contains a relatively small proportion of the heirs of the 'greater Barons' who were summoned to early parliaments. This is partly because comparatively few ever existed—eighty summoned in 1307 was a high figure for the period—and partly because the families concerned destroyed one another in early feuds such as the Wars of the Roses, or have otherwise died out. In later days peerages were created by the King by letters patent, and were usually restricted to descendants in the male line. Many of these also died out by degrees and were replaced by others, so that the number of extremely old creations is small. For instance, although a number of ancient baronies are concealed in senior ranks of the peerage, of the 589 Barons existing in 1963 only 64[1] were of creations prior to 1800.

Apart from the hereditary question, however, an interesting form of

[1] This figure includes 7 Baronesses.

personal continuity exists in both Houses. The late Lord Wedgwood has stated that, at least from long before 1600, every House of Commons has contained Members who also sat in the preceding Parliament.[1] In the House of Lords, a similar unbroken chain of valuable experience probably stretches back indefinitely. So that, like a cask of ancient brandy constantly refreshed, the traces of our Parliament lead back into the infinite past.

The actual composition of the House of Lords in June, 1963, was as follows:

Peers of the Blood Royal	4
Archbishops	2
Dukes	22
Marquesses	26
Earls	137
Viscounts	109
Bishops	24
Barons	582
Baronesses	7
Scottish Representative Peers	16
TOTAL	929 (of whom 7 were minors who had not yet taken their seats).

As we shall see below (p. 151) this composition was altered in several interesting directions within a month; but since the details of the new composition are not yet clear it will be as well to explain how the above figures were arrived at.

The Bishops are those of London, Durham and Winchester and the twenty-one senior appointments among the remaining Bishops. The sixteen representative Peers from Scotland were elected for the life of each Parliament by all Scottish Peers, under the Act of Union of 1707. There are now no survivors of the twenty-eight Irish representative Peers who had been elected for life (under the Act of Union of 1801) before the Irish Free State Act of 1922 abolished the machinery for electing such Peers. Peeresses in their own right were not entitled to sit in the House of Lords unless under the Life Peerages Act, 1958. By one of the constitutional anomalies which will by now be expected

[1] Wing-Commander Sir A. W. James, M.C., *How Parliament Works*, 1944, p. 10.

by the reader, Irish Peers (but not Scottish) who were not elected representative Peers could, and can, serve as Members of the House of Commons. The 'father' of the 1945 and 1950 Houses of Commons, Earl Winterton, was one of these.

Let us visit the House of Lords in session. Their Chamber is splendidly refurbished and glittering with gold leaf after the damage of war years. The House sits for ordinary business in the afternoon, and debates rarely last for more than about four hours. The Lord Chancellor, who acts as Speaker of the House of Lords, will be seated in front of the empty Throne, not on a Chair but on the Woolsack—a square couch or ottoman, originally stuffed with sheep-shearings to serve as a constant reminder of England's staple trade, and nowadays filled with wool from all parts of the Empire. The Woolsack is not within the House and Peers may not speak from that part of the Chamber.

The Lord Chancellor's full-bottomed wig, court dress and gown are similar to the Speaker's, and the Clerk of the Parliaments and his colleagues at the Table resemble their counterparts in the Commons. But if the visitor expects to see any substantial proportion of the Peers seated on the scarlet benches of the Chamber or to see them in their robes, he will be disappointed. Robes are only worn on State occasions, or by a new Peer and his sponsors when he takes his seat. Some of the Peers are minors, others invalids. A great many rarely or never attend the House. Only about two hundred and fifty attend regularly and of these perhaps one hundred take an active part in its business. The quorum is three. Only on exceptional occasions do the 'backwoodsmen' turn out. In 1909 the Lords defeated the Liberal Budget by 350 votes to seventy-five, and in 1956 the Second Reading of the Death Penalty (Abolition) Bill was defeated by 238 votes to ninety-five.

On an average day, therefore, only a sprinkling of ordinary-looking gentlemen is to be seen on the Government and Opposition benches, and on the 'cross-benches' which face the Woolsack nearer to the Bar and denote the non-party attitude of their occupants. The Bar of the Lords forms a kind of large box or pen with standing room for 150 persons, where the Commons, headed by their Speaker, attend to hear the Speech from the Throne at the opening and closing of a Session and the Royal Assent given to Bills at intervals during its course. At the beginning of a new Parliament they are also summoned to receive the

Queen's direction (through a Commission) to appoint a Speaker and to recieve the Royal approbation of their choice.

In the House of Lords the Serjeant at Arms used to be an officer of the Lord Chancellor rather than of the House. The post is at present combined with those of Yeoman-Usher of the Black Rod and Secretary to the Lord Great Chamberlain. The duties carried out by the Serjeant in the Commons—including attendance at the Bar—are performed in the Upper Chamber by the Gentleman Usher of the Black Rod and his deputy the Yeoman-Usher. One of these officers is sent to summon the Commons to attend the Queen or Royal Commissions, and on every such occasion the ancient ceremony is repeated of barring the door of the Commons Chamber in his face until he has rapped three times—with his ebony 'Rod' in which a sovereign is embedded. The practice dates from the stormy period of our constitutional history, when the Commons often dreaded interruption, particularly from a royal messenger, in which capacity Black Rod comes, and it is intended to demonstrate the right of the Commons to close their doors and deliberations against all comers if they so wish. It has sometimes been suggested that this procedure of summons might be curtailed, at least on the majority of occasions, to save precious time.

There are many points of difference between the two Chambers. The Lord Chancellor, unlike the Speaker, is able to take part in party controversy, and to speak in debates. He is a member of the Government, and usually of the Cabinet. He is also head of the Judiciary and responsible for the administration not so much of a department as of a whole group of departments. Indeed his duties and responsibilities, as described to a Joint Committee of both Houses, are terrifying in their scope.[1]

It is interesting that although the Lord Chancellor is the Speaker of the House of Lords he has been granted no powers or authority with which to maintain order. He cannot direct his Serjeant at Arms to remove a recalcitrant debater, as is done in the Commons. Indeed, the only existing means of restoring order is for some Peer to move 'That the clerk at the Table do read the Order of the House relating to asperity of speech.' The order dates from 1626 and runs as follows:

[1] See evidence given before the Joint Committee on Accommodation in the Palace of Westminster (H.C. Paper 116-I of 1943–44).

> To prevent misunderstanding, and for avoiding of offensive speeches, when matters are debating, either in the House or at Committees, it is for honour sake thought fit, and so ordered, that all personal, sharp, or taxing speeches be forborn, and whosoever answereth another man's speech shall apply his answer to the matter without wrong to the person; and as nothing offensive is to be spoken, so nothing is to be ill taken, if the party that speaks it shall presently make a fair exposition or clear denial of the words that might bear any ill construction; and if any offence be given in that kind, as the House itself will be very sensible thereof, so it will sharply censure the offender, and give the party offended a fit reparation and a full satisfaction.

The most recent use of the Order was on 2nd May, 1950, and was purely precautionary. It is significant of the unruffled nature of debate in the Upper Chamber that the Order had not previously been read for almost eighty years, when a 'scene'—of a sort still quite common in the lower Chamber—threatened in connexion with the Ballot Bill. The reading of the Order was completely successful in calming the House. On a more recent occasion, when a Peer sought the leave of the House to ask two Questions, which other Peers considered were unfortunately phrased, a motion was made to refuse this leave; but the Peer at once withdrew the Questions.[1]

It will be correctly deduced from the above that proceedings in the Lords are simpler, quieter and shorter than in the Commons. The procedure has developed on much the same lines in both Houses, but since the Lords have never had to cope either with the sustained pressure of business or the systematic obstruction which have afflicted the Commons, there has been no necessity for the same number of restrictive rules, and the practice approximates much more to the leisured ways of the Commons a hundred years ago. There are very few Questions; many fewer Public Bills than in the Commons; practically no financial business; but far more short, privately initiated debates, founded on Motions 'for Papers', which are used because they entitle the mover to a right of reply. Usually no specific documents are required from the Government and the Motion is withdrawn. There is no form of closure, apart from the right which every Peer has to move that a brother Peer 'be no longer heard', but the House can at any time alter its rules, and in 1961 a closure motion was accepted by the Lord Chancellor and put without debate.

[1] Lords *Hansard*, 21st February, 1961.

Divisions are fewer than in the Commons—during the session 1961–1962 there were forty-six in the Lords as against 261 in the Commons—but the system is similar, with separate lobbies for the 'Contents' and 'Non-Contents'. The historian Burnet (1680) relates how Lords Grey and Norris were tellers in a division on the Habeas Corpus Act. 'Lord Norris, being a man subject to vapours, was not at all times attentive to what he was doing; so, a very fat lord coming in, Lord Grey counted him for ten, as a jest at first, but seeing Lord Norris had not observed it, he went on with his mis-reckoning of ten. So it was reported to the House, and declared that they who were for the bill were the majority, though it, indeed, went on the other side. And by this means the bill passed.'

The Committee system corresponds to that of the Commons, except that there are no Standing Committees or Committees of Supply or Ways and Means.

The composition of the active part of the House of Lords also profoundly affects the nature of its debates. It is formed partly of the most politically interested among the older creations of Peers, who are, of course, of all ages; and partly of new creations of politicians, diplomatists, governors and other eminent men, who are usually advanced in years. Also, although the House is organized in parties, with Whips and the usual machinery, the fact that there is a permanent Conservative majority, and a much larger independent element than in the Commons, and that Peers have no worries about re-election, has prevented the development of the party strife which is a feature of the other House. Together these conditions produce a staid and dignified atmosphere in their Lordships' debates which is seldom broken even by enthusiastic applause.

Before considering the work which the House of Lords actually does, let us see approximately what the functions of a Second Chamber ought to be. The authoritative Bryce Conference in 1918, composed of thirty Members drawn from all parties, held that they were to revise Bills from the House of Commons, to initiate non-controversial Bills, to delay a Bill long enough to secure the opinion of the nation, and fully to discuss important questions which the House of Commons has no time to investigate. It considered that the Second Chamber should not have the power to compel dissolution or to overthrow a Ministry, nor should it have equal rights with the Commons over finance. It should represent the views of the nation as a whole and should be so constituted that no party should have a permanent majority.[1]

It may be convenient to consider the functions of the House of Lords under the same headings as those of the House of Commons. The *critical* and *deliberative* function is exercised mainly by means of the small debates—on Motions 'for Papers'—already mentioned. Since the active 'inner circle' of Peers of all parties collectively commands vast experience and abilities on almost every subject, these debates are often of the highest quality, and provide a splendid (and cheap) education in public affairs for all who care to read them. They form one of the main tributaries to the ever-flowing stream of national wisdom and culture. A few of the subjects recently discussed have been as follows:

Rival Ideologies
Polish Ex-Servicemen's Pensions
The National Productivity Year
British Subjects' Egyptian Claims
Supersonic Civil Aircraft
The Moloney Report on Consumer Protection
The Refugee Problem
Road Accidents
Kenya

The *legislative* function of the Lords is seriously curtailed by the fact that they have no right to control finance and that Bills of major importance usually originate in the House which contains the country's elected representatives. About one-third of the less important Public measures and half the Private measures are, however, originally introduced in the Lords. In addition a great deal of 'tidying up' of Commons Bills is done by means of Amendments in the Lords (the London Government Bill of 1963 gave rise to lively and protracted controversy at this stage), and a legitimate complaint sometimes lies against the Commons for sending up too many Bills together at the end of the Session. Only a few Bills are initiated by Private Peers (*cf.* 'Private Members' Bills').

Theoretically the *financial* function of the Lords is non-existent. The Lords are not supposed even to initiate Bills or amend provisions in

[1] The summary is taken from the section on the subject in W. Edwards's *Crown, People and Parliament*, 1760–1935, 1937, p. 202.

Bills dealing with local rates—let alone public expenditure or revenue. But to enable them to take a larger share in the work of Parliament than they otherwise would, the Commons often waive their privileges in respect of Amendments, and there are various devices to enable lesser Bills containing financial provisions to originate in the Lords. The most common is to omit such provisions in the Bill which is sent down by the Lords; the blanks being filled in by the Commons in Committee.

Therefore, when rude things are said about the sittings of the House of Lords—such as the remark of the irreverent wit quoted by Erskine May: 'It has often been observed that when the Commons are sitting night and day, the Lords sit scarcely long enough to boil an egg'—it must be remembered that they are precluded by constitutional practice from taking a full share in public legislation and that they do in fact take their full share in the onerous and unspectacular tasks of private legislation. For these services they received until 1957 neither salary nor allowances (see p. 150).

The Lords also possess *judicial* functions of the highest importance, which the Commons do not. They come down from the Witenagemot and the Norman 'Great Council' and are the residue of the legal powers left over when the Common Law Courts were established. The most important part of these functions is to act as the supreme court of civil and (on points of law) criminal appeal—though it is interesting to note that the Appellate Jurisdiction of the House of Lords was abolished in 1873 and re-established in 1876. Theoretically all Peers have a right to hear appeals, but in practice the latter are heard at morning sessions, before professional judges drawn from among those who have served as Lord Chancellors or held high judicial office and from the 'Lords of Appeal in Ordinary', who are Life Peers. Perhaps it should be added that the House of Lords could on occasion until recently also act as a Court for the trial of a brother Peer accused of treason or felony. The last case was that of Lord de Clifford, who was acquitted after a trial attended by the usual ceremonial in 1935. The verdict was given in accordance with the advice of four judges acting as advisers. But this procedure had long been recognized as costly and out of date and it was abolished by the Criminal Justice Act, 1948.

Ought the House of Lords to be abolished? The general weight of opinion seems to be that a Second Chamber is a necessary and convenient part of the Constitution; convenient to assist in originating and revising legislation and as an auxiliary forum of debate; necessary to ensure (by interposing a minimum of delay) that public opinion really has declared itself concerning measures of fundamental importance which might be rushed through by a single Chamber.

But the problem has another important aspect. From earliest times the House of Lords has been identified with great wealth, but with something far greater, too. No thoughts of abolition should fail to take into account the other idea which has always been present—the idea of peerages as honourable rewards *distinct from wealth* for distinguished abilities and noble service. The House of Lords is still the visible focus of that idea. In continuation of the quotation at the beginning of this chapter, Bagehot wrote:

> This [the religion of gold] is the obvious and natural idol of the Anglo-Saxon. He is always trying to make money; he reckons everything in coin; he bows down before a great heap and sneers as he passes a little heap. . . . From this our aristocracy preserves us. . . . Money is kept down, and, so to say, cowed by the predominant authority of a different power.

Nevertheless, it is widely agreed that the present House of Lords ought to be reformed, though hitherto there has been no agreement among reformers as to their best policy. The main attack is, of course, directed against the hereditary principle, and the preamble of the Parliament Act of 1911 still records the intention 'to substitute for the House of Lords as it at present exists a Second Chamber constituted on a popular instead of a hereditary basis'. The reader, in comparing the functions exercised by the House of Lords with the requirements of a Second Chamber as described by the Bryce Conference, may have noticed that the main discrepancy lies in the fact that the House of Lords invariably has a large Conservative majority and cannot be said always to reflect the views of the whole nation. The result is that, although the House of Lords lost its legislative veto by the Parliament Act, its 'braking' power is liable to be exercised much more powerfully when the majority in the House of Commons is anything other than Conservative.

Let us glance at a few of the most notable proposals for reform which have been advanced from time to time:

1. In 1888 the Earl of Rosebery suggested that some members of a

reformed House of Lords should be elected by the Peers themselves and others by County and Borough Councils.

2. In 1918 the Bryce Conference proposed that 246 members should be elected by the House of Commons in thirteen 'natural geographic areas' and eighty-one by a Joint Committee of Lords and Commons.

3. In 1933 a Bill was introduced by the Marquess of Salisbury, leader of the Conservative Party in the House of Lords, containing suggestions for a reformed Chamber composed in the main of 150 Peers elected by their own order and 150 members from outside according to a method to be prescribed by resolutions of both Houses.[1] The Bill passed its Second Reading but went no further.

The object of the indirect elections which these proposals require is to avoid the danger of the Second Chamber becoming simply a rival of the House of Commons.

4. The Labour Party manifesto for the general election of 1945, *Let Us Face the Future*, stated that '. . . we give clear notice that we will not tolerate obstruction of the people's will by the House of Lords'.

5. The question of reform was brought to a head by the Bill which became the Parliament Act, 1949. On 27th January, 1948, it seemed to face certain rejection by a tense House of Lords in the close-packed little Robing Room, but the general desire for a comprehensive settlement persuaded the Government to enter into conference. Consideration of the Bill was therefore adjourned, while leading members of the parties met to discover whether a basis of agreement existed for a full-scale Conference upon both the composition and powers of a reformed House of Lords.

On 4th May, 1948, a White Paper[2] announced the failure of the negotiations by a narrow margin. An understanding had quickly been arrived at on the question of *composition*. Granted a parallel agreement on *powers*, all parties consented to take as the basis for detailed discussions the conception of a Second Chamber complementary to, but not rivalling, the Lower House, and in which no party would be assured of a majority. Members of the modified House of Lords, who could be of either sex, would be called 'Lords of Parliament'. Apart from certain

[1] These proposals are summarized in W. Edwards's *Crown, People and Parliament, 1760–1935*, 1937, p. 199 *et seq.*, and dealt with at length in Sir W. Ivor Jennings's *Parliament*.

[2] *Cmd.* 7380.

The House of Lords in February, 1742. Mr. Speaker Onslow and Members of the House of Commons attending to hear the Royal Assent to a Bill. *From a print by John Pine*

The present House of Lords: the State Opening of Parliament by H.M. the Queen

descendants of the Sovereign, and Spiritual and Law Lords, they would be appointed on grounds of personal distinction or public service from among hereditary Peers, or from commoners who would be created Life Peers. Lords of Parliament would receive salaries and would be disqualified in case of neglect of duty or incapacity. Thus, the present hereditary right to attend and vote would disappear, but hereditary Peers who were not appointed Lords of Parliament would be entitled to vote at elections, or to stand for election, to the House of Commons.

The question of *powers* was limited to considering what should be a reasonable time for the due performance of its functions by a Second Chamber. As explained on p. 31, the new Parliament Bill sought to reduce from two years to one (dating from the first Second Reading in the House of Commons) the period during which a disputed Bill may be prevented from passing by the Second Chamber. The Government were prepared to concede, as part of a general settlement, an alternative period of nine months from the first Third Reading, whichever was the longer. The Opposition stood upon a period of eighteen months from Second Reading, or, as a final concession, one year from Third Reading; and thus, the difference upon which the conversations foundered was whittled down to three months.

But both sides admitted an underlying difference of fundamental principle. The Government claimed that a longer period than nine months would jeopardize most Bills introduced in the fourth (and of course the fifth) session of a quinquennial Parliament, and might enable a Second Chamber, not directly responsible to the people, to impose its will upon the elected House of Commons, and force the Government to seek a general election. The Opposition, on the other hand, contended that the period of nine months was barely sufficient to ensure full parliamentary consideration by both Houses, whereas there must also be an interval for reflection by the country, after debate in Parliament had clearly defined the matters at issue between the Houses. Without this additional period they believed that the Second Chamber would lose its value as a balancing factor in the Constitution, a situation which would tend towards single-chamber government and endanger the liberties of the people. The Liberals sided with the Socialist Government and deplored the rupture on the narrow difference of three months. On 9th June, 1948, the Lords rejected the Parliament Bill by

177 votes to eighty-one. It was then reintroduced and forced through under the provisions of the Parliament Act of 1911.

So the main matter of reform still stands.[1] In February, 1953, a proposal was again put forward for an informal, All-Party Conference to consider the vexed question and once again the attempt came to nothing.

It seems that the dispute centres more upon the significance of the power of delay still allowed to the Lords than upon its duration. Is the famous 'brake' only to produce a warning shriek and a shower of sparks, or may it, exceptionally, bring some hurtling legislative project to a standstill for inspection by the owners of the railway? If the outstanding difference were split, the disparity would be no more than six weeks on either side. Perhaps such a narrow gap may still be bridged. 'I believe,' said Viscount Samuel on the eve of the discussions:

> that it would be quite possible for the leaders of the three Parties at this moment to agree upon a scheme which would command the assent of four-fifths of the nation. That would be a sign of great moral and political strength in our ancient Constitution, and especially in this House. Its long centuries of service to Britain would culminate in an act of statesmanship which would live for ever in history. It would be brought to a conclusion at the cost of self-sacrifice on the part of individual Members, but your Lordships' House would be able to provide for its own continuance in a finer form, able to render to the people better service, while embodying still, as I hope and believe may be provided, what is best in its ancient traditions and its present membership.

Meanwhile there have been various developments. In July, 1957, the Peers were at last granted modest remuneration for their legislative services in the shape of an expenses allowance of three guineas for each day of attendance, in addition to their railway fares, allowed in 1946.

Next, the Conservative Government's Life Peerages Bill was passed in April, 1958. Its object was to strengthen the House of Lords by widening the area from which men and women of distinction in all walks of life could be recruited to take an active part in its business, since many such are thought nowadays not to desire hereditary peerages. So, for the first time women were enabled to enter the House of Lords. Parallel with this Bill, a Standing Order of the House of Lords was drafted to enable peers who are unable to join effectively in

[1] See P. A. Bromhead, *The House of Lords and Contemporary Politics*, 1911–57, 1958.

its work to apply for leave of absence and thus 'sign off' for a stated period. Opposition to the Bill came from those who wished to abolish the House of Lords, to alter it radically or to make no change at all.

Finally, in November, 1962, a Joint Committee of both Houses was set up to consider the rights of all the territorial classes of peers to sit in the House of Lords and to vote at parliamentary elections; and also to consider under what conditions, if any, they should be permitted to renounce their peerages. This inquiry resulted from the plight of certain Members of the House of Commons who became known to the public as 'the Reluctant Peers' because upon the deaths of their fathers they were obliged to leave the Commons, where they desired to stay in order to continue their political careers.

Three 'Reluctant Heirs' of an earlier generation, St. John Brodrick, George Curzon and William Palmer (Viscount Wolmer), had the same intentions. But in 1895 a Select Committee of the Commons decided that in the first case to arise, that of Palmer, he could not avoid the succession to the position of his father, Lord Selborne. In recent times the Hon. Anthony Wedgwood Benn has waged a more protracted struggle. Among other steps he tried unsuccessfully in 1955, by means of a Personal Bill, to renounce irrevocably his succession to his father's title. When Viscount Stansgate died in 1960 Mr. Benn (not a 'Reluctant Peer' but 'a Persistent Commoner', he claimed) petitioned Parliament, but the Committee of Privileges of the Commons reported against him and were supported by the House. When a new writ was moved for his constituency of Bristol South-East he stood again and was re-elected by a large and increased majority, only to be excluded from the House on the Speaker's orders in view of the earlier decision of the House that he had ceased to be eligible for membership. Finally his unsuccessful opponent petitioned against his election before an Election Court and Mr. Benn was unseated.

The Joint Committee reported on 5th December, 1962, within a month of their appointment. Both Houses debated the Report on 28th March, 1963, and since it became apparent that all parties were broadly in favour of its conclusions the necessary short bill was introduced to implement them and received the Royal Assent on 31st July, 1963. Briefly, the provisions of the Peerage Act are as follows:

Surrender of peerages. A peer is now entitled at his own discretion and within a time limit to execute an irrevocable instrument to surrender his peerage for life and for no other period. If he does so he is eligible for election to the Commons. (This in effect creates a new type of status of 'Life Commoner'.) The peerage remains dormant until his death, when his heir will enjoy the same choice.

The periods within which he may exercise his choice are as follows:

1. Being already a peer	12 months after the passing of the Act
Upon succeeding to a peerage—	
2. While a Member of the House of Commons	1 month after succeeding
3. While a parliamentary candidate . .	1 month after election
4. While not being an M.P. but being over 21 years of age	12 months after succeeding
5. While being under 21 years . . .	12 months after attaining 21 years

Provision is made for a suspension of choice in cases of illness, suitably certified.

Peerages of Scotland. All peers of Scotland (instead of only 16 heretofore elected) and peeresses of Scotland in their own right are entitled to sit in the Lords.

Peerages of Ireland. All peers of Ireland and peeresses of Ireland in their own right are eligible to sit in the Commons and to vote in the parliamentary constituencies where they have the appropriate residential qualifications.

Peeresses in their own right. All (except those of Ireland) are admitted to the House of Lords and have the same choice of surrendering their peerages as male peers.

The effect of these partial changes remains to be seen. Will they precipitate further alterations or postpone them? All that can be said is that for the moment the future composition and status of the Second Chamber still remain very open questions.

As to Lord Stansgate, he availed himself of his right to become Mr. Wedgwood Benn literally the moment after the Act was passed.[1] Upon the resignation of the sitting member under a 'gentleman's agreement' he was re-elected for Bristol South-East with a large majority on 20th August, 1963. As the *Annual Register of World Events for* 1961 aptly

[1] Lord Altrincham, the Earl of Home and Viscount Hailsham also renounced their peerages soon after the passing of the Act.

remarked, 'Whatever his political future, he has already secured immortality in the constitutional textbooks on a level with John Wilkes and Charles Bradlaugh.' This claim is borne out by the fact that the Earl of Home has since been able to disclaim his peerage in order to take his place, as Prime Minister, in the House of Commons.

Chapter XII
CRITICISM OF PARLIAMENT

'Democracy is on trial in the world, on a more colossal scale than ever before.'
C. F. Dole, *The Spirit of Democracy*.

'In each decade, the question is worth reframing: is the British democratic system falling out of balance?'
Nigel Nicolson, *People and Parliament*.

No sketch of Parliament would be complete without some mention of the criticisms which are levelled against it. We must know about its weaknesses, real or alleged, if we are to judge of its strength.

Critics of the British Parliament have always existed, of course, and there has been no lack of such criticism since the end of the Second World War. Works like Professor G. W. Keeton's *The Passing of Parliament* (first published in 1952) and Mr. Christopher Hollis's pamphlet *Has Parliament a Future?* (1960) furnish serious, if somewhat melancholy evidence of the prevailing mood in certain quarters. But the reader is warned against concluding from the following pages—which emphasize, of necessity, the supposed defects of Parliament—that 'everything's wrong, and nothing's right' at Westminster. For there are many witnesses who are eager to speak of the continuing vitality and importance of Parliament: side by side with Professor Keeton's book, for example, there is Mr. Harry Boardman's account of *The Glory of Parliament* (1960).

With this encouraging thought in mind, let us briefly consider some of the major criticisms of Parliament, and in particular of the House of Commons. These strictures may be broadly grouped and summarized as follow:

1. Under modern conditions Parliament can no longer cope with the enormous volume and complexity of its tasks.
2. Instead of controlling the Executive the House of Commons is little more than a rubber stamp for all-powerful Governments, and parliamentary government has given way to Cabinet government.
3. Many of the decisions which ought to be taken in the House of Commons are taken instead outside Parliament by bodies such as the Trades Union Congress and the Federation of British Industries, or by technical experts and 'Managers' who are able to dominate the politicians by means of their specialized knowledge.
4. Political power is so far monopolized by the great parties as virtually to prevent the entry into the House of Commons of independently minded candidates (even under party labels) of the type who in the past have contributed so much to the prestige of Parliament. Further, even if such men should reach Westminster, they would find the time of the House monopolized by every Government to such an extent that their drive and initiative would soon be stultified.
5. Parliament has largely delegated its legislative powers to the Civil Service.
6. The existing system of voting does not accurately reflect the opinion of the electorate since it exaggerates majorities and depreciates or suppresses minority opinions.
7. All the above factors are tending to transform the House of Commons into a helpless puppet and have already gravely damaged its reputation in the eyes of the public.

It so happens that these charges have been examined by a number of authorities, of all parties and of no party, in books or speeches of exactly the type which in this country serve to educate public opinion and eventually to determine constitutional development. Let us glance at each charge in turn. For the sake of brevity a few quotations will suffice, but in fairness to the authors students are recommended to refer to the full sources.[1]

I. CAN PARLIAMENT DO ITS JOB?

Mr. Christopher Hollis, a former Member, does not mince matters:

> Parliamentary Government has already very largely perished. The Member is the obedient servant of the party machine. He tramps into the division lobby voting for or against he knows not what on subjects upon which as a general rule no opinion save that of the specialist is of the least value. The matters which were the subject of legislation in Victorian days were matters upon which any educated man could form an opinion.... As things are now, it would really be simpler and more economical to keep a flock of tame sheep and from time to time to drive them through the division lobbies in the appropriate numbers. Absurd and excessive hours of meeting, constant all-night sittings, do not prove, as is sometimes superficially claimed, that Parliament is working hard; they prove that Parliament is not working at all.[2]

Not every informed observer would agree with such harsh strictures. Indeed, a glance at some of the activities of individual Private Members mentioned on pp. 168–169 will show that Mr. Hollis takes a very gloomy, extreme view of the situation. But many people believe that the House of Commons in its present form cannot deal satisfactorily with the enormous variety, complexity and technical or scientific difficulty of the subjects it often has to discuss. It may be argued, for instance, that few Members have the specialized knowledge needed to debate Telecommunications Satellites. Other critics point out that parliamentary control over the vast network of our nationalized industries is quite inadequate.[3]

One suggested remedy is a system of *departmental committees*, such as exist in the United States of America, in France and in our own local government, composed of Members of Parliament already experienced or interested in the work of one or more Departments of State. The conception is that the House would grow to trust these specialist committees to the extent of devolving many of its burdens upon them.

[1] See also *Parliamentary Reform*, 1933–60, published by Cassell for the Hansard Society, 1961.

[2] *Can Parliament Survive?*, 1949, pp. 64–5; B. Crick, *Reform of the Commons*, Fabian Tract 319, 1959.

[3] For a full discussion of this question see A. H. Hanson, *Parliament and Public Ownership*, 1961.

Though the idea is attractive and has won much distinguished support, it is criticized on the grounds (1) that the House has hitherto naturally not shown itself ready to delegate its supreme authority; (2) that such committees, which must obviously be all-party, could not help the House in the duty of controlling a Minister unless they shared his responsibility, which could hardly be arranged; (3) that no Minister would consent thus to share his responsibility, even if it could be arranged, for example in framing his budget or his Estimate; and (4) that if the committees were purely advisory they would often impede the Minister (e.g. in the matter of foreign negotiations) and probably clash with him.

A related form of proposal is that the House of Commons should delegate more work to its own Standing and Select Committees. Progress has already been made in this direction: for example, there is now a Welsh Grand Committee as well as the older 'Scottish Grand'; and, since 1955, a permanent Select Committee has examined the reports and accounts of the Nationalized Industries. In their pamphlet *Change or Decay* (1963), a group of Conservative Members of Parliament proposed that economic business of a specialized or technical kind should be dealt with by Standing Economic Committees of the House, composed mainly of back-bench Members with industrial and business experience. Other critics point out that such specialist Committees (and indeed the House of Commons in general) should be given better research and information facilities than those at present available to Members.[1] Opponents of increased delegation of this kind argue that the House *as a whole* must safeguard its rights, especially in matters of finance; in April, 1963, for example, the Select Committee on Procedure recommended that no part of the Finance Bill should be committed to a Standing Committee, even as an experiment.

Other critics advocate some form of *regional devolution* as a cure for Parliament's real or supposed shortcomings. It is said that the Parliament of Northern Ireland has worked successfully. Why should there not be similar regional Parliaments for Scotland and Wales, therefore, to deal with all matters concerned exclusively with those two coun-

[1] The case for 'more research facilities' was expressed on several occasions during the debate of 31st March, 1960, on House of Commons Accommodation, when the House debated Parliamentary Reform on 15th March, 1963, and again during the debate on Accommodation on 1st August, 1963.

tries? Opponents of the scheme maintain that the different countries which make up Great Britain are now so closely integrated economically that devolution would in fact produce more confusion than order, especially in the realm of finance. Supposing too, they ask, that a Tory Government ruled at Westminster, a Labour in Edinburgh and a Liberal in Cardiff, how would the clash of policies be resolved?

An expedient which at one time found considerable favour was an *Industrial Parliament*, to lift some of the ever-increasing problems of our modern industrial organization from the shoulders of the Political Parliament. Among the first to propound such a scheme of *functional devolution* were Mr. and Mrs. Sidney Webb and Mr. G. D. H. Cole, while Mr. Winston Churchill developed the idea in his Romanes Lecture of 1930. It is visualized as a Third House of Parliament, either equal in authority to the House of Commons, or only slightly subordinate. Mr. Hollis has suggested that some such body might be endowed with powers similar to those of the Church Assembly. He sees it dealing, by virtue of its specialist personnel, with all the intricate problems of our industrialized civilization, and submitting measures in final form for the agreement or veto of the existing Legislature. To this scheme the late Professor Laski demurred in general as follows:

> The proposal . . . leaves wholly unsolved the means by which the Parliament with the taxing power can be prevented from assuming an immediate supremacy over its rival, and the impossible difficulties in which we should become involved if there were a difference in the party complexion of the two Parliaments, with the result that the Government in each of them proceeded upon different postulates of action from the other.[1]

To Mr. Hollis's particular scheme he raised two objections:

> The first is how he would safeguard the interests of consumers in a legislature of which the very essence is that it is concerned with the interests of producers. . . . The second is the difficulty—I should myself say the impossibility—of constructing a 'House of Industry' without giving equal representation to employers and workers in each of the electoral units created. But if you once do this . . . you give special weight to the claims of property not to be adversely affected by the power of numbers.[2]

The ideas behind all these suggestions are being daily discussed and

[1] *Reflections on the Constitution*, 1951, p. 48.
[2] Ibid., pp. 49–50.

developed, for it is a commonplace of criticism of Parliament that it tries to do too much.

2. PARLIAMENT VERSUS THE EXECUTIVE

This subject has already been touched on in Chapter III.

In his Chichele Lectures some years ago the Rt. Hon. L. S. Amery explained how much the power of the Executive had increased lately at the expense of Parliament. In his summing up he said:

> The central directing instrument of government, in legislation as well as in administration, is the Cabinet. It is in Cabinet that administrative action is co-ordinated and that legislative proposals are sanctioned. It is the Cabinet which controls Parliament and governs the country. In no other country is there such a concentration of power and such a capacity for decisive action as that possessed by a British Cabinet, provided always that it enjoys the support of a majority in the House of Commons.[1]

The matter was raised in the House of Lords on 17th May, 1950, when Viscount Cecil of Chelwood moved to resolve 'That the growing power of the Cabinet is a danger to the democratic constitution of the country', and an interesting debate ensued. After sketching the decreasing individuality and independence of Members of recent years Viscount Cecil said:

> It seems to me that if this state of things goes on, we are bound to have an increasing concentration of power in the hands of the Administration—that is to say, the Cabinet—which will tend more and more to be an oligarchy consisting of individuals who, by political docility, have earned the approval of those who have control of the Party organization.
>
> The position really is this. The Cabinet, appointed by the Prime Minister, have dictatorial powers over the whole administrative functions of the Government, and the Prime Minister is answerable only to the majority of the House of Commons. Further, the membership of that majority owe their position to the political organization of the Party of which the Prime Minister is the chief. If they show any disposition to take an independent line, intimation is conveyed to them that they will not be the Party candidates at the next Election.

He was answered by the Lord Chancellor (Viscount Jowitt):

> It is of the essence of the whole conception that the Cabinet should listen to

[1] *Thoughts on the Constitution*, 1947, p. 70.

what the House of Commons are thinking and saying, and should listen to what the electorate are thinking and saying. It listens and it learns. In very truth I may apply to such a body Carlyle's witty saying: 'I am the leader, therefore I must follow.' Consider what control Parliament has in making its opinion felt. It has the admirable system of Parliamentary Questions. I am told that there are something like 15,000 to 16,000 Questions every year. There is the Adjournment debate, and there is the possibility of Motions on the Adjournment. . . . If we are realists about this, we shall agree that it is the fact, certainly in my lifetime, that the Cabinet has always occupied substantially the position which it occupies today.

The Marquess of Salisbury remarked:

What seems to me vital is that the authority both of the House of Commons and of the House of Lords should be maintained *vis-à-vis* the Cabinet and the Executive machine, if a balance of liberty and authority, which is the basis of ordered freedom, is to survive. That seems to me the one vital point.

In summing up the debate the late Viscount Addison declared:

I should say—and I have watched Cabinets for a considerable period—that the Cabinets of today are more sensitive to public opinion than I have ever known them to be in the past. . . . Today we have the radio, the newspapers, an exceedingly alert House of Commons, and hundreds of questions being asked in Parliament every week; and really it is a fact that if Ministers were inclined to do unfair, tyrannical or unreasonable things, they would have great difficulty in getting away with it.

As the above quotations show, opinions vary as to how far a proper, healthy relationship has been preserved between Parliament and the Executive. Many Members are disturbed at the growth of the power of the Executive, and one speaker in a debate on Private Members' Time in the House of Commons on 28th October, 1959, insisted that 'Parliament was not intended simply as a machine to ratify measures proposed by the Executive'. The ideal envisaged by most critics embodies a strong Executive *and* a strong Parliament. The late Lord Campion, who as sometime Clerk of the Commons was a professionally unbiased witness, observed that:

Strong government balanced by strong popular control through a representative body is the underlying principle of the English system. The democratic party system has upset the balance. To their authority as servants of the King, wielding the powers of the prerogative, Ministers have added a second source of power, the power of Parliament itself. Through their command of a devoted Party majority they have to a large extent in practice reversed the constitutional relation of the Executive to the House of Commons. As Ministers, they may be subject to the control of the House of Commons; as Party leaders, they are in a position to control the controllers.[1]

An interesting pendant to this subject is the much debated question of 'the mandate', which is of course connected with the principle that Members of Parliament are representatives and not delegates. How far may a Government in power put policies into practice which have not been specifically endorsed by the electorate?[2] In earliest times, as we have seen, Members were delegates, who often received strict instructions from their constituents. Gradually the position changed, and certainly for a long period before 1832 no theory of mandated instructions through Members to a Government existed. The problem may be said to have arisen since the great Reform Bill, when representative government in its modern sense started. Sir Robert Peel, for his own purposes, issued the first detailed modern election programme in the shape of the Tamworth Manifesto. He also reversed his mandate by repealing in 1846 the Corn Laws which he had been elected in 1845 to maintain. Here is what Viscount Simon ironically remarked about 'the mandate' in the House of Lords debate referred to above:

> As a matter of history, I think I am right in saying that this elaborate, complicated electoral manifesto, in which you try to tuck in all sorts of attractive items so as to secure that you have covered this section and that section of the population, is a fairly modern development in this country.
>
> The doctrine is current—and it has been maintained again and again by some speakers . . . that once a Government is installed in power after a General Election, the Government has an absolute unquestioned authority in all circumstances to carry out by legislation every item in that listed programme, however casually it may appear in the manifesto. . . . I think it is a mistake to treat the electorate, the sovereign power in this country, as though they acted on the day of a General Election in putting a particular Government into power, and that they then went to sleep until there is another General Election, when they suddenly wake up and, as often as not, reverse the decision they gave before.

[1] From *Parliament: A Survey*, by Lord Campion and others, 1952, pp. 25–6.

[2] See 'Parties and the People's Mandate' in *The British Party System*, edited by Sydney D. Bailey, Hansard Society, 1952.

It is a complicated question, depending largely upon circumstances and opinion. But broadly speaking it can be said that parties in power are apt to be a little debonair about their mandate, while parties in opposition are apt to view the matter with more conscientious scruple. As so often, however, each case must be judged on its merits and the best sanction against a seriously violated mandate is a sharp verdict from the electorate at the next general election.

One other proposal aimed at curbing excessive 'executive' control is that Britain should have a Parliamentary Commissioner (*Ombudsman*), somewhat on the Scandinavian model. This high-ranking independent official would have powers to examine and criticize the whole range of public administration. In particular, he would be expected to deal with individual grievances when it appeared that some serious injustice had been perpetrated (for example in the 'Crichel Down' case—see p. 38). Governmental and bureaucratic excesses and mistakes, it is argued, would be more speedily uncovered and remedied if members of the public had such an *Ombudsman* to whom they could appeal. The fate of this whole suggestion is uncertain: support for the idea, though strong in some quarters, is not overwhelming.

3. WHO GOVERNS THE GOVERNMENT?

In a healthy democracy the seat of real power is keenly scrutinized. Many today fear that our often transient Members cannot hope to grapple with the complexity of modern economic and industrial organization and must in fact, if not in appearance, be dominated by their permanent Civil Servants and technicians.

Mr. Hollis remarks apprehensively:

> Our Government, Mr. Amery argues, is a Cabinet Government. But may it not be that in Bagehot's time, with Parliament still in possession of its freedom we had Parliamentary government, that today in Mr. Amery's time we have Cabinet government, but that soon we shall have neither Parliamentary government nor Cabinet government, but that power will pass wholly out of the hands of those nominally responsible for it, and we shall have managerial government.[1]

Controversy is also constantly being excited by suggestions that the Executive is controlled, for instance, by various associations such as the Federation of British Industries or 'the City' if it is a Right-wing

[1] *Can Parliament Survive?*, pp. 62–3.

Government, or by the Trades Union Congress or some section thereof if it is a Left-wing Government.

Every enlargement of the scope and strength of such associations will insensibly take from the power of the House of Commons. It may be a matter for discussion whether the present tendency may not in time lead to a movement for the representation of interests instead of men.

The problem is even more acute in some of the Dominions, where the Labour caucus may dictate to the Prime Minister not only who shall be his Ministers but even which offices they shall fill. It is a difficult problem, of which the facts are hard to obtain and harder to disentangle.[1] In theory, of course, a Government can only govern honestly in the national interest if it is as free from sectional threats and bargains as the individual Members who compose it; but in practice the most idealistic Government could hardly govern without 'promises of support', which in political life are rarely to be found without strings attached.

4. PRIVATE MEMBERS VERSUS THE EXECUTIVE

The main problem of the House of Commons in action is one of time: how to reconcile the legitimate demands of the Government to get its growing volume of business through, with the legitimate demands of the Private Members of all parties to exercise their initiative in bringing forward Bills and Motions, and yet to avoid the danger of Parliament becoming an all-the-year-round machine. It is easy to claim that the former is the more important; but the contributions which Private Members desire to make are often extremely fresh and valuable; without them it is impossible for Parliament to be the full and free forum of debate which it ought to be for the discussion of all questions of national interest and importance. Moreover, the incessant struggle for freedom of action by Private Members (including many of the Government's own supporters) against the justifiable claims of the Administration, is but the counterpart of the tension which exists in the breasts of most of their constituents, where equal passions for freedom and for order wage battle constantly, to produce the independent yet law-abiding character of the average Briton.

[1] See S. E. Finer, *Anonymous Empire: A Study of the 'Lobby' in Great Britain*, 1958; J. D. Stewart, *British Pressure Groups: Their Role in Relation to the House of Commons*, 1958.

The power of the Executive has been continually growing during the last 150 years. In 1832 the Government had precedence for their Business on two days a week only, and that by courtesy. It was not till 1861 that a third day was given to them. By 1888 they were taking two complete days and about two-thirds of the sittings on the other three days. By 1939 Private Members, if they were lucky, had perhaps eight Wednesdays to bring forward Motions and thirteen Fridays for their Bills during a session. During many of the years since 1939 the Government have often absorbed the whole of the time except Questions, the few days for 'grievances before supply' Motions, and the daily minimum half-hour Adjournment Motion. But the diminution of actual time is no measure of the loss of debating opportunities. In the middle of last century the initiative of a Private Member was almost unrestricted. He could move the Adjournment at any moment and raise any subject upon it; or he could move an Amendment to the Motion for reading any Order of the Day and again talk upon any matter. Discussion was allowed to wander within wide limits. No amendment had need to be relevant to the main subject; in 1831, for instance, on a Motion for the Speaker to leave the Chair for the Committee on the Reform Bill, an Amendment was moved for the production of papers on the state of Poland. Nowadays, the scope of debate in various circumstances is strictly confined in accordance with a series of rulings from the Chair which have been worked out since the 1850s.

A short digression may be useful upon this question, which is a perpetual thorn in the flesh of Members and officials. Most of all it troubles the Speaker. The time of the House is limited. Its work continually increases. How can debate on any given matter be most fairly focused and restricted to the matter in hand? The earliest authoritative account of procedure, by Hooker in about 1570, lays it squarely down as one of the Speaker's duties that 'if any speak to a Bill, and he be out of the matter, he [the Speaker] shall put him in remembrance, and will him to come to the matter'. So far so good; that was an excellent first principle in an age whose triumph it was to establish such fundamental rules. Another was that no Member could speak more than once to the same Question except in Committee. But when the real pressure of business started after 1832 enemies closed in from all directions upon the discursive and irrelevant orator.

As mentioned above, opportunities for irrelevant interruption by

William Lenthall, Speaker of the Long Parliament

r John Trevor, the corrupt Speaker'

Lord Althorp, the perfect Parliamentarian

John Bellamy, proprietor of 'Bellamy's Kitchen'

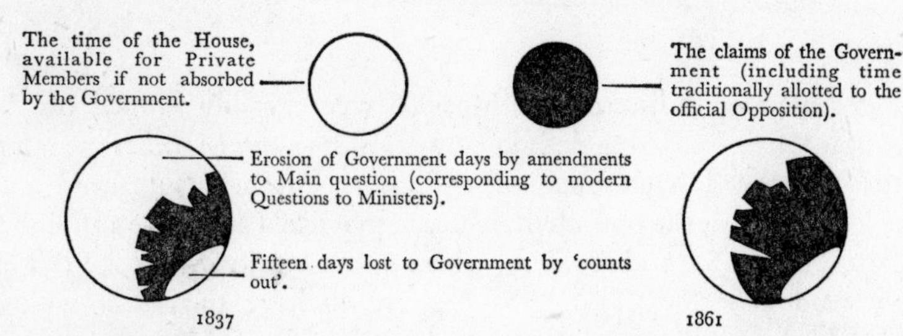

The Government have two days only, in theory, and much less in practice.

Another day for the Government but their time still eroded by irrelevant amendments and motions and by days lost through 'counts out'.

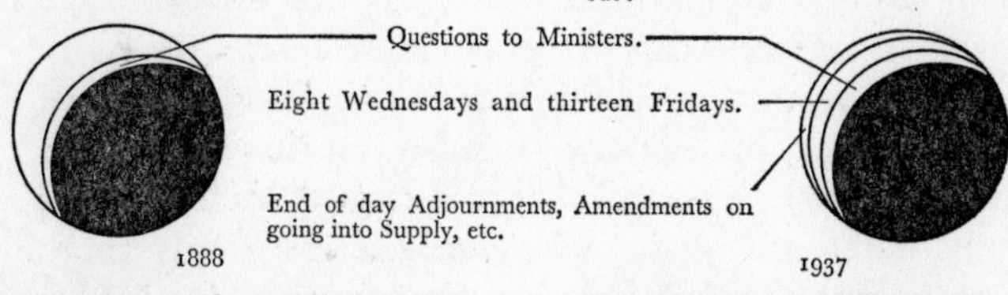

Government now control two whole days and about two-thirds of all the other sittings. *But*, this session there were 5,549 Questions to Ministers at the beginning of sittings as against 699 in 1860.

Private Members now lucky if they receive eight Wednesdays and thirteen Fridays per session for their Bills and Motions, apart from the Question hour (now firmly established) and a short, uncertain period just prior to the Adjournment of the House.

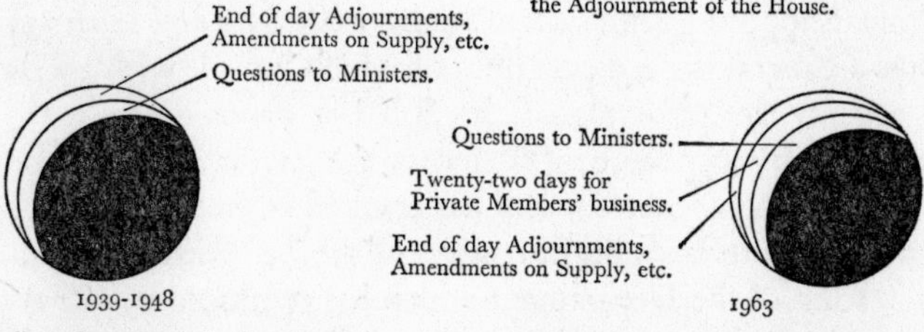

The eclipse almost total. In the crisis of war the Government absorbed the entire time of the House, except for the Question hour, Amendments upon going into Supply, and the small but important compensation of an assured half-hour before the Adjournment every day.

Back to normal: Questions, Amendments on going into Supply, an assured half-hour on the daily Adjournment, and twenty-two days for Private Members' business.

A THREATENED ECLIPSE WHICH MUST NEVER OCCUR

THE PRECIOUS INITIATIVE OF THE PRIVATE MEMBER

The right of Private Members (i.e. back-bench Members on both sides of the House) to get their own ideas debated in the form of Bills and Motions is a precious feature of our Parliament. During the past century they have waged a constant battle for time in face of the ever-increasing claims of Government and Opposition. This diagram shows how their fortunes have varied. The allocation to them of the whole of Question Time slightly exaggerates their success, since a small unascertainable proportion might fairly be attributed to the official Opposition and to 'sponsored' Questions.

Amendment or Adjournment Motions were steadily lopped off. In 1882 the Chair was given definite powers to stop any Member speaking with 'continued irrelevance or tedious repetition'. But more was needed to delimit the bounds of debate in practice. Let us take a straightforward case, a Second Reading, where to the Motion 'That the Bill be now read a Second Time' the Opposition have moved the usual Amendment to postpone the Second Reading for six months and the Question has been proposed 'That the word "now" stand part of the Question'. Only a limited time can be allotted for this stage of the Bill's progress, say one day or six hours of debate. The Minister in charge must have a reasonable time to explain his measure, say, forty-five minutes, and his opposite number in the Opposition thirty minutes to expose its principal alleged defects. A leader from each side will reply at the end of the debate, which leaves only time for say eleven 20-minute speeches from among over 600 Members, many of whom may wish to contribute. It will be readily agreed that this precious allotment of time must be protected against waste. Easier said than done. Supposing some Member in perfectly good faith (1) starts to discuss a general issue, a part only of which is dealt with by the Bill; or (2) accepts the principle of the Bill but proceeds to criticize its details clause by clause; or (3) quotes the evidence given before a Royal Commission when the Bill has resulted from that Commission's Report; or (4) interlards his discussion of the Bill with criticism of the administration of the Department which has produced it; or (5) makes a long and well-deserved eulogy of the Minister's work in preparing the Bill—would these various approaches be in order? If readers climbed in turn into the Chair each would probably give a different ruling.

In the practice of the House of Commons two protections are used. The first is the Speaker's 'eye', in fact his discretion as already described. The second is the body of precedents, gradually built up through the years, of experience of what is in fact relevant to the various matters discussed by Parliament. Here are a few from among the scores to be found in the pages of *Hansard* which bear upon the above points:

1. 16th March, 1870. Game Laws Amendment Bill—Second Reading. In the course of the debate an Hon. Member was proceeding to discuss the general question of the Game Laws.

Mr. Speaker Denison: 'The Hon. and Gallant Gentleman is not in order in discussing the general question . . . We have a Bill before us for a particular object, and the discussion must be confined to that Bill.'

2. 19th April, 1882. Poor Law Guardians (Ireland) Bill. Second Reading.

Mr. Speaker Brand: 'It is irregular on a motion for the Second Reading of a Bill to discuss the clauses, unless the clauses so discussed raise some principle of the Bill.'

3. 29th March, 1893. Evicted Tenants (Ireland) Bill. Second Reading.

Mr. Speaker Peel: 'It is perfectly in order, in discussing a Bill which depends entirely upon the Report of a Commission, to refer to the evidence upon which the Commission were induced to draw up their Report.'

4. 29th April, 1942. Ministry of Works and Planning Bill. Second Reading. A Member started to discuss details of the movements and work of personnel of the Ministry, the object of the Bill being to set up the new Ministry.

Mr. Deputy-Speaker (Sir Dennis Herbert): 'In case the Hon. and Gallant Member should go on in this way for some time, I should like to remind him that he must not discuss details of administration. He must bear in mind the objects of the Bill. This is not an opportunity for discussing the general administration of the Ministry.'

5. A good deal of latitude has been allowed, but if the eulogy proves very long and fulsome, Members are not slow by diverse signs to show their impatience.

Such is a fractional part of one only of the day-to-day technical problems which face the House of Commons. When a fresh one arises, the relevant precedents are considered by the Speaker. He suggests a course which is generally, but not necessarily, accepted by the House. Thus is procedure formed. It is tedious and worrying work, often unpleasantly near to the splitting of hairs, yet hairs upon which a great deal may sometimes hang.

To return to Private Members: a lively debate in the House of Commons on 28th October, 1959, led to the allocation of four extra half-days for the discussion of Private Members' Motions. Speaking generally, however, their rights to force the consideration of 'grievances before supply' and to secure a discussion on any subject—even against the convenience of the Government—have been seriously curtailed during the last hundred years owing to the ever-increasing quantity of Government business which must be transacted. But the essential importance of these rights, which are the foundation of the control of the House of Commons over the Executive, remains.

The position regarding Private Members' Bills depends upon two considerations: first, the opinion which the individual concerned may hold as to the necessity for much or little legislation—which is likely in turn to depend upon how far he tends to the Left or the Right in politics; and secondly, the fact that most modern legislation requires highly expert knowledge in its preparation. Since the Government alone possesses this knowledge through the staffs of the Departments, Private Members' Bills are likely to be of minor importance, though the handful which do get through in a normal year are generally of considerable interest. One of the most famous of all Private Members' Bills was the Matrimonial Causes Bill of 1937, which fundamentally altered the divorce law of the country. Other notable instances have been the Baking Industry (Hours of Work) Bill (1938), which at last abolished the evil system of permanent night baking, and the Hire Purchase Bill of the same year, which controlled the abuses which had grown up round the Hire Purchase trade. An interesting recent example of a successful Private Member's Bill was the Air Guns and Shot Guns Bill of 1962, which restricted the use and possession of air guns, shot guns and similar weapons.

As regards opportunities for raising particular topics, Sir Winston Churchill has emphasized that they exist in plenty if diligently sought out:

> Of course, anyone who chooses to learn parliamentary procedure will see that in the course of a session there are very few topics that he cannot find occasion to vent, but careful study of the rules of procedure is recommended to those who wish to find these opportunities.[1]

This view is constantly being confirmed by the sight of an active new Member asking Questions, diligently balloting, putting his name to 'Early Day' Motions,[2] applying regularly for the Adjournment, using

[1] Commons' *Hansard*, 29th November, 1944, c. 33.

[2] See Glossary. In *Backbench Opinion in the House of Commons, 1955–9*, 1961, S. E. Finer and others have shown the importance and interest of these Early Day Motions.

the 'Ten Minute' Bill procedure, and contriving somehow to get 'in' on specialized debates as well as the 'wide-open' ones such as the Address (see Glossary), Consolidated Fund Bills and the major Adjournments.

In conclusion, another short digression may be permitted in pious memory of a Member who, by indomitable perseverance and will-power, taught the House of Commons to exercise one of its functions and proved the eternal importance of the *individual* quality of membership under any system of procedure.

Joseph Hume was a retired Indian surgeon who, in the years before and after the Reform Bill of 1832, kept an office and a clerk at his own expense to examine the Estimates and to prepare his statements and facts. Very little interest was taken in the Estimates in those days; a sprinkling of Members attended, many of them dozing or lying sleeping on the benches. Hume was the most assiduous attender in the House, sitting every day from the meeting till the adjournment almost without interruption, and dining off a pocketful of pears as he sat, rather than leave his post of duty.[1] For almost forty years, with the help of a handful of supporters, he waged a ceaseless and disinterested war for economy in the national finances. Almost alone, he in some measure achieved what a hundred years later many witnesses stated to be impossible, even with all the professional aids which could be devised—a detailed control of the Estimates by Parliament. He procured the abolition of sinecure posts and pensions and the reduction of Mr. Speaker's allowances. No detail was too small for his scrutiny: even the gilt edging of the paper used for reports and notices was abolished at his behest. In a double sense Joseph Hume achieved an honourable niche in the temple of House of Commons fame. As a memorial to his labours, his bust stands in the Oriel Room of the House of Commons Library, while the following tribute was paid to his work by Mr. Gladstone: 'Mr. Hume did more, not merely to reduce the public expenditure as a matter of figures, but to introduce principles of economy into the management of the administration of public money, than all the men who have lived in our time put together. This is the kind of labour which we want above all things.'

[1] *Random Recollections of the House of Commons* (1st Series), 1830–5, by One of No Party, p. 7.

5. DELEGATED LEGISLATION

Delegated legislation means exactly what it says. Since the province of Government is nowadays so gigantic that Parliament has neither the time nor the detailed knowledge itself to make all the necessary laws and rules, it delegates by Act some of its legislating function to other authorities, who take the necessary powers by means of 'Statutory Instruments'. Some, but not all, of these have to be laid before Parliament and subjected to some degree of control. It is a very old practice, dating back to long before the Reform Bill of 1832, and has grown with the increase of the scope of government, until, in 1960, no fewer than 2,496 such Instruments were made. As a Member has remarked, that works out at almost one every three hours, day and night, throughout the year.

The outcry against bureaucracy and complaints about 'red tape' relate principally to this delegated legislation. For some time past a great deal of alarm has been voiced concerning what has been felt to be the increasing and, perhaps, undue power and discretion which this practice takes from Parliament and gives to the Ministers and officials in Government Departments who make most of these Statutory Instruments. A book on this subject, significantly called *The New Despotism*, was written in 1929 by the then Lord Chief Justice (Lord Hewart of Bury). A Committee which investigated the matter in 1932[1] found no evidence of any conspiracy on the part of the Civil Service to secure illicit powers such as was suggested in *The New Despotism*, but it recommended a number of safeguards. Nothing definite was decided until, with the Second World War, the quantity of delegated legislation, particularly under the Emergency Powers (Defence) Acts, still further increased and provided inevitable examples of irritating regulations and unsatisfactory drafting. The point was reached when a citizen could not even drop a bus-ticket in the street without infringing the law. A debate in the House, on 17th May, 1944, resulted in the setting up of a scrutinizing Committee of the Commons to examine all Instruments or Orders of a certain class, and the working of this Select Committee on Statutory Instruments, which has the advice of the Speaker's Counsel, has been attentively watched.[2]

[1] The Departmental Committee on Ministers' Powers, Cmd. 4060 (The 'Donoughmore' Committee).

[2] See Special Report from the Select Committee on Statutory Instruments dated 25th February, 1958, for the standards of clarity which the Committee seeks to maintain.

Powerful indictments of the whole system continue to appear. But the conclusion seems to be that, although there is no cause for general alarm, the large measure of minor legislation which it is essential for Parliament to delegate to the Departments does result in instances of mistakes and delays which can profitably be exposed by a vigilance committee of the type which was set up nearly twenty years ago.

6. PROPORTIONAL REPRESENTATION

We have seen in Chapter V how at Westminster the narrow interests of a constituency must give way to the broader interests of the nation. Our present problem is to judge how faithfully the various sections of opinion in the country should be mirrored at Westminster.[1]

The words 'Proportional Representation' (referred to hereafter as P.R. for short) sound almost as daunting as 'Bimetallism' or the 'Theory of Relativity', but it is not in fact difficult to grasp their meaning.

Most people in this country agree that voting for Members of Parliament ought to be secret and that what they loosely think of as 'the majority of votes' should decide the result. They are equally ready to agree that the House of Commons should 'fully and fairly represent the views of the people', or some such sentiment; and many would unthinkingly claim that this result is achieved by the existing system of voting. Let us see what does in fact happen.

Today each of the 630 constituencies in the United Kingdom elects a single Member. A result selected almost at random from the 1959 elections shows the following votes cast at Kingston-upon-Hull (North) in round thousands:

J. M. Coulson (Conservative) . .	23,000
J. Foord (Labour)	22,000
A. Butcher (Liberal) . . .	5,000

The winner happens to have been a Conservative but there were many similar results where the Labour candidate won and the argument is the same whichever party came out on top. That is the 'simple majority' or 'first past the post' method of voting which is at present in force in Britain and which satisfies a great many people. Others, however, object to the system on several grounds.

[1] For a full discussion of the present position regarding electoral reform, see Chapter I of *Parliamentary Reform*, 1933–60, 1961.

They point out that the winner got in on a *minority vote*, which they claim is wrong in principle, for although 23,000 people voted for the Conservative candidate 27,000 voted against him. If it was also what is called a *split vote*, that makes the position worse. Supposing that a majority by over a thousand of Mr. Butcher's 5,000 supporters would have actually preferred to see the Labour candidate triumph rather than the Conservative—if it could not be their own Liberal—then, so runs the argument, their votes for Mr. Foord would have wiped out Mr. Coulson's majority and the former should have been elected.

Enemies of the present system maintain that when Members are elected upon minority votes all over the country, as often happens, they produce governments based upon a majority (often a huge majority) in the House of Commons but backed by only a minority of votes in the country. It follows, too, that radical changes of policy may be carried through Parliament on the basis of this minority of votes. (Much of the legislation of the last year or so of some Governments is passed against the will of the majority of the electorate—after the pendulum of opinion has swung against them but before the next general election has provided a fresh mandate.) This is naturally called a distortion of the true weight of opinion in the electorate. For instance, in 1924 the Conservatives polled less than half the votes cast at the general election, but they gained two-thirds of the contested seats. In 1945 the position was turned to the advantage of Labour. A corresponding disadvantage was bound to fall upon the other parties, notably the Liberals. In other words, a seat in the House of Commons cost Liberal voters far more votes per seat than it did Conservatives in 1924 or Socialists in 1945, which is repugnant to those who desire to push the doctrine of 'one vote, one value' as far as it will go.

A further result of the existing system of voting is that a small turnover of votes from one party to another in the country may produce a sweeping change in the composition of the House of Commons. For instance, in 1923, each of the main parties polled within one per cent. of its votes at the previous general election, yet the result was a loss of ninety Conservative seats and a change of Government.

A surprising consequence of the 'simple majority' system may be that *even though each Member secures an absolute majority*, a minority of votes in the whole country may obtain a majority of seats in Parliament. The voting in three constituencies might be as follows:

	Constituency I	II	III	*Total Votes*	*Seats*
Party A .	20,001	20,001	10,001	50,003	2
Party B .	20,000	20,000	30,000	70,000	1
	40,001	40,001	40,001		

An extreme case occurred in the South African general election of 1948, where, although no Member was returned on a minority vote, the final results were:

	Votes	*Contested Seats Won*
Smuts parties . .	547,437	60
Malan parties . .	442,338	78

From these figures it could fairly be claimed that the country as a whole voted for Smuts and got Malan.

Another objection to the 'simple majority' system is that it makes no effort to avoid the complete waste of many votes. This arises in two ways. Where a candidate is returned with a majority of say 10,000, since all he required was a majority of one, the weight of opinion represented by his 9,999 surplus supporters may be considered to have been wasted. Again, many electors live out their lives in single-Member constituencies where a Member of a different political complexion from their own is returned at election after election, so that their votes are utterly thrown away. Partisans of P.R. claim that in the great majority of both types of case the waste is unnecessary.

What are the remedies suggested for these alleged ills? Broadly speaking they are recommended by two classes of reformers. There are those who cling to single-Member constituencies on the ground that it is advisable to maintain the comparatively intimate relations which may there obtain between Members and their constituents; and those who are prepared to forfeit that advantage for the benefits of the system known as Proportional Representation, which requires much larger constituencies returning from three to eight Members.

Reformers who cling to the single-Member constituency can only aim to prevent Members being elected upon minority or split votes, by ensuring that they secure an absolute majority, i.e. at least one more than half the total votes cast. One method is by the *Second Ballot*, which may entail the expense of two elections, because when no candidate secures an absolute majority over all his opponents a second election is held to decide between the two leading candidates alone. The best remedy, however, is the *Alternative Vote*, which works very simply.

Instead of placing a cross against his or her choice, as at present, the voter marks the candidates in order of preference, 1, 2, 3, etc., but whichever preference is eventually used each person has only a single vote. Thus in the 1959 Hull election the first count would have shown the results we have seen, but since no candidate had an absolute majority, Mr. Butcher's second choices would be examined and added to the scores of the first two candidates. The winner at the second count would take his seat in the House of Commons with the added confidence of an absolute majority. An actual example will make this plain. At the West Donegal[1] by-election in 1949, candidate Brennan led candidate O'Donnell at the first count, but since he had no absolute majority the second preferences of the remaining candidate, Canning, were distributed, all but 271 being found to be valid. The final result reversed the positions of the first two candidates as follows:

	First Count		*Second Count*
Brennan (F.F.) . .	12,700	+ 163	12,863
O'Donnell (Inter-party) .	11,256	+2,378	13,634
Canning (C-na-P.) . .	2,812	—2,812	—
Non-transferable papers .		+ 271	271
	26,768		26,768

Nevertheless, it must be remembered that neither of these systems avoids the danger of a minority of votes in the country gaining a majority of seats in Parliament, as happened in South Africa. It is noteworthy that some advocates of P.R. favour the Alternative Vote if they cannot have their own remedy; others do not. They claim that though it may lead to increased polls (at the first count) for minority parties, who need no longer fear the complete waste of their vote, it would not necessarily lead to their greater representation.

We come therefore to P.R., which not only does all that the Alternative Vote will do, but obviates distorted results of the South African type and also, to a large extent, wasted votes. According to its

[1] A Bill providing for a return to single-member constituencies in Eire was passed by the Dáil in 1958, only to be rejected by the country in a referendum in June, 1959.

opponents there are 300 different systems of P.R., each more complicated than the last. In fact this number includes every smallest variant and we need only examine the two main methods.

Much is heard of the *Party List* systems used on the Continent, under which each party publishes a list of its candidates and seats are automatically allotted to the parties in proportion to votes gained.[1] This correctly reflects the opinions of the electors concerning party differences only, and not (except to the extent that the system may be modified to allow the voters a choice between individual candidates) concerning other differences—such as between the Right and Left wing of any one party. For that reason, and because British law at present does not recognize the existence of parties, it has no appreciable support in this country.

The solution which advocates of P.R. recommend under the conditions ruling in English-speaking countries is called the *Single Transferable Vote*. Its object is, as far as possible, to give some effective weight to every vote in respect of the candidates' parties or personalities, on the ground that if the great bulk of votes are effective then the result must reflect the wishes of the bulk of the voters. Like all forms of true P.R., as we have said, this method requires large constituencies, each electing several Members—to allow more than one body of opinion to secure representation and to provide a wider choice of personalities among the candidates than is available in the single-Member constituency.

Once again the voters mark their ballot papers in order of preference as far down the list as they like, whatever the number of seats to be filled. This time the place of the absolute majority is taken by a 'quota', calculated by dividing the total number of ballot papers by one more than the number of seats to be filled and adding one to the result. The reason for this at once becomes apparent if we take the simplest possibility as an example. Suppose only 20 constituents vote to elect a single M.P., as in very early times. 20 divided by 1 plus 1 seats is 10 and with one added = 11. Any candidate who secures this quota need evidently fear no rival, since only 9 votes remain. The method is the same for any number of seats and ballot papers.

Surplus votes above the quota must, by the theory of P.R., be used and not wasted, and second preferences therefore come into play. The

[1] See W. J. M. Mackenzie: *Free Elections*, 1958.

question at once arises, which particular papers should be counted as surplus, since thereupon would depend which candidates received the second preferences which those papers happened to bear. It would not do, for instance, simply to take those on the top of the pile. The only fair answer is to give to each not-yet-elected candidate in turn that proportion of the surplus votes which his total of second preferences among the elected candidate's papers bears to the total of votes cast for that candidate. Unless the addition of these surplus votes provides a quota for sufficient candidates to fill the required number of seats, then *all* the second preferences of the candidate at the bottom of the poll (who has no chance in any case) are distributed, and so on until the necessary number of seats are filled.

Let us look to Eire once again for an actual example. The first count for the 1948 election in the four-Member constituency of County Clare showed the following results:

de Valera (Fianna Fail) . .	12,574
Hogan (Labour) . . .	4,586
Burke, T. (Ind. Farmer) . .	4,576
Shanahan (Fianna Fail) . .	3,235
O'Grady (Fianna Fail) . .	3,020
Burke, C. (Fine Gael). . .	2,854
Brady (Fianna Fail) . . .	2,697
Burke, T. (Farmers) . . .	2,042
O'Loughlin (Clann na Poblachta)	1,732
Lillis (Clann na Poblachta) . .	1,612
Brennan (Fine Gael) . . .	1,183
Smythe (Clann na Poblachta) .	851
Monaghan (Fine Gael) . .	552
	41,514

In this case the quota was 8,303, showing de Valera the only candidate elected at the first count, with 4,271 surplus votes—votes which under P.R. must not be wasted but must be transferred to some other candidate who may profit by them. They were therefore transferred under the principles mentioned above and the second count showed these results:

	First Count		Second Count	
de Valera (F.F.) . .	12,574	—	4,271	8,303
Hogan (Lab.) . .	4,586	+	337	4,923
Burke, T. (Ind. F.) .	4,576	+	192	4,768
Shanahan (F.F.) . .	3,235	+	704	3,939
O'Grady (F.F.) . .	3,020	+	2,082	5,102
Burke, C. (F.G.) . .	2,854	+	34	2,888
Brady (F.F.). . .	2,697	+	691	3,388
Burke, T. (Farm.) .	2,042	+	69	2,111
O'Loughlin (C. na P.) .	1,732	+	62	1,794
Lillis (C. na P.) . .	1,612	+	37	1,649
Brennan (F.G.) . .	1,183	+	21	1,204
Smythe (C. na P.). .	851	+	12	863
Monaghan (F.G.) . .	552	+	30	582
	41,514			41,514

It should be noted that not all of those who made de Valera their first choice selected another candidate of the same party for their second. Since a quota was still required for three candidates the second (or in thirty cases the third, since the second had already been used for Monaghan) preferences on the bottom candidate's (Monaghan's) 582 papers were next distributed, and so on, taking the candidates in turn from the bottom, until the following four candidates secured a quota and were elected—de Valera and O'Grady (Fianna Fail), Burke (Ind. Farmer) and Hogan (Labour). The effect of making the single vote transferable by using this system of P.R. was to allow electors who gave their first preference to unsuccessful candidates some say in the result, and in particular to substitute O'Grady for Shanahan as a Member of Parliament.

Finally, a concise idea of the effect of the Single Transferable Vote has been given by a special correspondent of *The Times*.[1] Assuming five-Member constituencies, he finds that certain predictable results will follow. Firstly, more than five-sixths of the voters would help in the election of a Member. Secondly, less than a sixth would vote only for unsuccessful candidates. Thirdly, any organized body of political opinion exceeding a sixth of the voters in a constituency would obtain

[1] 27th March, 1950.

at least one Member and conversely no party would obtain a Member unless it was supported by over one-sixth of those voting.

The whole question of P.R. was exhaustively debated in the House of Commons on 10th October, 1944,[1] when the main attack was delivered by its enemies on the ground that wherever it had been tried abroad, and especially in France, it had tended to a multitude of 'splinter parties', and to unsavoury compromises between them to maintain unstable governments. Hear how Mr. Edmund Harvey resisted these charges:

> We know that it is right that there should be fair representation for every point of view in the House of Commons, and we have the advantage of having seen this system work. It has been working in Tasmania for over a generation, and in the troubled land of Eire, and we have the testimony of a Member of the old Unionist minority to the healing influence that Proportional Representation has brought into the politics of Eire. Political differences there would have been far more bitter had it not been known that there was a possibility of every view being heard. . . . The country where parliamentary institutions were in danger before the war is France, and France is the country which has never had a form of true Proportional Representation. Many parties existed in a Parliament based on single member constituencies, and just at the last moment, when the war was at hand, they realized too late the need for change.[2] [Mr. Harvey then quoted many countries where P.R. was in use]. . . . We have had the objection that there would be too many parties. The number of parties, in more than one case, has diminished when this system has been applied. In Tasmania there are only two parties although they have had it for some thirty years. Proportional Representation would not create new parties, but it would allow a real difference of opinion to come to the surface, and it would help all that is best in the party system. It would free opinion very much more than is at present possible from the power of the caucus. It would enable members of one party who were dissatisfied with the official choice of a little caucus to vote for somebody in their own party and not throw their vote away. The single transferable vote would give them an opportunity still to vote for the official nominee as a second choice, after voting first for the man or woman of their own choice. That I think would have a beneficial effect on the inner life of

[1] See *Hansard* for that date, cc. 1642–1708.

[2] Partisans of P.R. claim that under the Party List system of P.R. used in 1945 and 1946 the number of parties in the Assembly slightly decreased (from fourteen to ten) and the influence of small parties was less.

> parties and would help in the choice of the very best candidates when constituencies were contested....

Now for the counter-attack by the opponents of P.R. Let us start from the common ground between the contestants, which is that P.R. does indeed reflect the political feelings in the country with far more truth than does the existing system. Here is Mr. (later Lord) Pethick-Lawrence speaking:

> .... I challenge the basic argument in favour of Proportional Representation. Those who want Proportional Representation claim it as a great reform and tell us that the present system is to be condemned because the House of Commons does not meticulously reflect the multi-coloured views of the country. They suggest that that is an axiomatic desideratum, and that the nearer the House of Commons comes to reproducing . . . the electorate, the more perfect would be our system of parliamentary representation.
>
> That seems to me to be entirely fallacious. It is not my view of the object of democracy. Our democracy is designed, not to achieve some mathematical proportion sum, but to create a Parliament that will work, a Parliament that will sustain a Government in the prosecution of a settled and consistent policy. I will add this further—that our democracy, as we know it, depends upon a firmly-knit Opposition, and I do not believe that either of these objects will be equally well achieved by Proportional Representation as by our present system, and it is for that reason that I have a fundamental opposition to it....

The same speaker maintained that our parliamentary system, if it was to work, required sharp issues leading to the execution of contrasting policies, not blurred issues resulting in a succession of similar Governments fusing into one continuous policy. All this is more likely to be secured by a system which, as ours does, magnifies in the House of Commons discrepancies of voting strength in the country. Under this conception the 'strangle-hold of the party caucuses' is the necessary discipline for the proper functioning of our Constitution.

To an impartial observer it might seem safer to ignore arguments drawn from foreign experience. It does not at all follow that what suits or does not suit a parliamentary climate abroad necessarily agrees with our own. Some States adopt and retain P.R.; others try it and reject it. The evidence has become as confused and contradictory as that which is adduced from all parts of the world for or against the use of capital punishment. Argument has raged in this country for decades.

Speakers' Conferences in 1918 and 1930 recommended a trial use of P.R. Parliament rejected the idea, but the Single Transferable Vote was in fact used in most of the University constituencies before their abolition in 1948. It is a curious commentary on P.R. that although at one of these elections in 1945 one of the candidates would normally have forfeited his deposit, since he gained fewer than one-eighth of the votes on the first count, he was actually elected at a subsequent count. The explanation is perhaps that our law is not adjusted to P.R. candidates. In Eire, for instance, the deposit is only lost if the candidate fails to poll one-third of the quota *by the time he is eliminated.*

The Speaker's Conference of 1944 rejected the proposal for P.R., which was again decisively negatived on a division in the House of Commons at the conclusion of the debate mentioned above. Neither of the major parties at present favours the system, though not long ago Sir Winston Churchill suggested the possibility that a Select Committee might re-examine it as a means of breaking the political deadlock produced by the 1950 general election. It is true that any fresh sign of a Liberal revival, such as the increase of votes at by-elections which led up to the capture of Torrington in March, 1958, and of Orpington in March, 1962, renews public interest in P.R. and especially in the Alternative Vote, because of its suitability for single-Member constituencies. For the moment, however, the last word rests with the opponents of Proportional Representation.

7. PRESTIGE OF PARLIAMENT

What is the upshot of the battle? Do the people trust Parliament as much today as they did fifty or a hundred years ago? The answer lies locked in the minds and hearts of the people. On the one hand are the considered doubts of the writers quoted above, and a great deal of discontented and cynical criticism everywhere (often stimulated by the visible decline of parliamentary institutions in certain other countries). On the other are the evidence of the undoubted popularity of parliamentary broadcasts, including television; the widespread excitement revealed at general elections; the ready sale of books about every aspect of Parliament; the respect accorded to leading parliamentarians; and above all the never-failing queues for seats in the gallery of the House of Commons. Perhaps the answer is that although our constitutional machinery has been tested through the ages and enjoys high repute in the world, no machinery will run for ever without periodic overhaul and re-design. This certainly seems to be the meaning underlying a recent debate on Parliamentary Reform,[1] at the end of which the House of Commons resolved 'to maintain Parliament as the paramount forum of the nation and to bring its practices and procedures into harmony with this end and in accord with the needs of 1963'. Hitherto our thinkers and rulers have fortunately enjoyed the necessary calm and sagacity to adapt the machinery enough to meet every crisis with relative success, yet never so much as to threaten the stability of the ancient, well-tried conception. Are substantial alterations required today? It is for the reader to judge: he has no easy task.

[1] Commons' *Hansard*, 15th March, 1963.

Chapter XIII
BENEFITS AND RESPONSIBILITIES

'Sweet is the Name of Liberty, but the Thing itself a Value beyond all inestimable Treasure.'

Peter Wentworth, M.P., 1575.

The intelligent elector may by this time be saying, 'This is all very well. You have told me a great deal about Parliament and in a sort of a way answered some important questions. I admit that it is an ancient and honourable institution. But the biggest question remains. How do *I* come into it? Once in a while I am allowed a vote and after that, especially if my candidate is beaten, I don't seem to have the least influence on anything to do with the government of the country. Besides, how does the existence of a Parliament secure my personal liberty? Surely a Parliament which can do everything but turn a man into a woman can take away my liberty tomorrow?'

A facile reply would be to ask 'How much influence do you expect?' In an electorate of over 35 millions, if the power of government were to be equally divided, each person's share would be just under $\frac{1}{35,000,000}$, which is not substantial, and the casting of one vote every few years is a not unreasonable expression of its weight. But the real answer is that government in this country is always keyed to public opinion, not directly, as by the referendum,[1] but in the sense that it does really

[1] A practice in use in France, Eire, Switzerland, Australia and other countries, by which

depend upon the consent and the support of the people. The influence which any elector has in addition to his vote varies therefore in proportion to the interest he takes in politics. The more he thinks, writes, argues and persuades about political matters, the greater his political influence is likely to be. Moreover, he can bring legitimate pressure to bear on a Member by letter or interview, or by enlisting the Press, or a Member's other constituents, in support of his cause.

The answer to the second part of the question is that Parliament has the greatest possible importance in preserving our liberties. The Acts of Parliament of 1679 and 1816 made the right to writs of Habeas Corpus effective and secured the right to *personal freedom*. The essence of the whole Habeas Corpus transaction, says Dicey, 'is that the Court can by writ of Habeas Corpus cause any person who is imprisoned to be actually brought before the Court and obtain knowledge of the reason why he is imprisoned; and then having him before the Court, either then and there set him free or else see that he is dealt with in whatever way the law requires, as, for example, brought speedily to trial'. Any imprisoned person can thus, through counsel, a relation, or a friend, apply to a court for a writ of Habeas Corpus and in any case of reasonable doubt the judge will issue the writ. That is the procedure which alone stands between the ordinary citizen and the concentration camp, and the necessary suspension, during the war, of this protection, to enable the Home Secretary to imprison citizens whose activities *might* endanger the country, caused Parliament grave concern and many long debates.

The right to *freedom of discussion* depends more on an absence of the common law's restraints—a freedom from licence and censorship. As Dicey says: 'Freedom of discussion is, then, in England little else than the right to say anything which a jury, consisting of twelve shopkeepers, think it expedient should be said or written.' But the important point is that the principle of absolute freedom of speech has been incessantly repeated and maintained in and by the House of Commons.

The *freedom of public meeting* is nothing more than a combination of the individual freedoms of liberty of the person and of speech.

Sometimes, as in the cases of Wilkes and Bradlaugh, the House of

an issue (generally a Bill) is placed directly before the electors, who vote 'Yes' or 'No'. Sir Winston Churchill suggested in May, 1945, that it might be used to ascertain the country's wishes regarding the necessity for a general election.

Commons, instead of speaking for the people, has, by adopting an unfair and illiberal attitude, come into collision with the public; but the quarrels were openly thrashed out, and, after serving a useful purpose, they remain on record as public precedents of great value.

It should be remembered, as has already been pointed out, that although Parliament is primarily responsible for their maintenance, our liberties also receive an indispensable protection from the scrupulous fairness of the independent judges who administer the law in the courts.

Since the House of Commons has complete power to alter its own procedure, the majority could (perhaps by stigmatizing criticism as obstruction and obstruction as disorderly conduct) by a simple Resolution expel the Opposition. With the help of a majority in the House of Lords they could repeal the Habeas Corpus Act, and consign their victims to prison. With a sufficient following outside to overawe the judges, they could usurp the sovereign power and maintain a tyranny. 'We can never be really in danger', said 'Junius' in his 'Letters', 'till the forms of Parliament are made use of to destroy the substance of our civil and political liberties: till Parliament itself betrays its trust, by . . . employing the weapons committed to it by the collective body to stab the Constitution.' The safeguard against such events is the fact that with all their failings—and these have been many—Members who have sat in the House of Commons have never been persons who, in the final issue, put personal power before the welfare of the country. The responsibility for the continuance of this parliamentary tradition rests ultimately upon the ordinary voter.

We have been fortunate in England to have enjoyed, with one short interruption, six and a half centuries of democratic progress. Across the Channel, however, even in recent times, democracy has all too often been strangled by the tyranny of an individual or an ideology. In 1947 the Communists had seized power in Bulgaria. They were confronted in Parliament by a united opposition of a hundred deputies under Nikola Petkov, who had well earned the description of 'one of the greatest democrats of all time' by his fight against the Nazis.

On the afternoon of 5th June, 1947, Petkov arrived to find the Parliament building surrounded by police and the atmosphere electric. One of Petkov's best friends, also a Member, tells what happened in the packed Chamber when the President rose amid a tense silence:

'I have today received a letter from the Prosecutor of the Sofia Court, requesting me to ask your authorization for the detention of the member Nikola Petkov.'

The whole Communist majority rose on its feet with terrific shrieks of 'Bravo!' 'Approved!' 'Hurrah!' They had been told in advance what to do.

We all looked at Nikola. His face was pale. He turned and said: 'Well, it might have been expected.'

The shouts of the Communists grew less deafening, and the President announced that he would dismiss the Assembly for twenty minutes, during which time the Parliamentary Committee for the Ministry of Justice could deal with the case.

Then Nikola stood up. 'This is unconstitutional!' he cried. But his words were lost in shouts of 'Out!' 'Traitor!' 'Spy!' 'To the gallows!'

We rose to our feet as one man and shouted, 'Shame, this is terror!'

The Communists, however, were nearly three times as numerous as we were and they outshouted us. . . .

Finally the moment came when Nikola had to speak. His was the last word before the actual voting. After so many hours of strain, of emotion, of shouting, our nerves were stretched to the breaking point, but we gave him a great ovation. We decided to listen to him standing.

He had naturally not prepared anything in advance. His voice was uneven, sometimes trembling. He spoke very slowly, forcing his words out at shouting pitch because immediately he began speaking the loudspeaker system was disconnected, with the exception of the microphones on the Communist benches. So Nikola, alone, with no loudspeakers to magnify his voice, had to struggle with 300 shouting Communists whose voices roared through every loudspeaker in the hall. The stenographers had stopped taking notes, in obedience to what obviously had been an order. Afterwards they reported the whole speech as 'inaudible'.

But he went on shouting:

'It is only by brute force that you stay in power. The gun and the gallows are your only argument. I am in favour of another argument—free speech. And this is an argument which you Communists fear more than anything else. . . .

'We are democrats, we are against conspiracy, we believe in freedom. We will remain democrats and shall go on believing in freedom in spite of the horror of the terror machine which is now being thrown against us.'

This was too much for the Communists. They began their final barrage to silence him, shouting, 'Death to the traitor!' He stopped and looked at us. Sweat and tears were streaming down his face. He grasped the speaker's rostrum with his two hands and shouted to us:

'*Da ji-vee svo-bo-da-ta*' (Long live freedom!)

He repeated it again and again, syllable by syllable. We understood what he wanted. It had been a trick of the Communists in Parliament to chant slogans at the top of their voices, usually 'Long live Dimitrov' or 'Stalin, Tito, Dimitrov'. Nikola now wanted us to do the same with 'Long live freedom'.

We started shouting at once. Once, twice, ten times, twenty times. We were now completely carried away. I felt we had all become, all one hundred Opposition deputies, one single soul and body. Nothing else could be heard but 'Long live freedom!' 'Long live freedom!' . . .

Then the Communists raised their hands. This was the voting, later described in the official communiqué as the 'unanimous approval of the majority'. The 'tough guys' of the Communist majority, about twenty of them, hurried towards the speaker's rostrum. We left our seats, jumping over the benches, over fallen papers, over fallen deputies, and surrounded the rostrum. Someone started singing, 'He falls in the battle for freedom,' and we all joined in. This infuriated the Communists more than anything else, for it was the Resistance song, sung during the underground fight against the Germans and loved by Communists and non-Communists alike.

The first Communist attempt to get through the human barricade around Nikola was not successful. But they persisted. Soon they drew their revolvers and were finally reinforced by armed militiamen. Our resistance was broken.

That's how he was dragged away. We followed him through the Chamber and then through the corridors to the entrance. When he was thrown into the police car we started shouting again, syllable by syllable, 'Long live freedom!' Then the car vanished at top speed with many other military cars in its wake.[1]

Less than four months later, Petkov was hanged. In such a fashion does a free Parliament perish.

How then can a citizen who desires to benefit from and maintain the freedoms so painfully gained in the past, honestly discharge his responsibilities? In six ways at least.

1. *By voting*: which in fairness to those who submit themselves to his choice should entail reading the slender literature of each candidate, attending at least one meeting of each of them, and following the national campaign in the press and on television and sound radio.

2. *By paying a visit to Westminster*: which entails a pleasant saunter round Westminster Hall and meditation on the twenty generations of Lords and Commons who have trodden the ground before us.

[1] Condensed from M. Padev, *Dimitrov Wastes No Bullets*, 1948, pp. 58–63.

3. *By attending debates*: all of which—even the dullest—may affect the life of the individual citizen.

4. *By reading Hansard*:[1] 'Let me tell you,' said Disraeli, 'how to get on in the House of Commons. When the House is sitting, be always in your place. When it is not sitting read *Hansard*.' Certainly the voter cannot be expected always to be reading *Hansard*. But if he will read it sometimes; know his way about it; refer to it when something of particular interest to himself has been discussed: that is the closest bond with Parliament he can have, next to personal visits. There is a sense of satisfaction, a feeling of getting to the heart of the matter, in reading the verbatim report, which the abridged newspaper accounts, excellent though they are, can never provide. Indeed, it is hard to exaggerate the importance which this contrast may have for the future of democracy. How many British subjects live and die without hearing or reading a parliamentary debate in full? Without realizing the fact that, although a Press report may be accurate, lucid and even of sensational interest, it lacks by its very nature the completeness and the personal touches which invest the speaking Members with living personalities—whether sympathetic or the reverse—and draw the listener (or reader) intimately towards an appreciation of democratic government as nothing else can? Moreover, it will probably surprise most people who conscientiously read through—or better, sit through—a number of debates, to find that before the end of each one, some Member has expressed their exact feelings and desires upon the subject under discussion—probably far more clearly than they could themselves do.

'White Papers' can be good reading, too, and provide the same sense of getting at the pith of a subject. Some interesting items from recent years have been:

The proposed Underwater Crossing and Forth Road Bridge [Cmd. 9741]
Child Migration to Australia [Cmd. 9832]
Full Automation of the Telephone System [Cmnd. 303]
Report of the 'Bank Rate Tribunal' [Cmnd. 350]
Compensation for victims of crimes of violence [Cmnd. 1406]
Security Procedures in the Public Service [Cmnd. 1681]
Security at the National Gallery [Cmnd. 1750]
Noise from Motor Vehicles [Cmnd. 1780]

[1] Daily issues of Lords and Commons *Hansards* each cost 1*s*. 6*d*.

Report of the Tribunal appointed to Inquire into the Vassall Case and Related Matters [Cmnd. 2009]

Lord Denning's Report (on Circumstances leading to the Resignation of Mr. J. D. Profumo) [Cmnd. 2152]

5. *By reading some of the many books about Parliament intended for the general reader.* A short list is given on pages 249–251. It seems that at Westminster the onlooker has often seen most of the game, and of these doorkeepers and reporters have been particularly happy in their sketches. Among the former Joseph Pearson in the eighteenth century and William White in the nineteenth: and among the latter, Dickens, Grant, Whitty, O'Connor, Jeans, MacDonagh, the incomparable Lucy ('Toby, M.P.'), Arthur Baker and Harry Boardman have all written highly entertaining descriptions. In addition, there are, of course, innumerable interesting memoirs written by Members themselves.

If you wish to savour the rollicking humour of the Edwardian House of Commons, Earl Winterton has described it all admirably in *Pre-War* and his other books. Sir Alan Herbert exactly catches the atmosphere of a Standing Committee and the practical difficulties of piloting a Bill through Parliament in *Independent Member* and *The Ayes Have It.* Sir Dennis Herbert, later Lord Hemingford, illustrates his official life, grave and gay, as Chairman of Ways and Means in *Back-bencher and Chairman.* Lord Dalton in his three volumes of memoirs exposes much of the hinterland of politics, as well as its potholes. Lloyd George, Sir Winston Churchill and Earl Attlee have all told of their careers at Westminster. So have Addison, L. S. Amery, Bevan, Boothby, Clynes, Duff-Cooper, Kirkwood, Morrison, Snowden and Swinton: fortunately the list is endless.

Finally, for those who prefer their history in fictional form, there is a small but valuable group of novels dealing with Parliament, including those of Disraeli, Galt, Trollope, Belloc, Mason, Arnold Bennett, Fienburgh and Edelman.

6. *By discussing Parliament* sometimes, and perhaps, instead of taking the easy line of attacking and deriding it, by taking the much more rewarding line of defending and upholding it. Thirty years ago, Peter Wentworth's words sounded archaic and superfluous to those who praised the realism of dictators; today they ring out like silver bells against the ghastly horrors of the Europe that did away with 'talk' and took to 'action'.

For generations Parliament has efficiently controlled the affairs of the nation and guided those of an Empire which has become a Commonwealth. For hundreds of years it has remained the admiration of the world. The secret of its success is the idea of fairness and of regard for the rights of others (amounting almost to a mania) which inspires the whole of its procedure.

The nation will do well to ensure that none but its finest representatives come to Westminster to use in its service the matchless political instrument which is the heritage and responsibility of seven centuries of Freedom.

APPENDIXES
GLOSSARY
READING LIST

COMPOSITION OF THE HOUSE OF LORDS

Appendix I

Number of Members Summoned at Different Periods

Date	*Sovereign and regnal year*	*Remarks*	*Dukes*	*Marquesses*	*Earls*	*Viscounts*	*Barons*	*Representing Scotland*	*Representing Ireland*	*Archbishops and Bishops*	*Abbots and Priors*	*Masters of Orders*	*Total*
1295	23 Edward I	The 'Model' Parliament. At this period the spiritual outnumbered the lay peers.			8		41			20	67	3	139
1307	1 Edward II				9		71			19	55	2	156
1327	1 Edward III				6		46			21	23	1	97
1377	1 Richard II	Edward, the Black Prince, was created the first English duke (of Cornwall) 1337.	1		12		47			21	25		106

NOTE:—It should be emphasized that the above figures (which are approximate) refer to those who were *summoned*, and that owing to political considerations, expense, illness, the state of the roads and other causes, the numbers who actually took their seats were probably very much smaller.

Appendix I—*continued*

1399	1 Henry IV	Richard II created Robert de Vere the first Marquess in England, 1385.	5	1	10		34			20	26	1	97
1422	1 Henry VI		2		5		16			21	25		69
1425	3 Henry VI	Henry VI created John, Lord Beaumont, the first English Viscount in 1440.	2		5		19			21	26	1	74
1485	1 Henry VII	The noble families were reduced by the Wars of the Roses.	2		10	2	20			17	26	1	78
1509	1 Henry VIII		1	1	8		26			21	26	1	84
1547	1 Edward VI	After suppression of the Monasteries in 1539.	1	2	12		32			27			74
1558	1 Elizabeth I		1	1	12	2	27			26			69
1625	1 Charles I		1	1	37	11	47			26			123

Appendix 1—continued

Date	*Sovereign and regnal year*	*Remarks*	*Dukes*	*Marquesses*	*Earls*	*Viscounts*	*Barons*	*Representing Scotland*	*Representing Ireland*	*Archbishops and Bishops*	*Abbots and Priors*	*Masters of Orders*	*Total*
1685	1 James II		14	3	66	8	67			26			184
1702	1 Anne		21	1	65	9	66			26			188
1714	1 George I	After the Union with Scotland in 1707.	23	2	74	11	67	16		26			219
1727	1 George II		31	1	71	15	62	16		26			222
1760	1 George III		25	1	81	12	63	16		26			224
1820	1 George IV	After the Union with Ireland in 1801.	25	17	100	22	134	16	28	30			372
1830	1 William IV		23	18	103	22	160	16	28	30			400
1837	1 Victoria		24	19	111	19	192	16	28	30			439
1881	44 Victoria		26	19	117	25	254	16	28	26			511

Appendix 1—*continued*

1906	6 Edward VII		28	23	123	40	332	16	28	26			616
1913	3 George V		24	25	125	47	357	16	28	26			648
1936	1 Edward VIII	Machinery for electing Irish representative peers abolished 1922.	25	30	131	80	441	16	16	26			765
1951	14 George VI		24	27	133	93	529	16	5	26			853
1958	7 Elizabeth II		25	27	132	109	536	16	2	26			873
1963 (June)	12 Elizabeth II	Life Peerages Act, 1958	26	26	137	109	589[1]	16[2]		26			929[2]

[1] Including 46 Life Peers and Peeresses.

[2] The Peerage Act of July, 1963, enacted since these figures were compiled, now permits hereditary Peers to renounce their titles for life, and admits *all* holders of Scottish (but not Irish) peerages, and all Peeresses in their own right, to the House of Lords.

COMPOSITION OF THE HOUSE OF COMMONS

Appendix 2

Number of Members Returned at Different Periods

Date	*Remarks*	*County Members*	*Borough Members*	*University Members*	*Total*	*Distribution*				*Population of countries represented (Millions)*
						England	*Wales*	*Scotland*	*Ireland*	
1295	Edward I's 'Model' Parliament.	74	332		**406**[1]	406				
1377–99	Richard II: a period of transitory influence for the Commons but the number of borough members was declining.	74	Up to 226		**Up to 300**[1]	Up to 300				2[2]
1435	Henry VI: a low ebb of interest in parliamentary representation, but tide beginning to turn.	74	188		**262**[1]	262				

[1] The figures are estimates of the numbers of names returned in answer to writs for election. It must be remembered that during these periods not only did the towns which received writs of summons and those which made returns thereto vary, but that many elected members, principally from the boroughs, failed to attend. As a result, the total who sat was usually less than half the total shown, and the influence of the Knights of the shire predominated.

[2] This can only be a rough estimate.

1547	End of reign of Henry VIII: increasing desire to represent and to be represented. Wales and Calais enfranchised.	90	253		**343**	319	24			$3\frac{3}{4}$[1]
1625	End of reign of James I: many new boroughs created by now to satisfy increased desire for representation.	90	395	4	**489**	465	24			6[1]
1707	After Union with Scotland.	122	432	4	**558**	489	24	45		$6\frac{3}{4}$
1801	After Union with Ireland.	186	467	5	**658**	489	24	45	100	$16\frac{1}{2}$
1832[2]	After Representation of the People Acts, 1832 ('The First Reform Act').	253	399	6	**658**	471	29	53	105	24
1867–8	After Representation of the People Acts, 1867–8.	283	366	9	**658**	463	30	60	105	$30\frac{1}{4}$
1885	After Redistribution of Seats Act, 1885.	377	284	9	**670**	465	30	72	103	36

[1] This can only be a rough estimate.

[2] For principal changes in the electorate, 1831–1951, see the chart on pp. 50–51.

Appendix 2—continued

Date	*Remarks*	*County Members*	*Borough Members*	*University Members*	*Total*	*Distribution*				*Population of countries represented (Millions)*
						England	*Wales*	*Scotland*	*Ireland*	
1918	After Representation of the People Act, 1918.	372	320	15	**707**	492	36	74	105	$46\frac{1}{2}$
1920	After Government of Ireland Act, 1920: Home Rule and partition of Ireland, leaving only Northern Ireland represented.	300	303	12	**615**	492	36	74	13	$43\frac{3}{4}$
1944	After House of Commons (Redistribution of Seats) Act, 1944.	302	326	12	**640**	517	36	74	13	39
1963	Under Representation of the People Act, 1948, separate representation of Universities and City of London was abolished.	335	295	–	**630**	511	36	71	12	53

IN ANCIENT TIMES

The earliest Parliaments were the shortest and, before the expedients of prorogations and adjournments were hit upon, several were often summoned in a year. Here is a list of six of the Parliaments of Edward I (1272–1307):

Date	*Place of meeting*	*Period*	*Duration in days*
1300	Westminster	March 6–20	15
1301	Lincoln	January 20–30	11
1302	Westminster	October 14–21	8
1305	Westminster	February 28–March 20	21
1306	Westminster	May 30	1
1307	Carlisle	January 20–March 19	59

The main legal requirements concerning the duration of Parliament have changed as follows:

Date	*Sovereign*	*Title of Enactment*	*Effect of Enactment*
1330	Edward III	4 Ed. III, *c.* 14	'That a Parliament shall be holden every year once.'
1640	Charles I	Parliament Act 16 Cha. I, *c.* 1	(*a*) That Parliament should be summoned at least once every three years. Safeguards provided to ensure implementation. (*b*) That Parliament should not be dissolved or prorogued without its own consent within fifty days of meeting. (*c*) That Parliament should be dissolved after three years.
1664	Charles II	Triennial Parliaments Act 16 Cha. II, *c.* 1	Parliament Act repealed but (*a*) re-enacted without safeguards.
1694	William and Mary	Meeting of Parliament Act 6 & 7 Will. & Mary, *c.* 2	Provisions of Triennial Parliaments Act repeated with provision that no Parliament should last for more than three years.
1715	George I	Septennial Act 1 Geo. I, St. 2, *c.* 38	Maximum duration of Parliament extended to seven years.
1911	George V	Parliament Act 1 & 2 Geo. V, *c.* 13	Maximum duration of Parliament fixed at five years. This provision in the Act was temporarily suspended by further Acts during the two World Wars.

SOVEREIGNS, PRIME MINISTERS AND PARLIAMENTS SINCE 1715

Sovereign, regnal year and calendar year of summons	*Prime Minister (age in brackets) and Date of Administration*[1]	*Party*	*Parliament*			
			Date fixed for Assembly[2]	*Date of Dissolution*	*Duration (to nearest month) Yrs.*	*Mths.*
1 George I: (1715)	3 April 1721. Sir Robert Walpole, recognized as our first 'Prime Minister' (44)	Whig	17 Mar. 1715	10 Mar. 1722	7	0
8 George I: (1722)	,, (45)	,,	10 May 1722	5 Aug. 1727	5	3
1 George II: (1727)	24 June 1727 ,, (51)	,,	28 Nov. 1727	17 April 1734	6	5
8 George II: (1734)	,, (57)	,,	13 June 1734	27 April 1741	6	10
15 George II: (1741)	,, (64)	,,	25 June 1741	18 June 1747	6	0
	16 Feb. 1742. Earl of Wilmington (69)	,,				
	25 Aug. 1743. Henry Pelham (48)	,,				

[1] The exact date when a Prime Minister formed his Cabinet often remains in doubt. Wherever possible, the dates given are those on which he first accepted the commission of the Sovereign to form an administration. For simplicity, cases where a Prime Minister resigned and was almost immediately reappointed are ignored.

[2] The duration is reckoned from the date appointed by the Writ of Summons for the new Parliament to meet till the Dissolution, although the first meeting for the dispatch of business was in early years often postponed.

Appendix 5—continued

Sovereign, regnal year and calendar year of summons	*Prime Minister (age in brackets) and Date of Administration*	*Party*	*Parliament*			
			Date fixed for Assembly	*Date of Dissolution*	*Duration (to nearest month)* *Yrs.*	*Mths.*
21 George II: (1747)	14 Feb. 1746. Henry Pelham (51)	Whig	13 Aug. 1747	8 April 1754	6	8
27 George II: (1754)	6 Mar. 1754. Duke of Newcastle (60) 16 Nov. 1756. Duke of Devonshire (36) 29 June 1757. Duke of Newcastle (63)	,, ,, Coalition	31 May 1754	20 Mar. 1761	6	10
1 George III: (1761)	26 May 1762. Earl of Bute (49) 10 April 1763. George Grenville (50) 10 July 1765. Marquess of Rockingham (35) 30 July 1766. Earl of Chatham (57) Sept. 1767. Duke of Grafton (31)	Tory Whig ,, Coalition ,,	19 May 1761	11 Mar. 1768	6	10
8 George III: (1768)	,, (32) 28 Jan. 1770. Lord North (37)	,, Tory	10 May 1768	30 Sept. 1774	6	5
15 George III: (1774)	,, (42)	,,	29 Nov. 1774	1 Sept. 1780	5	9

21 George III: (1780)	28 Jan. 1770. Lord North (48) 27 Mar. 1782. Marquess of Rockingham (51) 1 July 1782. Earl of Shelburne (45) 2 April 1783. Duke of Portland (45) 19 Dec. 1783. William Pitt (24)	Tory Coalition ,, ,, Tory	31 Oct. 1780	25 Mar. 1784	3	5
24 George III: (1784)	,,	Tory	18 May 1784	11 June 1790	6	1
30 George III: (1790)	,, (31)	,,	10 Aug. 1790	20 May 1796	5	9
36 George III: (1796)	,, (37)	,,	12 July 1796	[1]	6	0
41 George III: (1801)	,, (41) 14 Mar. 1801. Henry Addington (44)	,, ,,	22 Jan. 1801	29 June 1802		
42 George III: (1802)	7 May 1804. William Pitt (44)	,,	31 Aug. 1802	24 Oct. 1806	4	2
47 George III: (1806)	11 Feb. 1806. Lord Grenville (46)	Whig	15 Dec. 1806	29 April 1807		4
47 George III: (1807)	7 April 1807. Duke of Portland (69) 4 Oct. 1809. Spencer Perceval (46)	Tory ,,	22 June 1807	29 Sept. 1812	5	3

[1] By Proclamation dated 5 Nov., 1800, the Members then sitting for England were summoned to meet as United Kingdom Members on 22 Jan., 1801.

Appendix 5—continued

Sovereign, regnal year and calendar year of summons	Prime Minister (age in brackets) and Date of Administration	Party	Parliament			
			Date fixed for Assembly	Date of Dissolution	Duration (to nearest month) Yrs.	Mths.
53 George III: (1812)	20 May 1812. Earl of Liverpool (41)	Tory	24 Nov. 1812	10 June 1818	5	7
58 George III: (1818)	,, (48)	,,	4 Aug. 1818	29 Feb. 1820	1	7
1 George IV: (1820)	,, (49)	,,	21 April 1820	2 June 1826	6	1
7 George IV: (1826)	,, (56) 10 April 1827. George Canning (56) 8 Aug. 1827. Viscount Goderich (44) 22 Jan. 1828. Duke of Wellington (58)	,, ,, Coalition Tory	25 July 1826	24 July 1830	4	0
1 William IV: (1830)	16 Nov. 1830. Earl Grey (66)	Whig	14 Sept. 1830	23 April 1831		7
1 William IV: (1831)	,, (67)	,,	14 June 1831	3 Dec. 1832	1	6

Appendix 5—continued

3 William IV: (1833)	16 Nov. 1830. Earl Grey (68) 16 July. 1834 Viscount Melbourne (55) 15 Nov. 1834. Duke of Wellington (65) 9 Dec. 1834. Sir Robert Peel (46)	Whig Liberal Tory Conservative	29 Jan. 1833	29 Dec. 1834	1	11
5 William IV: (1835)	15 April 1835. Viscount Melbourne (56)	Liberal	19 Feb. 1835	17 July 1837	2	5
1 Victoria: (1837)	,, (58)	,,	11 Sept. 1837	23 June 1841	3	9
5 Victoria: (1841)	30 Aug. 1841. Sir Robert Peel (53) 30 June 1846. Lord John Russell (53)	Conservative Liberal	19 Aug. 1841	23 July 1847	5	11
11 Victoria: (1847)	,, (55) 22 Feb. 1852. Earl of Derby (52)	,, Conservative	21 Sept. 1847	1 July 1852	4	9
16 Victoria: (1852)	,, (53) 19 Dec. 1852. Earl of Aberdeen (68) 3 Feb. 1855. Viscount Palmerston (70)	,, Coalition Liberal	20 Aug. 1852	21 Mar. 1857	4	7
20 Victoria: (1857)	,, (72) 20 Feb. 1858. Earl of Derby (58)	,, Conservative	30 April 1857	23 April 1859	2	0

Appendix 5—continued

Sovereign, regnal year and calendar year of summons	*Prime Minister (age in brackets) and Date of Administration*	*Party*	*Parliament*			
			Date fixed for Assembly	*Date of Dissolution*	*Duration (to nearest month.) Yrs.*	*Mths.*
22 Victoria: (1859)	17 June 1859. Viscount Palmerston (74)	Liberal	31 May 1859	6 July 1865	6	1
29 Victoria: (1865)	20 Oct. 1865. Earl Russell (73) 2 June 1866. Earl of Derby (67) 26 Feb. 1868. Benjamin Disraeli (63)	,, Conservative ,,	15 Aug. 1865	11 Nov. 1868	3	3
32 Victoria: (1868)	3 Dec. 1868. William Ewart Gladstone (59)	Liberal	10 Dec. 1868	26 Jan. 1874	5	2
37 Victoria: (1874)	18 Feb. 1874. Benjamin Disraeli, created Earl of Beaconsfield 1876 (69)	Conservative	5 Mar. 1874	24 Mar. 1880	6	1
43 Victoria: (1880)	23 April 1880. William Ewart Gladstone (70) 13 June 1885. Marquess of Salisbury (55)	Liberal Conservative	29 April 1880	18 Nov. 1885	5	7
49 Victoria: (1886)	1 Feb. 1886. William Ewart Gladstone (76)	Liberal	12 Jan. 1886	26 June 1886		5

Appendix 5—*continued*

50 Victoria: (1886)	26 July 1886. Marquess of Salisbury (56)	Conservative	5 Aug. 1886	28 June 1892	5	11
56 Victoria: (1892)	15 Aug. 1892. William Ewart Gladstone (82) 2 Mar. 1894. Earl of Rosebery (46)	Liberal ,,	4 Aug. 1892	8 July 1895	2	11
59 Victoria: (1895)	26 June 1895. Marquess of Salisbury (65)	Conservative	12 Aug. 1895	25 Sept. 1900	5	1
64 Victoria: (1900) and 1 Edward VII:	,, (70) 14 July 1902. Arthur James Balfour (54) 5 Dec. 1905. Sir Henry Campbell-Bannerman (69)	,, ,, Liberal	1 Nov. 1900	8 Jan. 1906	5	2
6 Edward VII: (1906)	,, (69) 8 April 1908. Herbert Henry Asquith (55)	,, ,,	13 Feb. 1906	10 Jan. 1910	3	11
10 Edward VII: (1910)	,, (57)	,,	15 Feb. 1910	28 Nov. 1910		9

Appendix 5—continued

Sovereign, regnal year and calendar year of summons	Prime Minister (age in brackets) and Date of Administration	Party	Parliament			
			Date fixed for Assembly	Date of Dissolution	Duration (to nearest month) Yrs.	Mths.
1 George V: (1911)	8 April 1908. Herbert Henry Asquith (58)	Liberal	31 Jan. 1911	25 Nov. 1918 (Extended owing to war)	7	10
	25 May 1915. Herbert Henry Asquith (62)	Coalition				
	7 Dec. 1916. David Lloyd George (54)	,,				
9 George V: (1919)	,, (57)	,,	4 Feb. 1919	26 Oct. 1922	3	9
13 George V: (1922)	23 Oct. 1922. Andrew Bonar Law (64)	Conservative	20 Nov. 1922	16 Nov. 1923	1	0
	22 May 1923. Stanley Baldwin (55)	,,				
14 George V: (1924)	22 Jan. 1924. James Ramsay MacDonald (57)	Labour	8 Jan. 1924	9 Oct. 1924		9
	4 Nov. 1924. Stanley Baldwin (57)	Conservative				
15 George V: (1924)	,, (57)	,,	2 Dec. 1924	10 May 1929	4	5

Appendix 5—continued

20 George V: (1929)	5 June 1929. James Ramsay MacDonald (62)	Labour	25 June 1929	8 Oct. 1931	2	3
22 George V: (1931)	24 Aug. 1931. James Ramsay MacDonald (64)	Coalition[1]	3 Nov. 1931	25 Oct. 1935	4	0
26 George V: (1935)	7 June 1935. Stanley Baldwin (67)	Coalition[1]	26 Nov. 1935	15 June 1945 (Extended owing to war)	9	7
	28 May 1937. Neville Chamberlain (68)	"				
	10 May 1940. Winston Spencer Churchill (65)	"				
	23 May 1945. Winston Spencer Churchill (70)	Conservative				
9 George VI: (1945)	26 July 1945. Clement Richard Attlee (62)	Labour	1 Aug. 1945	3 Feb. 1950	4	6
14 George VI: (1950)	" (67)	"	1 Mar. 1950	5 Oct. 1951	1	7
15 George VI (1951) and	26 Oct. 1951. Winston Spencer Churchill (76)	Conservative	31 Oct. 1951	10 May 1955	3	6
1 Elizabeth II:	7 April 1955. Sir Anthony Eden (57)	"				

[1] Also known as the 'National' Government.

Appendix 5—continued

Sovereign, regnal year and calendar year of summons	*Prime Minister (age in brackets) and Date of Administration*	*Party*	*Parliament*			
			Date fixed for Assembly	*Date of Dissolution*	*Duration (to nearest month)* *Yrs.*	*Mths.*
4 Elizabeth II: (1955)	7 April 1955. Sir Anthony Eden (57)	Conservative	7 June 1955	22 Sept. 1959	4	4
	10 Jan. 1957. Harold Macmillan (62)	,,				
8 Elizabeth II: (1959)	,, (65)	,,	20 Oct. 1959			
	19 Oct. 1963. Sir Alec Douglas-Home (60)	,,				

THE HOURS OF SITTING OF THE HOUSE OF COMMONS

Appendix 6

The House has frequently varied its working hours to suit its own convenience and the changing habits of the generations. The following chart shows the broadest alterations but omits variations of detail.

Period	*Usual hour of meeting*	*Usual hour of rising*	*Remarks*
1560	8 a.m.	11 a.m.	Afternoons for committee work.
1620	7 or 8 a.m.	noon	Afternoons for committee work. During this century the competition of the Law Courts, which also sat in the mornings, gradually pushed the hour of meeting of the House forward, but for long Members disliked candle-light debates.
1690	noon	2 or 3 p.m.	Candle-light sittings coming in.
1759–1832	1 or 2 p.m. extending even to 4 p.m.	Often till the early hours of the morning	Saturday sittings were practically abolished by Sir Robert Walpole—it is said to enable him to hunt. The hours of meeting and rising were now both advanced to match the later times of the midday meal, of business and of pleasure.
1833–4	5 p.m.	midnight	Even this late hour of rising was a relief after the still later hours of the previous generation. There was a 'Morning Sitting' for Private Business and Petitions from noon till 3 p.m., and an interval known as 'the Speaker's Chop' for a meal before the 'Evening Sitting' at 5 p.m.
1835	4 p.m.	midnight	Only one 'Morning Sitting' each week.

Appendix 6—continued

Period	*Usual hour of meeting*	*Usual hour of rising*	*Remarks*
1867	4 p.m. (sometimes 2 p.m.)	midnight or 1 a.m.	'Speaker's Chop', 7–9 p.m.
1906	2.45 p.m.	11.30 p.m. (often exceeded)	'Speaker's Chop' abolished.
1945 onwards	2.30 p.m.	10.30 p.m. (often exceeded)	One early day (now Friday, 11 a.m. till 4.30 p.m.) since 1846.

THE DECREASE IN THE BURDEN ON PARLIAMENT

Appendix 7

(I) Private Bills

Early records are imperfect but the following figures illustrate the decline in Private Bill Legislation. It must be remembered that during the past century much legislation of the Private Bill type has been dealt with by the House (at a great saving of time and money) in the form of Provisional Order Bills and, latterly, under the Statutory Orders (Special Procedure) Act, 1945. These do not figure in the following table:

Year	*Number of Private Bills which received the Royal Assent*
1801	277
1846 (at the height of the railway boom) ..	1,130
1901	196
1962	37

Note: It is said that in 1825 thirty Committees on Private Business met on a single day, nineteen being fixed to meet in one room. (W. C. Townsend, *History of the House of Commons*, 1843–4, Vol. II, p. 381.)

(II) Public Petitions

During the early part of the nineteenth century debates on public petitions occupied a great part of the time of the House of Commons. It was not until 1839 that these debates were discontinued and their place was gradually taken by Questions to Ministers (see Appendix 8 (II)), though the number of petitions presented remained high until the end of the century.

Session	*Number of Petitions Presented*	*Session*	*Number of Petitions Presented*
1785	298	1863	12,583
1801	192	1873	21,426
1812–13	1,699	1883	23,304
1827	3,635	1893–4	33,742
1833	10,394	1903	13,170
1843	33,898	1913	600
1852–3	11,164	1950–62 .. (Average of 13 Sessions)	20

THE INCREASING BURDEN ON PARLIAMENT *Appendix 8*

(I) SITTINGS OF THE HOUSE AND NUMBER OF DIVISIONS

Down to the Hanoverian succession, Parliament usually met in October or November, and sat until April. A normal Session was a few weeks before Christmas and two or three months after. The date of prorogation then gradually crept on to May, June, July and occasionally August. An entry in the diary of Mr. Speaker Abbot forms a useful landmark (Vol. II, p. 158):

> '1808. Monday, July 4th. Prorogation.
>
> The most laborious session for hours of sitting ever known within living memory of the oldest Members or officers of the House.
>
> There were 111 sitting days, amounting to 829 hours, averaging 7½ hours a day. Since Easter to the close of the Session rarely less than 10 or 11 hours every day.'

The number of hours after midnight in 1808 was 112 and the number of divisions during the Session 87.

From this starting point the comparison runs as follows:

Years	*Number of days of sitting*	*Total number of hours*	*Number of hours per day*	*Number of hours after midnight*	*Number of Divisions per Session*
1808	111	829	7½	112	87
		Averages for decennial periods			
1845–1854	129	1,010	8	94	207
1855–1864	116½	912	7h. 55m.	93	189
1865–1874	115	897	7h. 46m.	107	187
1875–1884	133	1,150	8h. 39m.	170	283
1885–1894	139	1,178	8h. 28m.	106	325
1895–1904	127	1,099	8h. 39m.	55	369
				After 11p.m.[1]	
1905–1914	145	1,177	8h. 6m.	95	441
1915–1924	144	1,092	7h. 32m.	71	226
1925–1934	149	1,156	7h. 44m.	84	432
1935–1944	144	1,050	7h. 12m.	(*See note*[2])	179
1944–1956 (Average of 13 Sessions)	155	1,196	7h. 58m.	195[3]	200
1957–1962 (Average of 6 Sessions)	160	1,292	8h. 3m.	192½[3]	208

[1] From 1907 to 1938–9 the hours are reckoned from 11 p.m., when business was normally interrupted.

[2] From the outbreak of war in 1939 the House usually met at 11 a.m. and sat mainly during hours of daylight.

[3] From 1946 the hours are reckoned from 10 p.m., when business was normally interrupted.

(II) QUESTIONS TO MINISTERS[1] *Appendix* 8—*continued*

Session	*Total number of Questions on the Notice Paper in each session*	*Session*	*Total number of Questions on the Notice Paper in each session*
1847	129	1905	6,244
1848	222	1906	11,865
1850	212	1907	10,147
1860	699	1908	13,811
1870	1,203	1909	12,251
1880	1,546	1910	8,201
1883	3,185	1911	15,439
1884	3,555	1912–13	19,913
1885	3,354	1913	8,936
1886	2,821	1914	7,705
1887	5,030	1914–16	12,976
1888	5,549	1916	15,743
1889	4,049	1917	19,146
1890	4,407	1918	12,025
1890–1	3,770	1919	20,523
1892 (1st)	2,889	1920	18,652
,, (2nd)	55	1921	14,133
1893–4	6,534	1922	12,869
1894	3,567	1923	12,370
1895 (1st)	3,304	1924	13,092
,, (2nd)	569	1924–25	14,035
1896	4,464	1926	10,713
1897	4,824	1927	10,536
1898	5,155	1928	7,559
1899 (1st)	4,290	1928–29	7,074
,, (2nd)	231	1929–30	18,327
1900 (1st)	4,792	1930–31	14,373
,, (2nd)	314	1931–32	9,657
1901	6,448	1932–33	7,559
1902	7,168	1933–34	8,768
1903	4,536	1934–35	8,449
1904	5,933	1935–36	10,215

[1] The total number of Questions on the Notice Paper each session does not provide an entirely fair picture of the trend over the years, since the length of sessions varies considerably. The *daily average* of all Questions on the Paper (e.g. ninety-six in 1908 as compared with 110 in 1958–9) shows that the increase is not so great as might have been expected.

Appendix 8—continued

Session	*Total number of Questions on the Notice Paper in each session*	*Session*	*Total number of Questions on the Notice Paper in each session*
1936–37	11,769	1948–49	17,334
1937–38	13,787	1950	9,861
1938–39	18,460	1950–51	15,720
1939–40	13,536	1951–52	14,192
1940–41	10,825	1952–53	13,878
1941–42	11,592	1953–54	15,990
1942–43	11,911	1954–55	7,262
1943–44	11,498	1955–56	18,285
1944–45	7,856	1956–57	14,259
1945–46	27,313	1957–58	12,734
1946–47	17,310	1958–59	14,518
1947–48	16,303	1959–60	13,471
1948	853	1960–61	13,778

(III) PUBLIC BILLS *Appendix 8—continued*

The number of Public Bills which have annually received the Royal Assent during the last 150 years has varied remarkably little, rarely falling below 90 or above 150, but in general there has been an increase in length, scope and complexity.

Year	*No. of pages of Public General Acts*	*Year*	*No. of pages of Public General Acts*
1900	198	1931	374
1901	178	1932	1,047
1902	147	1933	1,055
1903	256	1934	664
1904	103	1935	1,519
1905	82	1936	1,508
1906	348	1937	1,003
1907	354	1938	934
1908	736	1939	1,399
1909	282	1940	502
1910	214	1941	448
1911	458	1942	246
1912	92	1943	524
1913	354	1944	517
1914	523	1945	891
1915	311	1946	1,232
1916	277	1947	2,002
1917	183	1948	2,008
1918	695	1949	2,288
1919	564	1950	1,000
1920	560	1951	675
1921	569	1952	1,437
1922	696	1953	815
1923	481	1954	1,198
1924	581	1955	747
1925	1,691	1956	1,016
1926	543	1957	1,103
1927	593	1958	1,188
1928	493	1959	1,451
1929	833	1960	1,145
1930	798	1961	1,048
		1962	1,335

THE FATE OF PRIVATE MEMBERS' BILLS *Appendix 9*

The following Table shows the fate of the legislative attempts of Private Members:

Year	*Number of Public Bills introduced into Commons by Private Members*	*Number which received the Royal Assent*
1896	175	13
1897	191	14
1898	184	18
1899	158	10
1900	161	14
1901	152	3
1902	163	10
1903	166	12
1904	146	11
1905	165	6
1906	188	4
1907	168	13
1908	226	19
1909	205	15
1910	177	8
1911	223	14
1912–13	217	8
1913	185	16
1914	199	16
1914–16 (War years)	2	–
1916 (War years)	–	–
1917–18 (War years)	–	–
1918 (War years)	–	–
1919	34	5
1920	61	5
1921 (two sessions)	75	14
1922 (two sessions)	73	7
1923	94	10
1924–25	92	14
1926	82	17
1927	103	10
1928	94	16
1928–9	48	9
1929–30	97	5
1930–1	95	7

Appendix 9—continued

Year	*Number of Public Bills introduced into Commons by Private Members*	*Number which received the Royal Assent*
1931–2	27	9
1932–3	62	14
1933–4	60	10
1934–5	10	3
1935–6	45	12
1936–7	51	13
1937–8	79	21
1938–9	60	16
1939–40, 1940–1, 1941–2, 1942–3, 1943–4, 1944–5 *War years*	–	–
1945–6	–	–
1946–7	–	–
1947–8	–	–
1948	–	–
1948–9	23	5
1950	–	–
1950–1	31	9
1951–7 (Average of 6 Sessions)	29	10
1957–63 (Average of 6 Sessions)	48	20

A. Longest Parliaments

The two longest Parliaments in English history have been:

1. The *Long Parliament* of Charles I:
   Assembled 3rd November, 1640;
   Expelled by Cromwell 20th April, 1653 . $12\frac{1}{2}$ years
   or
   Recalled 25th April, 1660;
   Dissolved itself 20th December, 1660 . 20 years 2 months
2. The Long or *Pensionary Parliament* of Charles II:
   Assembled 8th May, 1661;
   Dissolved 24th January, 1679 . . . $17\frac{3}{4}$ years

B. Longest Sittings of the House of Commons

The three following continuous sittings of thirty hours and over have been recorded, and there have been several almost as long.

1. 4 p.m. Monday, 31st January to 9.30 a.m., Wednesday, 2nd February 1881—$41\frac{1}{2}$ hours.

   This was the celebrated occasion which led to the introduction of the 'closure'. The Irish Members under Mr. Parnell were sworn to prevent the introduction of the Protection of Person and Property (Ireland) Bill, known as the Coercion Bill. (See p. 96.)
2. 2.45 p.m. Wednesday, 22nd July to 1.04 a.m., Friday, 24th July, 1936—$34\frac{1}{4}$ hours.

   A debate on the Draft Unemployment Assistance (Determination of Need and Assessment of Needs) Regulations resulted in disorder and suspensions.
3. 2.30 p.m. Monday, 11th June to 10.16 p.m. on Tuesday, 12th June, 1951 —$31\frac{3}{4}$ hours.

   Debate on the Committee stage of the Finance Bill.

By contrast the longest sitting of the House of Lords was $13\frac{1}{2}$ hours on 2nd–3rd July, 1963, when the Report stage of the London Government Bill was being debated.

C. Longest Speeches in Parliament

William Pitt the elder introduced the fashion of long speeches into the House of Commons, and orations of 2 or 3 hours and even longer quickly became fashionable. In 1831 Lord Brougham spoke for six hours on Law Reform; Palmerston spoke for over $4\frac{1}{2}$ hours on a summer night in 1851, 'from dusk almost until dawn', defending his conduct of policy in the Don Pacifico affair; and Gladstone spoke for five hours when introducing his first Budget in 1853. In modern times the longest speech was delivered by Mr.

Appendix 10—*continued*

Lloyd George on 29th April, 1909, as Chancellor of the Exchequer when introducing his Budget. It lasted for 4 hours 51 minutes, less an interval of 30 minutes to relieve his voice. The longest speech by a back-bench Member since 1945 was made by Mr. Malcolm Macmillan, who spoke for 2 hours 37 minutes on the night of 15th–16th March, 1961.

D. Longest Debates in the House of Commons on single Bills

1. 1893–94. The Government of Ireland Bill:

	Days
Introduction	4
Second Reading	12
Committee stage	46
Report stage	14
Third Reading	3
Financial Resolution	3
Total	82

2. 1909: Budget Resolutions and Finance Bill:

	Days
Budget Resolutions: Committee stage	12
,, ,, : Report stage	4
Finance Bill, Second Reading	4
,, ,, Committee stage	42
,, ,, Report stage	9
,, ,, Third Reading	3
Total	74

The above was probably the most violent and protracted legislative struggle which Parliament has known. All-night sittings became almost a matter of course. The closure was moved 106 times. Divisions reached the enormous total of 549, which alone represents 90 hours spent in the division lobbies. This was parliamentary opposition at its toughest.

E. Divisions

1. *Largest and closest Divisions*

The largest division on record occurred on 11th August, 1892, on Mr. Asquith's amendment to the Motion for an Address in reply to Her Majesty's speech at the opening of Parliament. The numbers were Ayes, 350; Noes, 310—660, or, with the Speaker and 4 Tellers, 665 out of a total House of 670 Members—a record never likely to be repeated.

Appendix 10—continued

Other large or close divisions have been:

(i) 22nd March, 1831: the Second Reading of the Reform of Parliament (England) Bill was carried by 1 vote.

Ayes	302
Noes	301
Speakers and Tellers	5
	608 out of 658 Members

(ii) 4th June, 1841, a vote of want of confidence moved by Sir R. Peel on Lord Melbourne's Government was carried by 1 vote.

Ayes	312
Noes	311
Speaker and Tellers	5
	628 out of 658 Members

(iii) 21st April, 1893, Second Reading of the Government of Ireland Bill:

Ayes	347
Noes	304
Speaker and Tellers	5
	656 out of 670 Members

This led to a double record because the House of Lords, who are well-known for the smallness of most of their divisions, rejected the Bill by 419 to 41—a total with officers of 465 out of 560 Peers at that date. It is believed to be the largest recorded division in that House.

(iv) 27th July 1950: Mr. Churchill 'spied strangers', whereupon Mr. Speaker put the Question under Standing Order No. 105 'That strangers do withdraw'. Had the motion been carried a Secret Session would have followed:

Ayes	295
Noes	296
Majority	1

2. *Largest number of Divisions at one sitting*

This occurred on 20th–21st March, 1907, when the House of Commons divided 43 times on the Army (Annual) Bill and on other matters. On 14th–15th December, 1933, there were 33 divisions in Committee on the Newfoundland Bill and on other matters.

Appendix 10—*continued*

3. *Minorities*

There have been many minorities of 1 and even 0, the explanation of the latter being that the only two Members in the minority were employed as Tellers. For instance,

(i) 13th December, 1932, Second Reading of Rent and Mortgage Interest Restrictions (Amendment) Bill:

Ayes	326
Noes	0

4. *Equality of Votes*

Divisions in which the numbers were equal have taken place, for example, on 10th May, 1860, 7th June, 1866, 3rd April, 1905, 1st May, 1950 and 1st March, 1951.

F. 'Counting Out' of the House of Commons

The average number of occasions per session when the House has been adjourned for lack of a quorum (forty) was as follows:

1880–1913	7
1914–1949	3.5
1950–1961	2

1295	The 'Model' Parliament meets.
about 1340	The knights and burgesses start to meet apart from the Lords.
1376 or 1377	Election of first Speaker now recognized as such.
1388	Office of Clerk of the House of Commons established.
1396–7	Haxey's case—privilege of freedom of speech asserted by Commons.
1401	Commons ask Henry IV for confirmation that redress of grievances must precede the grant of supply.
1407	Henry IV agrees that money grants shall be initiated by the Commons.
about 1460	Legislation by Bill instead of by petition becomes customary.
1547	Journals of House of Commons date from this year.
about 1548	Commons first sit in St. Stephen's Chapel.
1547–1610	Many rules of procedure established and now known as the 'ancient usage', *e.g.*, three readings for Bills, method of putting questions, one speaker at a time to be heard, order in debate, Committees of Supply and of Ways and Means, Order Book.
1679	Last occasion on which Sovereign gave the Commons an express command as to the election of a Speaker.
1681	Votes and Proceedings regularly published from this date.
1694	Triennial Act (a fresh Parliament every three years).
1715	Septennial Act (maximum duration of Parliament extended to seven years).
1742	Journals first printed.
1727–1760	Speakership of Arthur Onslow (see p. 95).
1771	Publication of debates, secured by pressure of public opinion.

Appendix 11—continued

throughout 18th century	Multiplication and formalization of rules of procedure.
1803	Continuous series of reports of debates begun by William Cobbett and later reissued by T. C. Hansard.
1834	Destruction of the House of Commons by fire.
1837	Amendments on reading Orders of the day no longer permitted.
1838	Amendments to alter succession of Orders of the day no longer permitted.
1839	Debate on Public Petitions abolished (Standing Order in 1842).
1844	First edition of the *Law, Privileges, Proceedings and Usage of Parliament* by Sir T. Erskine May (1856, Clerk-Assistant; 1871, Clerk of the House of Commons; 10th May, 1886 created Lord Farnborough; 17th May, 1886, died).
1849	Rule of Progress (no debate on Question to go into Committee after first occasion).
1852	Division of week into 'Motion' and 'Order' days.
1852	Commons occupy Chamber designed by Sir Charles Barry.
1854	Many reductions in number of stages and questions on Bills.
1855	Chairman of Ways and Means first appointed.
1860	Gladstone's Bill to repeal the paper duties rejected by Lords.
1861	All provisions relating to taxes henceforward grouped in one Bill to make rejection more difficult.
1861	Public Accounts Committee first appointed.
1861	Committee of Ways and Means to be fixed for any day. Automatic adjournment Friday to Monday.
1872	Rule of Progress extended to Supply (no Amendments to be moved except on certain occasions on going into Committee of Supply).

Appendix II—*continued*

2nd Feb. 1881	Mr. Speaker Brand summarily closes debate after obstruction by Irish Members. (Termed his *coup d'état*.) Rule that strangers not to be ordered to withdraw without a Resolution of the House.
21 & 24 Feb. 1882	Allocation of Time Orders, or 'guillotines', first used.
1882	Introduction of the Closure.
1882	Restriction on Adjournment motions by Private Members before day's 'business' to 'a Definite Matter of Urgent Public Importance'. Powers to deal with obstruction or continued irrelevance. Powers granted to Chair to put dilatory motions forthwith. Relevancy of Amendments to main question now insisted on.
1882 and 1886	Standing Committees set up to consider Public Bills.
1888	'Twelve o'clock rule'—House normally to adjourn at 12.30 a.m.
1894	Annual Taxing Act, hitherto known as the Customs and Inland Revenue Act, becomes the Finance Act.
1896	Special days allotted to the business of Supply.
1902	Deputy Chairman of Ways and Means appointed.
1906	Mr. Balfour's Reforms: 'Eleven o'clock rule'—House normally to adjourn at 11.30 p.m. Standing Committees used extensively henceforward.
1909	Power to select Amendments (the 'Kangaroo') first conferred on Chair.
1909	Hansard becomes the Official Report:—'Substantially the verbatim report' of proceedings.
1911	Parliament Act—power of House of Lords to delay legislation restricted.
1912	Estimates Committee first appointed sessionally.
1941	Destruction of the House of Commons by bombs.

Appendix 11—*continued*

1946	'Ten o'clock rule'—House normally to adjourn at 10.30 p.m.
1947	Allocation of time orders ('guillotines') applied to Standing Committees.
1949	Parliament Act—power of House of Lords to delay legislation further restricted.
1950	Commons occupy Chamber designed by Sir Giles Gilbert Scott.
1958	Life Peerages Act authorizes the creation of life peerages for men and women.
1963	Peerage Act permits hereditary peers to renounce their peerages for life and admits *all* holders of Scottish (but not Irish) peerages, and all peeresses in their own right, to the House of Lords.

GLOSSARY OF PARLIAMENTARY TERMS IN COMMON USE

NOTE.—*Owing to the constantly evolving history of Parliament it is difficult and dangerous to try to define parliamentary terms with precision. They have meant different things at different times, and different things to different people at the same time. The following pages attempt to explain some of the expressions most frequently met with. They relate almost exclusively to the House of Commons.*

Address. The name given to a communication or representation made by either House to the Crown. See also *Queen's Speech*.

Adjournment, Motions for. 'That this House do now adjourn', or 'That the debate be now adjourned'. In Committee the corresponding Motions are 'That the Chairman do leave the Chair' and 'That the Chairman do report Progress and ask leave to sit again'. These are used (1) with the intention of bringing the proceedings to a close, often in order to postpone or avoid a decision, or to discuss an incidental matter (and in such cases are therefore known as 'dilatory Motions'); but if the object of the Motion appears to the Chair to be obstructive it is either not accepted or it is put without debate; (2) as a convenient peg on which to hang a general debate, especially when it is not desired to record a formal conclusion on the real subject of debate; and (3) at the end of each day's regular business, for debates of half an hour's duration upon subjects of which Members have given previous notice. Such subjects are usually of local interest, or complaints of administrative action. This half hour provides an opportunity for Private Members to ventilate matters affecting their constituents for which there is no other opportunity. Legislation may not be proposed.

Adjournment Under S.O. No. 9. A Member may at the end of the hour appointed for Questions claim to move the adjournment of the House *for* *the purpose of discussing a definite matter of urgent public importance.* If the Speaker considers the Motion to be in order and the Member secures the support of forty Members the Motion stands over for debate at a fixed hour later in the evening. The definition has in practice been strictly interpreted, and this procedure has tended to be reserved for occasions when immediate action was necessary or when grave injustice threatened an individual.

Admonition. A formal reproof of an offender by the Speaker, less grave than a Reprimand.

Affirmation. Members who object to swearing an oath have now a statutory right to affirm instead.

Allegiance, Oath of. See *Oath.*

Allocation of Time. See *Closure.*

Allotted Days. A maximum of twenty-six sitting days (of which at least eight must be taken before 31st March) are allotted before 5th August in each session for the consideration by the Commons of the annual Estimates, and a few kindred matters.

Alternative Vote, the. A system of voting applied in some countries to single-Member constituencies to ensure that the successful candidate has a majority of the votes polled. The elector places the candidates in order of preference. Should no candidate secure an absolute majority, the first preferences given for the lowest candidate are ignored and the second preferences of those voters distributed among the remaining candidates.

Amendments. Alterations proposed to be made to a Motion, Bill or other proposed Amendment. Amendments must be relevant to the matter to be amended.

Appropriation Bill, the. Authorizes the issue out of the Consolidated Fund of the main sums required for the annual Estimates (apart from the Vote on Account) and appropriates *all* sums issued out of the Consolidated Fund during the session to the specific purposes for which they were voted.

Appropriations in Aid. Payments received by a Department in connexion with the public service and set off against the gross amount of its Estimate, under Treasury sanction.

Back Bench Members or Private Members. Members who are neither Ministers nor, as a rule, ex-Ministers. They occupy any bench except the front two on the Speaker's right and the front one on his left, both as far as the centre gangway.

Ballots. The relative precedence of Private Members to introduce Bills at the beginning of a Session and to move certain Motions is decided by ballots, during which numbered slips of paper corresponding to the names of Members who desire to compete are drawn from a box by a Clerk at the Table.

Bar of the House, the. Forms one of the boundaries of the House proper inside the Chamber. Members may not speak from outside it.

'Behind the Speaker's Chair.' An expression denoting the frequent informal discussions and arrangements between parties which take place in the vicinity of the Chamber—often in fact behind the Chair—and by means of which a great deal of official business is substantially facilitated.

Bills. Drafts of Acts under consideration by either House, up to the time they receive the Royal Assent and become Acts.

Bills, Hybrid. Public Bills which are found to affect private interests. They are dealt with by a special procedure, following partly Public Bill and partly Private Bill practice.

Bills, Private. Drafts of Acts with a local, private or personal application only. Not to be confused with Private Members' Bills, which are Public Bills introduced by Private Members—instead of by the Government.

Bills, Provisional Order. Bills to confirm Orders which have been issued by a Government Department, often after the holding of a local inquiry. The procedure is a simplified and shortened scheme of Private Legislation, and takes an average of three months between presentation and Royal Assent.

Bills, Public. Drafts of Acts of a public and general character, usually affecting the whole country.

Black Rod. The Gentleman Usher of the Black Rod, or his deputy the Yeoman Usher, is sent by the Lords to summon the Commons to the Upper Chamber on ceremonial occasions. He carries a black wand of office.

Blocking of Bills or Motions. Opposed business may only be taken up to a fixed hour every day. Thereafter, by simply saying 'object!', any Member can force the postponement of any item. The same result is achieved by continuing the debate on the preceding item long enough to prevent a contentious Bill or Motion being reached.

Blue Books. A colloquial name for those official reports and other publications which are sufficiently bulky to be given a blue cover.

Blue Paper (or Vote), the. A composite mass of papers circulated to Members in the morning and formerly printed on blue-coloured paper. It comprises mainly (1) the Votes and Proceedings of the previous sitting; (2) notices given at the previous sittings of Questions, Motions and Amendments for future sittings; (3) the agenda for the day; (4) the proceedings of recent sittings of Standing Committees; (5) collected and marshalled lists of Amendments to be proposed to Bills soon to be considered; (6) Division lists.

Budget, the. The annual review made by the Chancellor of the Exchequer of the country's accounts for the past year and of his financial proposals for the current year. The word is an eighteenth-century slang term for a 'bag of papers'.

Budget Resolutions. The resolutions varying taxation which are passed originally in the Committee of Ways and Means and upon which the Finance Bill is founded.

Cabinet, the. The chief Ministers of the Government, who are selected by the Prime Minister and meet to deliberate in private under his chairmanship. All are appointed to the Privy Council (of which in theory the Cabinet is a committee) and in practice all must belong to one or other House of Parliament.

'Carpet-bagger'. A political candidate for a constituency in which he does not live and with which he has no connexion. (U.S. slang.)

Casting Vote. When the numbers in a division are equal the Speaker (or Chairman) gives a casting vote to secure a decision. To maintain the impartiality of the Chair the vote is exercised where possible so as to give the House another opportunity for decision. In the Lords the question 'is resolved in the negative'.

'Catching the Speaker's Eye'. In the Commons when two or more Members rise simultaneously to speak the Speaker is supposed to call the one who first catches his eye. This practice is often modified for the general convenience (see p. 121).

Chairman, Deputy. See *Deputy Chairman.*

Chairman of Committees of the House of Lords. His duties correspond closely to those of the *Chairman of Ways and Means* (q.v.)

Chairman of Ways and Means, the. A Member elected at the beginning of every Parliament, on a Government Motion, to act as Chairman when the House is 'in Committee'. He also acts as Deputy Speaker and has important duties connected with Private Bills. Though a party Member he carries out his official duties with complete impartiality.

Chairmen, Temporary. A panel of experienced Members appointed by the Speaker to act as temporary chairmen in Committee of the Whole House and as the regular chairmen of Standing Committees. They have no power to accept motions for the Closure, or to select Amendments, *in Committee of the Whole House.*

Chaplain, the. Reads prayers before every sitting. The appointment is in the gift of the Speaker, whose personal officer the Chaplain is.

Charge upon the People. Any tax or other burden charged on the people, the produce of which is payable into the Exchequer.

Charge upon the Public Revenue, or Public Funds. Any public expenditure, whether out of the Consolidated Fund or out of moneys to be provided by Parliament, but exclusive of local rates. See *Queen's Recommendation.*

Chiltern Hundreds. A Member who wishes to resign has to do so by the indirect method of applying for one of the Offices of Profit under the Crown, the holding of which automatically vacates his seat. The two sinecure appointments used for this purpose are those of steward or bailiff of Her Majesty's three Chiltern Hundreds of Stoke, Desborough and Burnham, or of the Manor of Northstead. These offices can if necessary be held by Members in quick succession. Though technically Offices of Profit, they carry no salary.

Clandestine Outlawries Bill. See *Outlawries Bill.*

Clerks. The officials responsible for keeping the records of the House, advising the Speaker and Members upon procedure, attending Committees and other duties.

Closure, the. Procedure for closing a debate by majority decision while Members still wish to speak. The question for the *simple closure* is 'That the question be now put'; for the *kangaroo closure*, e.g. 'That clause 10, down to the word "then" in line 7, stand part of the Bill'; while the *guillotine* (or closure by compartments) takes the form of a time-table allocating definite times to each part or stage of a Bill. In the first two cases a Member can only claim the closure; it remains with the Speaker or Chairman to decide whether the question 'That the question be now put' shall be put to the House; and for the House to decide whether it shall be carried.

Motions for the closure, to be effective, require the support of at least one hundred Members voting in the majority in the Chamber. In a Standing Committee it is seventeen, or one-third of the number of its members (excluding the Chairman), whichever is the less.

Such Motions may be accepted in the House by the Speaker (or, when his absence has been formally announced, by the Chairman of Ways and Means, and similarly, in the absence of both, by the Deputy Chairman); in Committee of the Whole House by the Chairman of Ways and Means or the Deputy Chairman; and in Standing Committees by all chairmen.

Command Papers. Documents presented to Parliament by a Minister, nominally by command of Her Majesty, and referred to by a number, e.g. Cmnd. 2150.

Committee of Privileges, the. The most experienced and authoritative Committee of the House, to whom are referred questions of breaches of its Privileges.

Committee of Selection, the. Is chosen from among the most experienced Members of the House and nominates Members of Standing Committees and Private Bill 'groups', etc.

Committee of Supply. A Committee of the Whole House (q.v.), but its business is to consider and vote all State expenditure (except those items charged directly upon the Consolidated Fund) in the form of Estimates, Supplementary Estimates, Votes on Account and Votes of Credit.

Committee of Ways and Means. A Committee of the Whole House (q.v.). Its business is to consider and vote all Resolutions imposing taxes and making good the Supply granted to the Crown and certain other payments into and out of the Consolidated Fund, excluding those payments (such as the Civil List, and salaries of judges, the Speaker and others) which are charged directly upon the Consolidated Fund by existing legislation.

Committee of the Whole House. The Whole House sitting (in the Chamber) as a Committee, generally to consider the Committee stage of a Bill or a Money Resolution. The atmosphere and conditions of debate are more informal than when the House sits as a House.

Committee on National Expenditure, the. Took the place of the Estimates Committee during both world wars and conducted investigations into possible economies in expenditure.

Committees, Joint. Select Committees formed of an equal number of Members from each House to consider a Bill or matter in which both Houses are interested. The procedure followed is that of the House of Lords.

Committees, Select. All Committees which are not Committees of the Whole House, or Standing Committees, viz. those set up to inquire into special matters or Bills, and the usual Sessional Committees.

Committees, Sessional. Certain Select Committees regularly set up at the beginning of every Session, such as those on Privileges, Public Petitions, Selection, Public Accounts, Estimates, Publications and Debates Reports, Private Bill Standing Orders, and Kitchen and Refreshment Rooms.

Committees, Standing. Committees of Members of Parliament set up to consider the Committee stage of Bills. The personnel is composed partly of Members nominated for the duration of the Session and partly of specialist Members added for particular Bills, but in both cases the representation strictly follows the party proportions in the House.

Committees on Unopposed Bills. Deal only with Private and Provisional Order Bills which are not opposed.

Consideration (**or Report**) **stage, the.** Occurs in the House after a Bill has been reported to the House from a committee: (1) when it has been amended in Committee of the Whole House; or (2) after it has been sent to any other committee, even if not amended there. Fresh amendments may be proposed at this stage.

Consolidated Fund, the. The general revenue account into which all public moneys are paid—the public purse.

Consolidated Fund Bill. A Bill authorizing the issue of a sum of money out of the Consolidated Fund for the payment of authorized services, pending the passing of the Appropriation Bill towards the end of the Session.

Count, a. Any Member may call attention to the fact that a quorum (forty members) is not present (except between 7.30 and 8.30 p.m., or, on Fridays, between 1.15 and 2.15 p.m.). A bell is rung forthwith all over the House, and if at the end of four minutes forty Members are not present, the Speaker adjourns the House till the next sitting (not before 1 p.m. on Fridays).

'Cross the Floor', to. See *Floor of the House.*

Crossbenches. The transverse benches in the House of Lords used by peers attached to no party.

Delegated Legislation. The power to make subsidiary laws which is delegated by Parliament to the Executive by statute (see p. 170). The expression is also used of these subsidiary laws themselves, most of which are now known as Statutory Instruments (q.v.).

Deputy Chairman, the. A Member elected at the beginning of every Parliament, on a Government motion, to act as deputy to the Chairman of Ways and Means and if necessary to the Speaker. Though a party Member he carries out his official duties with absolute impartiality. He is specially concerned with Private Legislation.

Dilatory Motions. See *Adjournment.*

Disorderly Conduct. See *Suspension of Members.*

Dissolution. The conclusion of a Parliament by Royal Proclamation. The same Proclamation summons the next Parliament.

Divisions. Votes of the House. Members desiring to vote 'Aye' or 'No' walk through separate Lobbies, where they are counted by pairs of Members called Tellers.

Dropped Orders of the Day. Orders which are reached and called by the Clerk, but neither disposed of nor postponed to a future day.

Dummy Bill, a. A form or sheet of paper on which are written the Title of the Bill and the names of the Members by whom it is introduced or prepared. The dummy is used at the first stage of legislation before the House orders the Bill to be printed.

Duration of a Parliament. Under the Parliament Act, 1911, must not exceed five years. In periods of emergency this limit is extended by Act, usually for a year at a time.

Early Day Motion. A Motion for which no day has been fixed or appears to be available. Often used to test the opinions of Members (who may add their names) or in the hope of securing time for a debate.

Eleven O'Clock Rule, the. Now the Ten O'Clock Rule (q.v.).

'Erskine May'. See '*May*'.

Estimates, the. The detailed annual statements of the sums of money required by each Government Department—divided into Classes, Votes, Sub-heads and Items.

Examiners of Petitions for Private Bills, the. Officials (not Members) of each House who examine Private Legislation and documents related thereto (e.g. Memorials, q.v.) at certain stages to ascertain whether the relevant Standing Orders have been complied with. See also *Select Committee on Standing Orders.*

Excess Vote, an. A Grant to make good an overspending by a Department in excess of the money appropriated to it.

Exempted Business. Certain items are normally exempted from the operation of the Ten O'Clock Rule and may be taken after 10 p.m., even though opposed. These include the proceedings:

1. On any Bill originating in Committee of Ways and Means (Consolidated Fund Bills, Appropriation Bills, Finance Bills and a few others).
2. On the reports of the Committee of Ways and Means.
3. On the report of a committee authorizing the expenditure of public money except a report from the Committee of Supply.
4. Of a committee on a motion authorizing expenditure in connexion with a Bill (this extension is limited).
5. In pursuance of any Act of Parliament dealing with the confirmation of Statutory Instruments. Proceedings dealing with the annulment of such S.I.'s are normally exempted for a limited period.

Explanatory or Financial Memorandum, an. is often prefixed to a Bill to explain its provisions in non-technical language. Any Bill involving expenditure of public money *must* carry a Financial Memorandum. It is not part of the Bill and the wording must be uncontentious. (These memoranda descend from the briefs or 'breviats' which used to be prepared to assist the Speaker in very old days in 'opening the substance' of a Bill to the House.)

'Father of the House', the. The Member who has been longest in the House without a break, even though he has sat for several constituencies.

Finance Bill, the. Embodies all the alterations of taxation in both directions, and all the consequential administrative changes which are required for the year.

Financial (or Money) Resolution, a. The motion which must be submitted to the House with the Queen's Recommendation (q.v.) and be agreed to both in Committee and on Report before any provision involving public expenditure in a Bill can be entertained.

Floor of the House. 'To cross the Floor' means to change one's political allegiance as evidenced by sitting on a different side of the Chamber.

Friday Sittings. The House meets at 11 a.m. on Fridays, when no Questions are as a rule taken. Opposed business cannot be taken after 4 p.m., and the House rises not later than 4.30 p.m., unless exempted business is to be taken.

Front Benches. The front bench on either side of the House, as far as the centre gangway. On the Speaker's right (the 'Treasury' bench) sit the Prime Minister and leading members of the Government; on the left (usually) the leading members of the Opposition who have formed or are likely to form the alternative Government.

Gangway, the. Divides the benches on both sides half-way down the House. Elder statesmen no longer in the Government and Members of independent views or alienated from their party often choose to sit 'below the gangway'.

Government Draftsmen. Expert barristers, also known as Parliamentary Counsel, employed by the Government to prepare Bills for presentation to Parliament.

Guillotine, the. See *Closure.*

Hansard. The name of the family which for so long reported the debates of Parliament that the two became identified (see p. 134). See *Official Report.*

Hybrid Bills. See *Bills, Hybrid.*

Instructions are given by the House to some of its Committees ordering or empowering them to do something they might not or could not otherwise have done, e.g., directing a Select Committee to report specifically upon some matter lying within their terms of reference; or empowering a Standing Committee to divide a Bill into two or more Bills.

Irrelevance or Repetition in Speeches. A Member guilty of persistent irrelevance or tedious repetition may, after a warning, be directed by the Chair to discontinue his speech.

Joint Committees. See *Committees, Joint.*

Journal, the. The official record of the proceedings of the House, which dates back to 1547. It is fuller than the Votes and Proceedings, and has a useful index.

Kangaroo, the. See *Selection of Amendments.*

Kangaroo Closure, the. See *Closure.*

Leader of the Opposition, the. The leader of the largest party in opposition to the Government, in either House. In the Commons he is paid a salary of £3,000 a year, plus £750 allowance as an M.P. (see p. 80).

Legislation by Reference. The practice of altering the law by referring to, and amending, an old Act in a new one; instead of by repealing the old measure and re-enacting it in amended form (see p. 115).

Lobby Correspondents. Newspaper correspondents whose special passes entitle them to mingle with Members in the Members' Lobby.

Locus Standi. The ground or right of a petitioner against a Private Bill, etc., to be heard upon his Petition. See *Referees, the Court of.*

Lords of the Treasury. The Prime Minister is nowadays invariably the First Lord and the Chancellor of the Exchequer the Second. The Junior Lords are Whips.

Mace, the. The symbol of the Royal authority delegated to the Speaker. The House is not properly constituted and cannot sit unless the Mace is lying on the Table. In Committee the Mace is placed on brackets below the end of the Table. If an offender is to be reprimanded at the Bar the Serjeant at Arms stands upon his right hand with the Mace. The Mace does not enter the House of Lords but is left outside.

Maiden Speech, a. A Member's first speech in the House. By courtesy a maiden speech is not subject to interruptions and takes precedence of others. The Member is expected to show diffidence, and is customarily congratulated by the next Member to speak.

Manor of Northstead. See *Chiltern Hundreds.*

'May'. The standard treatise on parliamentary procedure. It was originally written in 1844, by Thomas Erskine May (at that time Assistant Librarian of the House of Commons) and entitled *A treatise upon the Law, Privileges, Proceedings and Usage of Parliament.* He held the appointment of Clerk of the House from 1871 to 1886, and was created Lord Farnborough shortly before his death in the latter year.

The book has been constantly revised in succeeding editions, of which the sixteenth is the latest.

Members, Disorderly Conduct of. See *Suspension of Members.*

Memorials. Notices of objection taken by interested parties to Private Legislation, on the ground of non-compliance with Standing Orders. See also *Examiners of Petitions.*

Minister, a. A term used colloquially for anyone holding Office in the executive Government. In addition to the Ministers so called (e.g. of Power, of Health, etc.), it covers the Secretaries of State, a number of Ministers with individual titles (e.g. Chancellor of the Exchequer, President of the Board of Trade, Postmaster-General), the Under-Secretaries, Law Officers and (generally in the form 'Junior Minister') the Whips. A Minister is almost invariably a member of one or other House.

Ministers without Portfolio. Members of the Government without Departmental responsibilities.

Money Bills are of two kinds:

1. 'Parliament Act Money Bills', which contain *only* provisions dealing with the imposition or repeal of taxation, public expenditure, or certain other exclusively financial matters. They receive the Speaker's certificate and the benefit of the provisions of the Parliament Acts.
2. Ordinary Money Bills, whose *main* object is to authorize expenditure or

to impose taxation. It used to be obligatory to introduce those authorizing expenditure upon a Money Resolution, with the Recommendation of the Crown. But since 1938 they have, to provide for a wider debate than the old procedure allowed, been presented and proceeded with under Standing Order No. 84 in the same manner as Bills in which the imposition of a charge is subsidiary to the main purpose. The old procedure is still available.

Money Resolution. See *Financial Resolution.*

Monk Resolutions, the. The detailed schedules moved in Committee of the Whole House to sanction the *virement* (q.v.) between votes (generally for each) of the fighting services. Mr. Monk was the Member who first moved for these Resolutions, in 1879.

Mother of Parliaments, the. An expression first used (of England) by John Bright at Birmingham in 1865. With the possible exceptions of the Hungarian and Icelandic Parliaments the English is the oldest surviving in the world. Some of its features were copied in the United States Congress. Some, owing to a description sent by Romilly to Mirabeau about 1790, found their way into French parliamentary law, and thence into several other nineteenth-century European Parliaments. The Dominion Federal and State Legislatures closely follow the British model.

Motion, a. A form of words containing a proposal which a Member wishes to submit to the House. If agreed to, it becomes an Order, by which the House gives an instruction to someone (from the Speaker downwards) or a Resolution, by which the House expresses its corporate opinion.

Motions, Notices of. Notice has normally to be given to the House of an intention to move a Motion.

Naming a Member. The power given to Mr. Speaker under Standing Orders Nos. 23 and 24 to indicate a Member who has disregarded the authority of the Chair, abused the rules of the House or been guilty of grossly disorderly conduct, by calling upon him by name. The Leader of the House then moves that the Member be suspended. (See p. 103.)

Notice Paper, or Order Paper. That part of the *Vote* (see *Blue Paper*) which comprises the agenda for the day's sitting, including all relevant notices.

Oath of Allegiance, the. The promise of loyalty required of all Members when they take their seats. They must either swear as follows: 'I swear by Almighty God that I will be faithful and bear true allegiance to Her Majesty Queen Elizabeth, her heirs and successors, according to law, so help me God'; or they may make an affirmation of allegiance. Heavy penalties, including the vacating of his seat, attach to a Member who sits or votes without having taken the oath or made an affirmation.

Official Report, the. The verbatim report of the daily debates in the Lords and Commons—known also as *Hansard*.

Opposed Business. After 10 p.m. (4 p.m. on Fridays) the objection of even one Member to items of business proposed halts their progress unless they are Exempted Business (q.v.).

Order Book, the. A chronological list, published daily, of the items of business of all kinds so far appointed to be taken in the House on future days.

Order Paper, the. See *Notice Paper*.

Order, a Point of. A point raised for the decision of the occupant of the Chair or the House itself relating to the rules and Orders which the House has made for the regulation of its business, including the orderly conduct of debate. This is one of the most misused of all parliamentary terms.

Orders. All Orders of the House originate or are assumed to have originated as Motions and to have been put as questions. When agreed to they become directions to be carried out by its Members, Committees or officers. They are of the following types:

1. Standing, i.e. permanent until repealed or modified. There are 117 regulating Public Business and about 250 regulating Private Business.
2. Sessional, i.e. valid for the duration of the Session, e.g. the order relating to free passage for Members through the streets leading to Westminster, mentioned on pp. 60–61.
3. Specific, such as those made for the attendance of a witness or the production of a document.
4. Orders relating to business and Orders of the Day (q.v.).

Orders in Council. See *Privy Council* and *Statutory Instruments*.

Orders of the Day. The ordinary business of the House is divided into Notices of Motions and Orders of the Day. The former consist of new proposals to be submitted by Members, the latter of matters of business appointed by the House to be considered on that day: usually, but not invariably, Bills or adjourned debates.

Outlawries Bill, the. A Bill which is given its First Reading (and never gets any further) at the beginning of every Session, before the Queen's Speech is taken into consideration. The ceremony dates from before 1603 and serves to show that Parliament has a right to deliberate without reference to the immediate cause of its summons.

Pairs. Two Members of opposed parties who agree to be absent from the House together and thus to neutralize each other's votes. (Members who 'paired' were defined by an eighteenth-century doorkeeper of the House of Commons as 'Two sneaking scoundrels, not worth a piece of dog's meat to either party!'[1])

[1] Joseph Pearson, *A Political Dictionary*, 1792, p. 40.

Parliament Acts, 1911 and 1949, the. The Acts which limit the powers of the House of Lords. (See pp. 31 and 148.)

Parliamentary Agents. Persons, usually solicitors, who act professionally for the promoters or opponents of Private Bills.

Parliamentary Bar. Those barristers who represent the promoters or opponents of Private Bills before committees in both Houses. (To be distinguished from Parliamentary Counsel who are servants of the Government.)

Parliamentary Counsel. See *Government Draftsmen*.

Parliamentary Papers. Documents of different types, printed and unprinted, which are deposited by Ministers and other authorities for the information of Members.

Personal Explanations are occasionally made after Questions, by an ex-Minister to explain his reasons for resignation, or by any Member to explain his conduct or to remove misunderstandings.

Petitions, Public, are decreasing in importance, having been largely superseded by Questions. They must be presented by a Member, either orally or dropped into a bag behind the Speaker's Chair, and they must be drawn up in conformity with certain prescribed rules. Except in the case of present personal grievance or privilege, where immediate action is necessary, no debate on the presentation of a petition is allowed. Petitions stand referred to the Committee on Public Petitions, whose powers are very limited.

Petitions Relating to Private Bills. Every Private Bill is still founded upon a petition to Parliament for leave to bring in a Bill. Other petitions are directed against such Bills, or for or against alterations in them.

Prayer. A colloquial term covering a Motion or an Address for the annulment of a Statutory Instrument.

Prayers are read in both Houses before each sitting: in the Lords by a bishop or the Lord Chancellor; in the Commons by the Chaplain.

Preamble, a, to a Public Bill is now rare. Its former purposes—to state the reasons and intended effects of proposed legislation—are now filled by an explanatory memorandum. In a Private Bill the Preamble sets forth—often at length—the reasons why the Bill is required.

Precedence of Private Members' Bills and Motions. See *Ballots*.

Prerogative, the. A word with complicated and disputed meanings. It is used here for the rights and powers, apart from those conferred by Statute, which the law recognizes as belonging to the Crown. Almost all, e.g. the right to declare war, to make treaties, to pardon offenders, are now exercised in the Sovereign's name by Ministers responsible to Parliament. In a few cases, such as the dissolution of Parliament or the dismissal of Ministers, the Sovereign's personal discretion is almost completely dormant; while in still fewer, such as the choice between alternative Prime Ministers, it is still in use.

Previous Question, the. A method of shelving the question before the House, once popular but now rarely used. The Motion is 'That the Question be *not* now put'. If carried, the House passes to the next business, but the superseded question may be put on a future day. If the motion is negatived the Question has to be put immediately.

Private Bills. See *Bills, Private.*

Private Members. See *Back Bench Members.*

Private Members' Bills. Public Bills introduced by Private Members (not by the Government).

Private Notice Questions. See *Questions.*

Privilege. Part of the law of the land, which by protecting the rights and dignities of Members inside Parliament enables them to serve and protect the interests of their constituents outside.

Privilege, Breach of. Questions of breach of Privilege in the House of Commons should be raised at the earliest opportunity and they take precedence of all other business. They are decided by the House itself, usually after reference to the Committee of Privileges. No Privilege not already existing may be claimed.

Privy Council, the. Originally the Sovereign's private advisory and executive council, it has lost most of its advisory functions to the smaller Cabinet (q.v.). Many formal acts of government are still exercised in the shape of Proclamations, and of Orders in Council. The connexion with Parliament is that all Cabinet Ministers become Privy Councillors and the oath of secrecy which they swear as such binds them in Cabinet. Privy Councillors are entitled to the prefix of 'The Right Honourable'.

Progress, Motions to Report, in Committees of the Whole House (or Supply or Ways and Means) correspond to Motions in the House for the Adjournment of the debate. When a Bill has been partially considered in Committee of the Whole House, for instance, the Chairman is directed to report Progress and to ask leave to sit again; or the Motion may be used to interrupt a debate in order to clear up some matter.

Proportional Representation. An electoral system designed to ensure that every substantial party or section of opinion shall be represented in proportion to its numerical strength. It requires large constituencies containing several seats. (See pp. 171–180.)

Prorogation. The termination by the Crown of a Session of Parliament (not to be confused with Dissolution, which ends a Parliament). It is effected by an announcement in the House of Lords by the Sovereign or a Royal Commission, and kills all Bills which have not passed through all their stages in both Houses. (The Government statement which used to detail those Bills for which time could not be found was known as the 'Slaughter of the Innocents'.)

Protest. Peers may dissent from a vote of the House and have their 'protest' entered in the Journal.

Provisional Order Bills. See *Bills, Provisional Order.*

Public Bills. See *Bills, Public.*

Putting the Question. Every matter is decided in the House of Commons upon a question put from the Chair, which is either affirmed or negatived or withdrawn (see p. 94).

Queen's Consent, the, is required to certain Bills, Public or Private, which concern the Royal Prerogative, the hereditary revenue or the personal property or interests of the Crown or Duchy of Cornwall. It is signified by a Privy Councillor. (If the Prince of Wales is of age it is given on his behalf in respect of the Duchy of Cornwall.) In the case of Public Bills a communication from the Crown is sometimes received, 'placing its interest at the disposal of Parliament'. The Queen's Consent should not be confused with the Royal Assent or the Queen's Recommendation.

Queen's Recommendation, the, must be given (under Standing Order) by the Crown (the Executive) to every motion involving public expenditure. It is signified by a Minister of the Crown before the Committee Stage of the Resolution.

Queen's Speech, the. A statement of policy framed by the Cabinet and delivered at the beginning of every session by the Sovereign in person or by the Lord Chancellor or a Royal Commission. Except for a reference concerning Supply, which is made to the Commons alone, the speech is addressed to both Houses of Parliament. The first part deals with foreign relations and policy, the second with home policy and contains a summary of the proposed legislative programme. It is answered by 'an humble Address' which affords an opportunity for a wide debate in both Houses, lasting, in the Commons, for several days. A somewhat similar speech at the end of the session summarizes the legislation which has been carried through.

Questions, Parliamentary, to Ministers. These are of several types:

1. 'Oral', requiring an oral answer in the House.
2. 'Non-Oral' or 'Written', requiring a written reply.
3. 'Private Notice', in effect 'oral' questions of an urgent nature, which, by special permission from the Speaker, receive a reply at the end of the Question hour, even on the day when first raised.
4. 'Supplementary', which follow replies to 'oral' questions, out of which they are supposed to arise impromptu, though in fact they are often previously prepared. An experienced Member is an adept

at using supplementaries to drive home a point or to twist a knife in a wound.

Quorum. In the House of Commons, forty; in the House of Lords, three. In the House of Commons, no business can be transacted if, upon the appeal of a Member to the Speaker, it is found that a quorum is not present. See *Count.*

Readings of Bills are among the stages through which Bills must proceed on their way to the statute book. (See p. 118.)

Recess. The adjournment which follows a Prorogation—also colloquially used of vacations within a session.

Re-committal of Bill. Since no Charge may be imposed or increased except in Committee, if it is desired to move an amendment containing such a Charge after the Bill has emerged from Committee, it must be re-committed. A Bill may also be re-committed for other reasons, e.g. to be divided into two Bills, or to have its provisions extended to another part of Great Britain, under an Instruction (q.v.) from the House.

Referees, the Court of. The Members who (together with Mr. Speaker's Counsel) determine whether a petitioner against a Private Bill has a sufficient *locus standi*—or right to be heard.

Regnal Year. Any year of a Sovereign's reign reckoned from his or her accession. Statutes were formerly cited by regnal years as well as by title. Thus the National Assistance Act, 1948, which received the Royal Assent on 13th May, 1948, was cited as '11 and 12 Geo. 6 c.29' being the Act called chapter, or number 29, passed in the parliamentary session which occupied part of the 11th and 12th regnal years of the reign of King George VI who acceded on 11th December, 1936. Since January, 1963, Acts have been cited by reference to the calendar year (e.g. 1963, c.53).

Report Stage. Colloquially used for the Consideration stage (q.v.), since it occurs after a Bill is reported to the House.

Reprimand. A formal reproof by the Lord Chancellor or Speaker of an offender against the privileges, etc., of Parliament, etc.

Reserved Speech. A Member may move an Order of the Day, or second a Substantive Motion, by raising his hat or by some other sign, and reserve his speech until later in the debate.

Resignation of Members. See *Chiltern Hundreds.*

Right of Reply, a, belongs to the mover of a Substantive Motion.

Royal Assent, the. The Sovereign's Assent given in the House of Lords (almost invariably nowadays by a Commission) to Bills which, having passed through all their Stages in both Houses, are thereby converted into Acts of Parliament. The last occasion when the Royal Assent was refused was in 1707 when Queen Anne refused it to the Scottish Militia Bill.

Royal Commissions (apart from those representing the Sovereign in Parliament) are appointed by the Crown, sometimes as a result of an Address from Parliament, to inquire into matters of great importance. The persons best qualified to consider the subject, whether inside or outside of Parliament, are invited to be members of the Commission.

Scope of Debate, the. One of the most important uses of procedure is to delimit the scope of debate upon different stages of Bills and items of business and so save time. Until about a hundred years ago the scope of debate was very much wider than the pressure of business nowadays permits. Since then a series of carefully worked out rulings has been given from the Chair and their effect is laid down in the manuals of procedure. (See pp.164–167.)

Second Speech, a, by the same Member (apart from a Right of Reply), on a question before the House, may be allowed only by general assent.

Secret Session. See *Spying Strangers*.

Secretaries. The **Secretaries of State** are among the principal Ministers of the Crown, each responsible for his own Department of State. **Under-Secretaries of State, Parliamentary Secretaries** and **Financial Secretaries** are junior Ministers. **Permanent Secretaries, Permanent Under-Secretaries of State** and **Permanent Under-Secretaries** (with Second Secretaries, Deputy Secretaries, Under Secretaries, Principal Assistant Secretaries and Assistant Secretaries below them) are the Civil Servants at the head of the corresponding Departments. **Parliamentary Private Secretaries** are Members who act as unpaid assistants to Ministers, in a semi-official capacity. **Private Secretaries** are not Members; they are personal assistants to individuals and may be either private persons or officials.

Select Committee on Standing Orders, the. Deals exclusively with the Standing Orders relating to Private Business, and decides all cases of non-compliance with Standing Orders which are reported by the Examiners; and recommends dispensations.

Select Committee on Statutory Instruments, the. The so-called 'scrutinizing committee' (see p. 170) which examines all delegated legislation which is subject to parliamentary proceedings. The committee is concerned more with the form than with the policy of the Statutory Instruments.

Select Committees. See *Committees, Select*.

Selection of Amendments. The power given to the Speaker (in the House), to the Chairman and Deputy Chairman in Committee of the Whole House and to all chairmen in Standing Committees, to select which Amendments they shall call from those on the Paper (known as 'the Kangaroo').

Serjeant at Arms. An official appointed by the Crown and lent to the House of Commons to act in the House upon such orders as he may receive from the Chair for the preservation of order and decorum among Members and strangers. He is, by statute, Housekeeper of the House, and supervises the departments of the police, door-keepers and attendants.

In the House of Lords the Serjeant at Arms was formerly exclusively a personal attendant upon the Lord Chancellor. His post is at present combined with those of Secretary to the Lord Great Chamberlain and Yeoman-Usher of the Black Rod.

Session, a, is a period of parliamentary sittings which is terminated by command of the Crown in the form of a Prorogation. It is usually broken up by adjournments, as the parliamentary vacations are called. The necessities of annually renewing certain Acts and securing financial supplies nowadays require annual Sessions, but a year may contain more than one Session. The duration of a Session used to be from February to August, with autumn sittings if required to complete business. Lately the session has begun and ended in the autumn.

Unless all stages of a Bill in both Houses are completed within one Session, the Bill is lost.

Sessional Orders. See *Orders*.

Short Title of a Bill, the. See *Title of a Bill*.

Single Transferable Vote, the. A method of voting which secures Proportional Representation (q.v.) when used in constituencies returning three or more Members. The elector has one vote only, transferable in accordance with his preferences, which he indicates on his ballot paper. To secure election, a quota, not a majority, of the votes cast is required, and the Returning Officer distributes the surplus votes (above the quota) of successful candidates (and if necessary all the votes of the least successful candidates) among the others until all the seats are filled. (See pp. 175–178).

Snap Division, a. A sudden division (usually carefully engineered) by which the Opposition hopes to catch the Government at a disadvantage and thus inflict a defeat.

Speaker, the, is the presiding officer of the House of Commons. He is a Member elected at the beginning of a Parliament for its duration, but generally remains in office for longer (see pp. 71–75).

Speaker's Conference, a. A Committee of Members of both Houses, under the Chairmanship of the Speaker, which is from time to time set up to make recommendations on questions of electoral reform and other matters.

Special Procedure Orders. Private legislation of the Provisional Order type, which is dealt with by Parliament under the shortened and cheaper procedure laid down by the Statutory Orders (Special Procedure) Act, 1945.

Speech from the Throne, the. See *Queen's Speech*.

Speeches. Members ought not to read their speeches, but may refresh their memory from notes. Speeches are supposed to reply to preceding arguments and so form part of a continuous debate, not to be set and independent orations. (See also *Irrelevance.*)

Spying Strangers. The method in use to clear the House for a debate in private is still for a Member to rise and state that he 'spies strangers', when the House may—if necessary upon a division—order all strangers to withdraw. A further Resolution is required to convert the sitting into a 'Secret Session', which is the machinery for bringing into operation any existing statutory sanctions against the disclosure of proceedings.

Standing Committees. See *Committees, Standing.*

Standing Orders, the. See *Orders.*

Statutes. Bills which have become Acts of Parliament, by passing both Houses and receiving the Royal Assent.

Statutory Instruments. Subsidiary laws made (by virtue of an Act of Parliament) principally (1) by Her Majesty in Council (2) by a Government Department or (3) in relation to a court of law. They are known as 'Delegated Legislation'.

Statutory Rules and Orders. Now known (except for Northern Ireland Orders) as *Statutory Instruments.*

Strangers. Technically includes all persons (including the Press) who are not Members or Officers of one or other House.

Substantive Motion or Resolution, a, is a self-contained proposal submitted for the approval of the House, and drafted to express a decision of the House.

Supplementary Estimates are presented for sums found to be required in addition to those already asked for.

Supplementary Questions. See *Questions.*

Supply. See *Committee of Supply* and *Allotted Days.*

Suspension of Members. A Member guilty of disorderly conduct may be ordered by Mr. Speaker to withdraw from the House for the remainder of the sitting. In worse cases the House may order his suspension for varying periods.

Suspension of Sitting. Mr. Speaker has power to suspend a sitting in case of grave disorder, or (with general assent) for convenience, e.g. to provide an interval in an unusually long ministerial speech.

Table of the House, the, at which the Clerks sit and upon which the Mace rests, occupies the space before the Speaker and between the Front Benches.

Tellers. Two Members from each side of a question who count the voters as they emerge from the Division Lobbies. They work in pairs and so act as a check upon each other.

Temporary Chairmen of Committees. See *Chairmen, Temporary.*

Ten Minute Rule Bills, are brought in under Standing Order No. 13, if the House gives its permission after hearing a brief explanatory statement from the Member in charge of the Bill, and from one opponent if the Bill is opposed.

Ten O'Clock Rule, the. On Mondays, Tuesdays, Wednesdays and Thursdays all opposed business except certain exempted items must end at 10 p.m., unless the rule has been suspended by the House.

Test Roll, the. The roll of parchment which a Member subscribes after taking the oath or making an affirmation.

Title of a Bill, the. There are at least two titles to a Bill:

1. The Long Title, which defines the purposes of the Bill. It may be amended to cover an extension of these purposes, within certain limits.
2. The Short Title, or Citation Title, which is quoted at the end of the Bill ('this Act may be cited as the Act, 19 ') and by which the Act will be known and cited.

   The Title by which the Bill is known during its passage through the House, called the 'Tag', is usually, but not invariably, the same as the Citation Title.

Tories. Originally seventeenth-century Irish outlaws who subsisted by killing and plundering. A nickname applied about 1680 to those who opposed the exclusion of James, Duke of York, from the throne; and thereafter to the great political party which sprang from the Royalists and Cavaliers. Used at first contemptuously by opponents it was soon adopted, in true British fashion, by the party itself. The word is still current for those holding conservative principles.

Treasury Bench, the. See *Front Benches.*

Unopposed Bills, Committees on. See *Committees on Unopposed Bills.*

Unopposed Business. Business to which no Member raises any objection.

Unparliamentary Language. Offensive words or expressions which are not permitted in debate.

'Usual Channels', through the. Negotiations conducted through and between the Whips' offices. They are often used to ascertain the general consensus of opinion of the various groups of Members in the House on different matters. (See also '*Behind the Speaker's Chair*'.)

Virement. The statutory power given to the Admiralty, War Office and Air Ministry (but not to the Civil Departments) to transfer surpluses arising in some of the votes of their Estimates to meet deficiencies in others. The virement must receive Treasury sanction at the time; and parliamentary approval subsequently, first by means of Resolutions in Committee (see *Monk Resolutions*) and later by the Appropriation Act.

Vote, the. See *Blue Paper.* Also used, of course, in the sense of a Division.

Vote on Account, a. An instalment granted annually in advance to the Crown before the main Civil Estimates are voted.

Vote of Censure, a, is usually moved by the official Opposition. The Government invariably find time for the debate and, if beaten as a result of it, must in practice resign or ask for a dissolution.

Vote of Credit, a, is a sum (generally large) demanded by the Government for the public service at a time when, as in war, only the total sum required can be named, without details.

Votes and Proceedings. The itemized record of the business transacted in the House—to be distinguished from the Official Report (*Hansard*) which is the verbatim report of the debates. (See also *Journal.*)

Ways and Means. See *Committee of Ways and Means.*

Whigs. Originally 'Whiggamores', seventeenth-century insurgent Presbyterians from the West of Scotland. A nickname applied about 1680 to those who favoured the exclusion of James, Duke of York, from the throne, and thereafter to the great political party opposed to the 'Tories' (q.v.). Used at first contemptuously by opponents it was soon adopted by the party itself but is now largely superseded by the name 'Liberals'.

Whips. Members who are party officials and, on the Government side, the holders of minor Treasury or Household posts (see p. 85).

The same word is used for the weekly circulars issued to Members by their Whips, detailing the programme of business and the relative necessity for their attendance during the week (see pp. 86–87).

White Paper. The name is colloquially used for Government and official statements, reports and other publications not sufficiently bulky to be given a blue cover and to become 'blue books'. The same name was applied to the revised version of the blue Notice Paper (or Order Paper) which used to be issued in the afternoon just before the House met.

'Who Goes Home?' The cry which is echoed round the precincts by policemen at the close of each sitting. It dates back for centuries to the time when Members walked home in groups for mutual protection against footpads.

Writs of Summons are issued from the Crown Office directing the election of Members to a new Parliament. To fill casual vacancies during the Session the Speaker issues his warrant for a new Writ to the Clerk of the Crown upon the order of the House. During recesses he has power under Statute to do so himself.

SELECT READING LIST

The following select list consists mainly of books suitable for the general reader. For a fuller bibliography, readers are referred to *Government and Parliament in Britain: A Bibliography*, by John Palmer, published by the Hansard Society for Parliamentary Government in 1960 at 3*s*. 6*d*.

I. HISTORICAL AND GENERAL

1. Abraham, L. A. and S. C. Hawtrey: *A Parliamentary Dictionary*. Butterworth, 1956, 21*s*. 0*d*.

   A useful reference book.

2. Bagehot, Walter: *The English Constitution*. World's Classics Series, Oxford Univ. Press, 1928 (reprinted 1949, 1952, etc.) 8*s*. 6*d*.

   In his introduction (written in 1927) to this book, which was first published in 1867, the Earl of Balfour said: 'Constitutional treatises are not usually regarded as light reading, yet surely he who thinks Bagehot's *English Constitution* dull must have brought a dull mind to its perusal.'

3. Ilbert, Sir Courtenay: *Parliament, its History, Constitution and Practice*. 3rd ed., revised by Sir C. Carr, Oxford Univ. Press, 1956, 10*s*. 6*d*.

   A short, readable and authoritative work by a former Clerk of the House of Commons.

4. Jennings, Sir W. Ivor: *Parliament*, 2nd ed., Cambridge Univ. Press, 1957, 65*s*. 0*d*.

   A comprehensive study of a vast subject, prepared by a well-known authority.

5. Mackenzie, K. R.: *The English Parliament*, revised ed., Penguin Books, 1963, 5*s*. 0*d*.

   A concise introductory history of Parliament.

6. Powell, Rt. Hon. J. Enoch, M.P.: *Great Parliamentary Occasions*. Herbert Jenkins, 1960, 13*s*. 6*d*.
Twelve descriptions of famous happenings in Parliament, ranging from the fourteenth century to the twentieth.

II. House of Lords

1. Bromhead, P. A.: *The House of Lords and Contemporary Politics*. Routledge, 1958, 35*s*. 0*d*.
Although overtaken by recent developments, this work is a readable and reliable survey of events up to its date of publication.
2. Joint Committee on House of Lords Reform: *Report, with proceedings and Appendices* (House of Commons Paper 38 of 1962–63). Obtainable from H.M. Stationery Office, 4*s*. 6*d*.

III. House of Commons

1. Campion, Lord: *An Introduction to the Procedure of the House of Commons*. 3rd ed., Macmillan, 1958, 24*s*. 0*d*.
An advanced detailed study of procedure, invaluable to the specialist but not designed for the general reader.
2. Chester, D. N. and N. Bowring: *Questions in Parliament*. Oxford Univ. Press, 1962, 35*s*. 0*d*.
The most recent study of an important aspect of the work of Parliament.
3. Hanson, A. V. and H. V. Wiseman: *Parliament at Work*. Stevens, 1962, 35*s*. 0*d*.
Readable and informative.
4. James, R. V. R.: *An Introduction to the House of Commons*. Collins, 1961, 12*s*. 6*d*.
The author, a Senior Clerk in the House of Commons, says in his Preface: 'My endeavour is to provide a photograph . . . of the House of Commons today.'
5. Lindsay, Sir Martin A., Bt., M.P.: *The House of Commons*. Collins, 1947.
An introductory illustrated account in the 'Britain in Pictures' series.
6. Richards, Peter G.: *Honourable Members: a Study of the British Backbencher*. Faber & Faber Ltd., 1959.
The first full-scale study of the 'Backbencher' in British politics.
7. Taylor, E.: *The House of Commons at Work*. 5th ed., Penguin Books, 1963, 4*s*. 0*d*.
A concise introduction to the procedure of the House of Commons.

IV. Elections

1. Butler, D. E.: *The electoral system in Britain*, 1918–1951. Oxford Univ. Press, 1953, 30*s*. 0*d*.
   The best book of its kind.
2. Butler, D. E. and R. Rose: *The General Election of* 1959. Macmillan, 1960.
   A lively and detailed study.
3. Ross, J. F. S.: *Elections and Electors*. Eyre & Spottiswoode, 1955, 42*s*. 0*d*.
   The author supports Proportional Representation. His book is informative and interesting.

V. The Palace of Westminster

Fell, Sir Bryan H.: *The Houses of Parliament: an illustrated guide to the Palace of Westminster*. 9th ed. revised by K. R. Mackenzie. Eyre & Spottiswoode, 1961.

VI. Political Parties

Jennings, Sir W. Ivor: *Party Politics*. 3 vols., Cambridge Univ. Press, 1960–1962, 45*s*. 0*d*. each.

INDEX

Well-known parliamentary terms not included in the index will be found in the Glossary commencing on page 228

Index

Index

Index

Index

Index